Financial Econometrics

D1564257

This excellent textbook – an overview of contemporary topics related to the modelling of financial time series – is set against a backdrop of rapid expansions of interest in both the models themselves and the financial problems to which they are applied.

Financial Econometrics covers all major developments in the area in recent years in an informative as well as succinct way. Subjects covered include:

- unit roots, co-integration and other comovements in time series
- time-varying volatility models of the GARCH type and the stochastic volatility approach
- analysis of shock persistence and impulse responses
- Markov switching
- present value relations and data characteristics
- state space models and the Kalman filter
- frequency domain analysis of time series.

Refreshingly, every chapter has a section of two or more examples and a section of empirical literature, offering the reader the opportunity to practise right away the kind of research going on in the area. This approach helps the reader develop interest, confidence and momentum in learning contemporary econometric topics.

Graduate and advanced undergraduate students requiring a broad knowledge of techniques applied in the finance literature, as well as students of financial economics engaged in empirical enquiry, should find this textbook to be invaluable.

Peijie Wang is Professor of finance at IESEG School of Management, Catholic University of Lille. He is the author of *An Econometric Analysis of the Real Estate Market* (Routledge, 2001).

Financial Econometrics
Methods and models

Peijie Wang

Routledge
Taylor & Francis Group

LONDON AND NEW YORK

First published 2003
by Routledge
11 New Fetter Lane, London EC4P 4EE

Simultaneously published in the USA and Canada
by Routledge,
29 West 35th Street, New York, NY 10001

Routledge is an imprint of the Taylor & Francis Group

© 2003 Peijie Wang

Typeset in Times New Roman by
Newgen Imaging Systems (P) Ltd, Chennai, India
Printed and bound in Great Britain by
MPG Books Ltd, Bodmin

British Library Cataloguing in Publication Data
A catalogue record for this book is available
from the British Library

Library of Congress Cataloging in Publication Data
A catalog record for this book has been requested

ISBN 0-415-22454-3 (hbk)
ISBN 0-415-22455-1 (pbk)

Contents

Detailed contents

7   State space models and the Kalman filter   118

8   Frequency domain analysis of time series   134

List of illustrations

Figures

Tables

Preface

This book focuses on time series models widely and frequently used in the examination of issues in financial economics and financial markets, which are scattered in the literature and are yet to be integrated into a single-volume, multi-theme and empirical research-oriented text. The book, providing an overview of contemporary topics related to the modelling of financial time series, is set against a backdrop of rapid expansions of interest in both the models themselves and the financial problems to which they are applied.

We assume that the reader already has knowledge of econometrics and finance at the intermediate level. Hence, basic regressional analysis and time series models such as OLS, maximum likelihood, ARIMA and VAR, while being referred to from time to time in the book, are not brought up as a book topic, and neither are the concepts of market efficiency and models for asset pricing. For the former, there are good books such as *Basic Econometrics* by Gujarati (1995), *Econometric Analysis* by Greene (1999), and *Introduction to Econometrics* by Maddala (1992); for the latter, the reader is recommended to refer to *Principles of Corporate Finance* by Brealey and Myers (2000), *Corporate Finance* by Ross *et al.* (2001), *Investments* by Sharpe *et al.* (1999), *Investments* by Bodie (2001), and *Financial Markets and Corporate Strategy* by Grinblatt and Titman (1998).

The book has two unique features – every chapter (except the first and final chapters) has a section of two or more examples and cases, and a section on empirical literature, offering the reader the opportunity to practise right away the kind of research in the area. The examples and cases, either from the literature or of the book itself, are well executed, and the results are explained in detail in simple language. This would, as we hope, help the reader get interest, confidence and momentum in learning contemporary econometric topics. At the same time, the reader would find that the way of implementation and estimation of a model is unavoidably influenced by the view of the researcher on the issue in a social science subject; nevertheless, for a serious researcher, it is not easy to make two plus two equal to any desired number she or he wants to get. The empirical literature reviewed in each chapter is comprehensive and up to date, exemplifying rich application areas at both macro and micro levels limited only by the imagination of human beings. The section demonstrates how a model can and should match practical problems coherently and guides the researcher's consideration on the rationale, methodology and factors in the research. Overall, the book is methods, models, theories, procedures, surveys, thoughts and tools.

To further help the reader carry out an empirical modern financial econometrics project, the book introduces research tools and sources of information in the final chapter. These include online information on and the websites for the literature on research in financial markets and financial time series; commonly used econometrics software packages for time series analysis; professional associations and learned societies; and financial institutions and organisations. A website link is provided whenever possible. The provision is based on our belief that, to perfect an empirical study, one has to understand the wider background of the business environment, market operations and institutional roles, and to frequently upgrade the knowledge base which is nowadays largely through internet links.

The book can be used in graduate programmes in financial economics, financial econometrics, international finance, banking and investment. It can also be used as doctorate research methodology material and by individual researchers interested in time series analysis, economic modelling, financial studies or policy evaluation.

References

Bodie, Z. (2001), *Investments*, 5th edn, McGraw-Hill.

Brealey, R.A. and Myers, S.C. (2000), *Principles of Corporate Finance*, 6th edn, McGraw-Hill.

Greene, W.H. (1999), *Econometric Analysis*, 4th edn, Prentice Hall.

Grinblatt, M. and Titman, S. (1998), *Financial Markets and Corporate Strategy*, Irwin/McGraw-Hill.

Gujarati, D. (1995), *Basic Econometrics*, 3rd edn, McGraw-Hill.

Maddala, G.S. (1992), *Introduction to Econometrics*, 2nd edn, Maxwell Macmillan International.

Ross, S.A., Westerfield, R.W. and Jaffe, J. (2001), *Corporate Finance*, 6th edn, McGraw-Hill.

Sharpe, W.F., Alexander, G.J. and Bailey, J.V. (1999), *Investments*, 6th edn, Prentice-Hall International.

Acknowledgements

The idea of writing a book in contemporary financial econometrics developed from my experience of advising doctoral and masters students in their research, to provide them with up-to-date and accessible materials either as research tools or as the advancement of the subject itself.

During the writing of this book, I received great encouragement and support from many individuals to whom I would like to express my gratitude. I am grateful to Bob Ward and James Freeman for reading through the chapters, correcting errors and making valuable suggestions which improved the manuscript. Some of my colleagues, including Yingmei Qin, Yun Zhou, Jingyin Hu, Karl Braun and Khelifa Mazouz, also made helpful comments on parts of the manuscript from various perspectives.

I would like to thank Stuart Hay, the economics and business editor at Routledge at the early stage of this project, for his insight and contribution in shaping the book. I appreciate Rob Langham, the present Routledge economics editor, for various discussions and consultations in finalising the book. I am indebted to Terry Clague and Heidi Bagtazo who have done excellent, efficient and effective editorial work – the book might never have been completed without their editorial assistance.

Finally, I thank the production and marketing teams of Routledge who bring the book to the reader.

Peijie Wang
May 2002

1 Stochastic processes and financial time series

1.1 Introduction

Statistics is the analysis of events and the association of events, with a probability. Econometrics pays attention to economic events, the association between these events, and between these events and human beings' decision making – government policy, firms' financial leverage, individuals' investment/consumption choice, and so on. The topics of this book, *Financial Econometrics*, focus on the variables and issues of financial economics, the financial market and the participants.

The financial world is an uncertain universe where events take place every day, every hour and every second. Information arrives randomly and so do the events. Nonetheless, there are regularities and patterns in the variables to be identified, effects of a change on the variables to be assessed, and links between the variables to be established. *Financial Econometrics* attempts to perform analyses of these kinds through employing and developing various relevant statistical procedures.

There are generally two types of economic and financial variables, one is the rate (flow) variable and the other the level (stock) variable. The first category measures the speed at which, for example, wealth is generated, or goods are consumed, or savings are made, at one point in time (continuous time) or over a short interval of time (discrete time). The second category works out the amount of wealth being accumulated over a period (continuous time) or in a few of short-time intervals (discrete time). Before we can establish links and chains of influence among the variables in concern, which are in general random or stochastic, we have to assess first their individual characteristics. With what probability may the variable take a certain value, that is, how likely is it that an event (the variable taking a given value) may occur? Such assessment of the characteristics of individual variables is made through the analysis of their statistical distributions. Bearing this in mind, a number of stochastic processes, which are commonly encountered in empirical research in economics and finance, are presented, compared and summarised in the next section. The behaviour and valuation of economic and financial variables are discussed in association with these stochastic processes in Section 1.3, with further extension and generalisation.

Independent identical distribution (i.i.d.) and normality in statistical distributions are commonly supposed to be met, though from time to time we would modify the assumptions to fit real world problems more appropriately. If the rate/flow variables are, as widely assumed, normally distributed (also i.i.d.) around a constant mean, then their corresponding level/stock variables would be log normally distributed around a mean which is increasing exponentially over time, and the level/stock variable in logarithms is normally distributed around a mean which is increasing linearly over time. This is the reason why we usually work with the level variables in their logarithms.

The classification of financial variables into rate variables and level variables gives rise to stationarity and non-stationarity in financial time series, though there might be no clear-cut match of the economic and financial characteristic and the statistical characteristic in empirical research. Related to this issue, Chapter 2 analyses unit roots and presents procedures for testing for unit roots. The chapter then introduces the idea of cointegration, where a combination of two or more non-stationary variables becomes stationary. This is a special type of link among stochastic variables, implying that there exists a so-called long-run relationship. The chapter also extends the analysis to cover common trends and common cycles, the other major types of links among stochastic variables in economics and finance.

One of the violations to the i.i.d. assumption is heteroscedasticity, that is, the variance is not the same for each of the residuals; and modifications are consequently required in the estimation procedure. The basics of this issue and the ways to handle it are a topic in introductory econometrics or statistics. What we introduce in Chapter 3 is specifically a kind of variance which changes with time, or time-varying variance. Time-varying variance or time-varying volatility is frequently found in many financial time series and so has to be dealt with seriously. Two types of time-varying volatility models are discussed, one is generalised autoregressive conditional heteroscedasticity (GARCH) and the other is stochastic volatility.

How persistent is the effect of a shock is important in financial markets. It is not only related to the response of, say, financial markets to a piece of news, but is also related to policy changes, of the government or of the firm. This issue is addressed in Chapter 4, which also incorporates impulse response analysis, a related subject which we reckon should be under the same umbrella. Regime shifts are important in the economy and financial markets as well, in that regime shifts or breaks in the economy and market conditions are often observed, but the difficulties are that regime shifts are not easily captured by conventional regressional analysis and modelling. Therefore Markov switching is introduced in Chapter 5 to handle these issues more effectively. The approach helps improve our understanding about an economic process and its evolving mechanism constructively.

Some economic and financial variables have built-in fundamental relationships between them. One of such fundamental relationships is that between income and value. Economists regard that the value of an asset is derived from its future income generating power. The higher the income generating power, the more valuable is the asset. Nevertheless, whether this law governing the relationship between income and value holds is subject to empirical scrutiny. Chapter 6 addresses this issue with the help of econometric procedures which identify and examine the time series characteristics of the variables involved.

Econometric analysis can be carried out in the conventional time domain as was discussed above, and can also be performed through some transformations. Analysis in the state space is one of such endeavours, presented in Chapter 7. What the state space does is to model the underlying mechanisms through the changes and transitions in the state of its unobserved components, and establish the links between the variables in concern, which are observed, and those unobserved state variables. It explains the behaviour of externally observed variables by examining the internal, dynamic and systematic changes and transitions of unobserved state variables, to reveal the nature and causes of the dynamic movement of the variables effectively. State space analysis is usually executed with the help of the Kalman filter, also introduced in this chapter.

State space analysis is nonetheless still in the time domain, though it is not the conventional time domain analysis. With spectral analysis of time series in Chapter 8, estimation is performed in the frequency domain. That is, time domain variables are transformed into frequency domain variables prior to the analysis, and the results in the frequency domain may be transformed back to the time domain when necessary. Such transformations are usually achieved through the Fourier transform and the inverse Fourier transform and, in practice, through the fast Fourier transform (FFT) and the inverse fast Fourier transform (IFFT). The frequency domain properties of variables are featured by their spectrum, phase and coherence, to reflect individual time series characteristics and the association between several time series, in ways similar to those in the time domain.

Financial econometrics is only made possible by the availability of vast economic and financial data. Problems and issues in the real world have inspired the generation of new ideas and stimulated the development of more powerful procedures. The last chapter of the book, Chapter 9, is written to make such a real world and working environment immediately accessible to the researcher, providing information on the sources of literature and data, econometric packages, and organisations and institutions ranging from learned societies, regulators to market players.

1.2 Stochastic processes and their properties

The rest of this chapter presents stochastic processes frequently found in the financial economics literature and relevant to such important studies as market efficiency and rationality. In addition, a few terms fundamental to modelling financial time series are introduced. The chapter discusses stochastic processes in the tradition of mathematical finance, as we feel that there rarely exist links, at least explicitly, between mathematical finance and financial econometrics, to demonstrate the rich statistical properties of financial securities and their economic rationale ultimately underpinning the evolution of the stochastic process. After providing definitions and brief discussions of elementary stochastic processes in the next section, we begin with the generalisation of the Wiener process in Section 1.3, and gradually progress to show that the time path of many financial securities can be described by the Wiener process and its generalisations which can accommodate such well-known econometric models or issues as autoregressive integrated moving average (ARIMA), GARCH, stochastic volatility, stationarity, mean-reversion, error correction and so on. Throughout the chapter, we do not particularly distinguish between discrete and continuous time series – what matters to the analysis is that the time interval is small enough. The results are almost identical, though this treatment does provide more intuition to real world problems. There are many stochastic processes books available, for example, Ross (1996) and Medhi (1982). For modelling of financial securities, interested readers can refer to Jarrow and Turnbull (1999).

1.2.1   *Martingales*

A stochastic process, X_n ($n = 1, 2, \ldots$), with $E[X_n] < \infty$ for all n, is a martingale, if:

$$E[X_{n+1} \mid X_1, \ldots, X_n] = X_n \tag{1}$$

Further, a stochastic process, X_n ($n = 1, 2, \ldots$), with $E[X_n] < \infty$ for all n, is a submartingale, if:

$$E[X_{n+1} \mid X_1, \ldots, X_n] \geq X_n \tag{2}$$

and is a supermartingale if:

$$E[X_{n+1} \mid X_1, \ldots, X_n] \leq X_n \tag{3}$$

1.2.2   *Random walks*

A random walk is the sum of a sequence of i.i.d. variables X_i ($i = 1, 2, \ldots$), with $E[X_i] < \infty$. Define:

$$S_n = \sum_{i=1}^{n} X_i \tag{4}$$

S_n is referred as a random walk. When X_i takes only two values, $+1$ and -1, with $P\{X_i = 1\} = p$ and $P\{X_i = -1\} = 1 - p$, the process is named as the Bernoulli random walk. If $p = 1 - p = \frac{1}{2}$, the process is called a simple random walk.

1.2.3   *Gaussian white noise processes*

A Gaussian process, or Gaussian white noise process, or simply white noise process, X_n ($n = 1, 2, \ldots$) is a sequence of independent random variables, each of which has a normal distribution:

$$X_n \sim (0, \sigma^2) \tag{5}$$

with the probability density function being:

$$f_n(x) = \frac{1}{\sigma\sqrt{2\pi}} e^{x^2/2\sigma^2} \tag{6}$$

The sequence of these independent random variables of the Gaussian white noise has a multivariate normal distribution and the covariance between any two variables in the sequence, $\text{Cov}(X_j, X_k) = 0$ for all $j \neq k$.

A Gaussian process is a white noise process because, in the frequency domain, it has equal magnitude in every frequency, or equal component in every colour. We know that light with equal colour components, such as sunlight, is white. Readers interested in frequency domain analysis can refer to Chapter 8 for details.

1.2.4 Poisson processes

A Poisson process $N(t)$ $(t \geq 0)$ is a counting process where $N(t)$ is an integer representing the number of 'events' that have occurred up to time t, and the process has independent increments, that is, the number of events that have occurred in interval $(s, t]$ is independent from the number of events in interval $(s + \tau, t + \tau]$.

Poisson processes can be stationary and non-stationary. A stationary Poisson process has stationary increments, that is, the probability distribution of the number of events occurred in any interval of time is only dependent on the length of the time interval:

$$P\{N(t + \tau) - N(s + \tau)\} = P\{N(t) - N(s)\} \tag{7}$$

The probability distribution of the number of events in any time length τ then is:

$$P\{N(t + \tau) - N(t) = n\} = e^{-\lambda t} \frac{(\lambda t)^n}{n!} \tag{8}$$

where λ is called the arrival rate, or simply the rate of the process. It can be shown that:

$$E\{N(t)\} = \lambda, \quad \text{Var}\{N(t)\} = \lambda t \tag{9}$$

In the case that a Poisson process is non-stationary, the arrival rate is a function of time, thereby the process does not have a constant mean and variance.

1.2.5   Markov processes

A sequence X_n $(n = 0, 1, \ldots)$ is a Markov process if it has the following property:

$$P\{X_{n+1} = x_{n+1} \mid X_n = x_n, X_{n-1} = x_{n-1}, X_1 = x_1, X_0 = x_0\}$$
$$= P\{X_{n+1} = x_n \mid X_n = x_n\} \tag{10}$$

The Bernoulli random walk and simple random walk are cases of Markov processes. It can be shown that the Poisson process is a Markov process as well.

A discrete time Markov process that takes a finite or countable number of integer values, x_n, is called a Markov chain.

1.2.6   Wiener processes

A Wiener process, also known as Brownian motion, is indeed the very basic element in stochastic processes:

$$\Delta z(t) = \varepsilon \sqrt{\Delta t}, \qquad \Delta t \to 0, \qquad \varepsilon \sim N(0, 1) \tag{11}$$

The Wiener process can be derived from the simple random walk, replacing the time sequence by time series when time intervals become smaller and smaller and approach zero. If $z(t)$ is a simple random walk such that it moves forward and backward by Δz in time interval Δt, then:

$$E[z(t)] = 0, \qquad \text{Var}[z(t)] = (\Delta z)^2 \frac{t}{\Delta t} \tag{12}$$

In a sensible and convenient way, let the distance of the small move $\Delta z = \sqrt{\Delta t}$. According to the central limit theorem, $z(t)$ has a normal distribution with mean 0 and variance t, and has independent and stationary increments. These are statistical properties described by equation (11).

1.2.7   Stationarity and ergodicity

These two terms have been frequently come across, and are relevant and important in financial and economic time series. Nonetheless, it is helpful here to provide simple definitions to link and distinguish them, and to clarify each of them. A stochastic process is said to be covariance stationary if:

1   $E\{X(t)\} = \mu$ for all t;
2   $\text{Var}\{X(t)\} < \infty$ for all t; and
3   $\text{Cov}\{X(t), X(t + j)\} = \gamma_j$ for all t and j.

This is sometimes referred to as weakly stationary, or simply stationary. Such stationary processes have finite mean, variance and covariance that do not depend on the time t, and the covariance depends only on the interval j.

A strictly stationary process has met the above conditions (1) and (3), and has been extended to higher moments or orders. It states that the random vectors $\{X(t_1), X(t_2), \ldots, X(t_n)\}$ and $\{X(t_{1+j}), X(t_{2+j}), \ldots, X(t_{n+j})\}$ have the same joint distribution. In other words, the joint distribution depends only on the interval j but not on the time t. That is, the joint probability density $p\{x(t), x(t + \tau_1), \ldots, x(t + \tau_n)\}$, where $\tau_i = t_i - t_{i-1}$, depends only on the intervals $\tau_1, \ldots, \tau_n$ but not on t itself. A second-order stationary process is not exactly covariance stationary as it is not required to meet condition (2). Therefore, a process can be strictly stationary while being not covariance stationary, and vice versa.

Ergodicity arises from the practical need to obtain ensemble moments values from a single realisation or observation of the stochastic process. A covariance stationary process is ergodic for the first moment if its temporal average converges, with probability 1, to the ensemble average. Similarly, a covariance stationary process is ergodic for the second moment if its temporal covariance converges, with probability 1, to the ensemble covariance.

1.3 The behaviour and valuation of security prices

A Wiener process has a mean value of zero and a unity variance. It is also a special type of random walk. The Wiener process can be generalised to describe a time series where the mean value is a constant and can be different from zero, and the variance is a constant and can be different from unity. Most financial securities' prices fall in this category when the financial market is efficient in its weak form. An Ito process further relaxes these conditions so that both the deterministic and stochastic parts of the generalised Wiener process are state and time dependent. Important relationships between stochastic variables and, in particular, between a financial security's price and the price of its derivative, are established by Ito's lemma. Ito's lemma is central to the valuation and pricing of derivative securities, though it may shed light on issues beyond the derivative arena.

1.3.1 Generalised Wiener processes

A Wiener process described by equation (11) is a special and rather restricted random walk. It can be generalised so that the variance can differ from $1 \times t$ and there can be a drift. A stochastic process or variable x is a generalised Wiener process if:

$$\Delta x = a\Delta t + b\Delta z \tag{13}$$

where a is the drift rate and b is the variance rate. Many financial time series can be subscribed to equation (13), especially in the context of so-called weak-form market efficiency, though equation (13) is a stronger claim to weak-form market efficiency than martingales.

1.3.2   Ito processes

If parameters a and b are functions of x and t, then equation (13) becomes the Ito process:

$$\Delta x = a(x, t)\Delta t + b(x, t)\Delta z \qquad (14)$$

Function $a(x, t)$ can introduce the autoregressive component by including lagged Δx. Moving average effects can be introduced by $b(x, t)$ when it has non-zero constant values at times $t - i$ ($i = 1, 2, \ldots$). Function $b(x, t)$ can generally introduce similar effects in the second moment, widely known as autoregressive conditional heteroscedasticity (ARCH), GARCH, variations and stochastic volatility. Both $a(x, t)$ and $b(x, t)$ can bring in time-varying coefficients in the first and second moments as well. Therefore, equation (14) can virtually represent all univariate time series found in finance and economics.

1.3.3   Ito's lemma

Ito's lemma is one of the most important tools for derivative pricing. It describes the behaviour of one stochastic variable as a function of another stochastic variable. The former could be the price of an option or the price of other derivatives, and the latter could be the price of shares.

Let us write equation (14) in continuous time:

$$dx = a(x, t)\, dt + b(x, t)\, dz \qquad (15)$$

Let y be a function of stochastic process x, Ito's lemma tells us that y is also an Ito process:

$$dy = \left(\frac{\partial y}{\partial x}a + \frac{\partial y}{\partial t} + \frac{1}{2}\frac{\partial^2 y}{\partial x^2}b^2 \right) dt + \frac{\partial y}{\partial x}b\, dz \qquad (16)$$

It has a drift rate of:

$$\frac{\partial y}{\partial x}a + \frac{\partial y}{\partial t} + \frac{1}{2}\frac{\partial^2 y}{\partial x^2}b^2 \qquad (17)$$

and a variance rate of:

$$\left(\frac{\partial y}{\partial x} \right)^2 b^2 \qquad (18)$$

Equation (16) is derived by using the Taylor series expansion and ignoring higher orders of zero, details of which can be found in most undergraduate level mathematics texts.

Ito's lemma has a number of meaningful applications in finance and econometrics. Beyond derivative pricing, it reveals why and how two financial or economic time series are related to each other. For example, if two non-stationary time series (precisely, integrated of order 1) share the same stochastic component, the second term on the right-hand side of equations (15) and (16), then a linear combination of them is stationary. This phenomenon is called cointegration in the sense of Engle and Granger (1987) and Johansen (1988) in the time series econometrics literature. The interaction and link between them are most featured by the existence of an error correction mechanism. If two non-stationary time series are both the functions of an Ito process, then they have a common stochastic component but may in addition have individual stochastic components as well. In this case, the two time series have a common trend in the sense of Stock and Watson (1988) but they are not necessarily cointegrated. This analysis can be extended to deal with stationary cases, for example, common cycles in Engle and Issler (1995) and Vahid and Engle (1993).

1.3.4 Geometric Wiener processes and financial variable behaviour in the short term and long run

We can ascribe a financial variable, for example, the share price, to a random walk process with normal distribution errors:

$$P_{t+1} = P_t + v_t, \quad v_t \sim N(0, \sigma_P^2) \tag{19}$$

More generally, the price follows a random walk with a drift:

$$P_{t+1} = P_t + \phi + v_t, \quad v_t \sim N(0, \sigma_P^2) \tag{20}$$

where ϕ is a constant indicating an increase (and less likely, a decrease) of the share price in every period. Nevertheless, a constant absolute increase or decrease in share prices is also not quite reasonable. A realistic representation is that the relative increase of the price is a constant:

$$\frac{P_{t+1} - P_t}{P_t} = \mu + \xi_t, \quad \xi_t \sim N(0, \sigma^2) \tag{21}$$

So:

$$\Delta P_t = P_{t+1} - P_t = \mu P_t + P_t \xi_t = \mu P_t + \sigma P_t \varepsilon, \quad \varepsilon \sim N(0, 1) \tag{22}$$

Notice $\Delta t = t + 1 - t = 1$ can be omitted in or added to the equations. Let Δt be a small interval of time (e.g. a fraction of 1), then equation (22) becomes:

$$\Delta P_t = \mu P_t \Delta t + \sigma P_t \varepsilon \sqrt{\Delta t} = \mu P_t \Delta t + \sigma P_t \Delta z \tag{23}$$

Equation (23) is an Ito process in that its drift rate and variance rate are functions of the variable in concern and time. Applying Ito's lemma, we obtain the logarithm of the price as follows:

$$\Delta p_t = p_{t+1} - p_t = \left[\mu - \frac{\sigma^2}{2}\right]\Delta t + \Delta z \tag{24}$$

where $p_t = \ln(P_t)$ has a drift rate of $\mu = \mu - (\sigma^2/2)$ and variance rate of σ^2. Equation (24) is just a generalised Wiener process instead of an Ito process in that its drift rate and variance rate are not the functions of P_t and t. This simplifies analysis and valuation empirically.

If we set $\sigma = 0$, the process is deterministic and the solution is:

$$P_t = P_0(1 + \mu)^t \approx P_0\, e^{\mu t} \tag{25}$$

and

$$p_t = p_0 + t \ln(t + \mu) \approx p_0 + \mu t \tag{26}$$

The final result in equations (25) and (26) is obtained when μ is fairly small and it is also the continuous time solution. From the above analysis, we can conclude that share prices grow exponentially while log share prices grow linearly.

When $\sigma \neq 0$, rates of return and prices deviate from the above-derived values. Assuming there is only one shock (innovation) occurring in the kth period, $\varepsilon(k) = \sigma$, then:

$$P_t = P_0(1 + \mu)(1 + \mu) \cdots (1 + \mu + \sigma) \cdots (1 + \mu)(1 + \mu)(1 + \mu) \tag{27}$$

for the price itself, and

$$p_t = p_0 + (t - 1)\ln(t + \mu) + \ln(1 + \mu + \sigma) \approx p_0 + \sigma + \mu t \tag{28}$$

for the log price. After k, the price level increases by σ permanently (in every period after k). However, the rate of change or return is $\mu + \sigma$ in the kth period only, after k the rate of return changes back to μ immediately.

The current rate of return or change does not affect future rates of return or change, so it is called a short-term variable. This applies to all similar financial and economic variables in the form of first differences. The current rate of return has an effect on future prices, either in original forms or logarithms, which are dubbed as long-run variables. Long-run variables often take their original form or are in logarithms, both being called variables in levels in econometric analysis. We have observed from the above analysis that adopting variables in logarithms gives rise to linear relationships which simplify empirical analysis, so many level variables are usually in their logarithms.

In the above analysis of the share price, we assume reasonably that the change in the price is stationary and the price itself is integrated of order 1, whereas under some other circumstances, the financial variables in their level, not in their difference, may exhibit the property of a stationary process. Prominently, two of such variables are the interest rate and the unemployment rate. To accommodate this, a mean-reversion element is introduced into the process. Taking the interest rate for example, one of the models can have the following specification:

$$\Delta r_t = a(b - r_t)\Delta t + \sigma r_t \Delta z, \qquad a > 0, \quad b > 0 \tag{29}$$

Equation (29) says that the interest rate decreases when its current value is greater than b and it increases when its current level is below b, where b is the mean value of the interest rate to which the interest rate reverts. A non-stationary process, such as that represented by equation (23), and a mean-reverse process, such as equation (29), differ in their statistical properties and behaviour. But more important are the differences in their economic roles and functions.

1.3.5 Valuation of derivative securities and beyond

In finance, Ito's lemma has been most significantly applied to the valuation of derivative securities, leading to the so-called risk-neutral valuation principle. It can also be linked to various common factor analyses in economics and finance, notably cointegration, common trends and common cycles.

Let us write equation (23) in continuous time for the convenience of mathematical derivative operations:

$$dP_t = \mu P_t \, dt + \sigma P_t \, dz \tag{30}$$

Let π_t be the price of a derivative security written on the share. According to Ito's lemma, we have:

$$d\pi_t = \left(\frac{\partial \pi_t}{\partial P_t} \mu P_t + \frac{\partial \pi_t}{\partial t} + \frac{1}{2} \frac{\partial^2 \pi_t}{\partial P_t^2} \sigma^2 P_t^2 \right) dt + \frac{\partial \pi_t}{\partial P_t} \sigma P_t \, dz \tag{31}$$

Now set up a portfolio which eliminates the stochastic term in equations (30) and (31):

$$\Omega_t = -\pi_t + \frac{\partial \pi_t}{\partial P_t} P_t \tag{32}$$

The change in Ω_t:

$$d\Omega_t = -d\pi_t + \frac{\partial \pi_t}{\partial P_t} dP_t = \left(-\frac{\partial \pi_t}{\partial t} - \frac{1}{2} \frac{\partial^2 \pi_t}{\partial P_t^2} \sigma^2 P_t^2 \right) dt \tag{33}$$

is deterministic involving no uncertainty. Therefore, Ω_t must grow at the risk-free interest rate:

$$d\Omega_t = r_f \Omega_t \, dt \tag{34}$$

where r_f is the risk-free interest rate. This shows the principle of risk-neutral valuation of derivative securities. It should be emphasised that risk-neutral valuation does not imply people are risk-neutral in pricing derivative securities. In contrast, the general setting and background are that risk-averse investors make investment decisions in a risky financial world.

Substituting from equations (32) and (33), (34) becomes:

$$\left(\frac{\partial \pi_t}{\partial t} + \frac{1}{2} \frac{\partial^2 \pi_t}{\partial P_t^2} \sigma^2 P_t^2 \right) dt = r_f \left(\pi_t - \frac{\partial \pi_t}{\partial P_t} P_t \right) dt \tag{35}$$

$$\frac{\partial \pi_t}{\partial t} + \frac{\partial \pi_t}{\partial P_t} r_f P_t + \frac{1}{2} \frac{\partial^2 \pi_t}{\partial P_t^2} \sigma^2 P_t^2 = r_f \pi_t \tag{36}$$

Equation (36) establishes the price of a derivative security as the function of its underlying security and is a general form for all types of derivative securities. Combining with relevant conditions, such as the exercise price, time to maturity and the type of the derivative, a specific set of solutions can be obtained. It can be observed that solutions are much simpler for a forward/futures derivative, or any derivatives with their prices being a linear function of the underlying securities. It is because the third term on the left-hand side of equation (36) is zero for such derivatives.

Consider two derivative securities both written on the same underlying security such as a corporate share. Then, according to Ito's lemma, the two stochastic processes for these two derivatives subscribe to a common stochastic process generated by the process for the share price, and there must be some kind of fundamental relationship between them. Further, if two stochastic processes or financial time series are thought to be generated from or partly from a common source, then the two time series can be considered as being derived from or partly derived from a common underlying stochastic process, and can be fitted into the analytical framework of Ito's lemma as well. Many issues in multivariate time series analysis demonstrate this feature.

References

Engle, R. F. and Granger, C. W. J. (1987), Co-integration and error correction representation, estimation, and testing, *Econometrica*, 55, 251–267.

Engle, R. F. and Issler, J. V. (1995), Estimating common sectoral cycles, *Journal of Monetary Economics*, 35, 83–113.

Jarrow, R. A. and Turnbull, S. (1999), *Derivative Securities*, 2nd edn, South-Western College Publishing, Cincinnati, Ohio.

Johansen, S. (1988), Statistical analysis of cointegration vectors, *Journal of Economic Dynamics and Control*, 12, 231–254.

Medhi, J. (1982), *Stochastic Processes*, Wiley Eastern, New Delhi.

Ross, S. M. (1996), *Stochastic Processes*, 2nd edn, John Wiley, Chichester, England.

Stock, J. H. and Watson, M. W. (1988), Testing for common trends, *Journal of the American Statistical Association*, 83, 1097–1107.

Vahid, F. and Engle, R. F. (1993), Common trends and common cycles, *Journal of Applied Econometrics*, 8, 341–360.

2 Unit roots, cointegration and other comovements in time series

The distinction between long-run and short-term characteristics in time series has attracted much attention in the last two decades. Long-run characteristics in economic and financial data are usually associated with non-stationarity in time series and are called trends, whereas short-term fluctuations are stationary time series and are called cycles. Economic and financial time series can be viewed as combinations of these components of trends and cycles. Typically, a shock to a stationary time series would have an effect which would gradually disappear, leaving no permanent impact on the time series in the distant future, while a shock to a non-stationary time series would permanently change the path of the time series; or would permanently move the activity to a different level, either a higher or a lower level.

Moreover, the existence of common factors among two or more time series may have such effect that the combination of these time series demonstrates no features which the individual time series possess. For example, there could be a common trend shared by two time series. If there is no further trend which exists in only one time series, then it is said that these two time series are cointegrated. This kind of common factor analysis can be extended and applied to stationary time series as well, leading to the idea of common cycles.

This chapter first examines the properties of individual time series with regard to stationarity and tests for unit roots. Then, cointegration and its testing procedures are discussed. Finally, common cycles and common trends are analysed to further scrutinise comovements amongst variables.

2.1 Unit roots and testing for unit roots

Chapter 1 has provided a definition for stationarity. In the terminology of time series analysis, if a time series is stationary, it is said to be integrated of order zero, or $I(0)$ for short. If a time series needs one difference operation to achieve stationarity, it is an $I(1)$ series; and a time series is $I(n)$ if it is to be differenced for n times to achieve stationarity. An $I(0)$ time series has no roots on or inside the unit circle but an $I(1)$ or higher order integrated time series contains roots on or inside the unit circle. So, examining stationarity is equivalent to testing for the existence of unit roots in the time series.

A pure random walk, with or without a drift, is the simplest non-stationary time series:

$$y_t = \mu + y_{t-1} + \varepsilon_t, \quad \varepsilon_t \sim N(0, \sigma_\varepsilon^2) \tag{1}$$

where μ is a constant or drift, which can be zero, in the random walk. It is non-stationary as $\mathrm{Var}(y_t) = t\sigma_\varepsilon^2 \to \infty$ as $t \to \infty$. It does not have a definite mean either. The difference of a pure random walk is the Gaussian white noise, or the white noise for short:

$$\Delta y_t = \mu + \varepsilon_t, \quad \varepsilon_t \sim N(0, \sigma_\varepsilon^2) \tag{2}$$

The variance of Δy_t is σ_ε^2 and the mean is μ.

The presence of a unit root can be illustrated as follows, using a first-order autoregressive process:

$$y_t = \mu + \rho y_{t-1} + \varepsilon_t, \quad \varepsilon_t \sim N(0, \sigma_\varepsilon^2) \tag{3}$$

Equation (3) can be extended recursively, yielding:

$$y_t = \mu + \rho y_{t-1} + \varepsilon_t$$
$$= \mu + \rho\mu + \rho^2 y_{t-2} + \rho\varepsilon_{t-1} + \varepsilon_t$$
$$\vdots$$
$$= \left(1 + \rho + \cdots + \rho^{n-1}\right)\mu + \rho^n y_{t-n} + \left(1 + \rho L + \cdots + \rho^{n-1}L^{n-1}\right)\varepsilon_t \tag{4}$$

where L is the lag operator. The variance of y_t can be easily worked out:

$$\mathrm{Var}(y_t) = \frac{1 - \rho^n}{1 - \rho}\sigma_\varepsilon^2 \tag{5}$$

It is clear that there is no finite variance for y_t if $\rho \geq 1$. The variance is $\sigma_\varepsilon^2/(1 - \rho)$ when $\rho < 1$.

Alternatively, equation (3) can be expressed as:

$$y_t = \frac{\mu + \varepsilon_t}{(1 - \rho L)} = \frac{\mu + \varepsilon_t}{\rho((1/\rho) - L)} \tag{6}$$

which has a root $r = 1/\rho$.[1] Comparing equation (5) with (6), we can see that when y_t is non-stationary, it has a root on or inside the unit circle, that is, $r \geq 1$; while a stationary y_t has a root outside the unit circle, that is, $r < 1$. It is usually said that there exists a unit root under the circumstances where $r \geq 1$. Therefore, testing for stationarity is equivalent to examining whether there is a unit root in the time series. Having gained the above idea, commonly used unit root test procedures are introduced and discussed in the following.

2.1.1   *Dickey and Fuller*

The basic Dickey–Fuller (DF) test (Dickey and Fuller 1979, 1981) examines whether $\rho < 1$ in equation (3), which, after subtracting y_{t-1} from both sides, can be written as:

$$\Delta y_t = \mu + (\rho - 1)y_{t-1} + \varepsilon_t = \mu + \theta y_{t-1} + \varepsilon_t \tag{7}$$

The null hypothesis is that there is a unit root in y_t, or $H_0 : \theta = 0$, against the alternative $H_1 : \theta < 0$, or there is no unit root in y_t. The DF test procedure emerged since under the null hypothesis the conventional t-distribution does not apply. So whether $\theta < 0$ or not cannot be confirmed by the conventional t-statistic for the θ estimate. Indeed, what the DF procedure gives us is a set of critical values developed to deal with the non-standard distribution issue, which are derived through simulation. Then, the interpretation of the test result is no more than that of a simple conventional regression.

Equations (3) and (7) are the simplest case where the residual is white noise. In general, there is serial correlation in the residual and Δy_t can be represented as an autoregressive process:

$$\Delta y_t = \mu + \theta y_{t-1} + \sum_{i=1}^{p} \phi_i \Delta y_{t-i} + \varepsilon_t \tag{8}$$

Corresponding to equation (8), DF's procedure becomes the Augmented Dickey–Fuller (ADF) test. We can also include a deterministic trend in equation (8). Altogether, there are four test specifications with regard to the combinations of an intercept and a deterministic trend.

2.1.2   *Phillips and Perron*

Phillips and Perron's (1988) approach is one in the frequency domain, termed the PP test. It takes the Fourier transform of the time series Δy_t such as in equation (8), then analyses its component at the zero frequency. The t-statistic of the PP test is calculated as:

$$t = \sqrt{\frac{r_0}{h_0}}\, t_\theta - \frac{(h_0 - r_0)}{2h_0\sigma}\sigma_\theta \tag{9}$$

where

$$h_0 = r_0 + 2\sum_{\tau=1}^{M}\left(1 - \frac{j}{T}\right)r_j$$

is the spectrum of Δy_t at the zero frequency,[2] r_j is the autocorrelation function at lag j, t_θ is the t-statistic of θ, σ_θ is the standard error of θ, and σ is the standard error of the test regression. In fact, h_0 is the variance of the M-period differenced series, $y_t - y_{t-M}$, while r_0 is the variance of the one-period difference, $\Delta y_t = y_t - y_{t-1}$.

Although it is not the purpose of the book to describe technical details of testing procedures, it may be helpful to present the intuitive ideas behind them. We inspect two extreme cases, one where the time series is a pure white noise process and the other a pure random walk. In the former, $r_j = 0$, $j \neq 0$ and $r_0 = h_0$, so $t = t_\theta$ and the conventional t-distribution applies. In the latter, $h_0 = M \times r_0$. If we look at the first term on the right-hand side of equation (9), t is adjusted by a factor of $\sqrt{1/M}$, and it is further reduced by value of the second term $\approx \sigma_\theta/2\sigma$. So, the PP test gradually reduces the significance of the θ estimate as ρ moves from zero towards unity (or as θ moves from -1 to 0) to correct for the effect of non-conventional t-distributions which becomes increasingly severe as ρ approaches unity.

2.1.3 *Kwiatkowski, Phillips, Schmidt and Shin*

Recently, a procedure proposed by Kwiatkowski *et al.* (1992), known as the KPSS test named after these authors, has become a popular alternative to the ADF test. As the title of their paper, 'Testing the null hypothesis of stationarity against the alternative of a unit root', suggests, the test tends to accept stationarity, which is the null hypothesis, in a time series. In the ADF test on the other hand, the null hypothesis is the existence of a unit root, and stationarity is more likely to be rejected. Many empirical studies have employed the KPSS procedure to confirm stationarity in such economic and financial time series as the unemployment rate and the interest rate, which, arguably, must be stationary for economic theories, policies and practice to make sense. Others, such as tests for purchasing power parity (PPP), are less restricted by the theory. Confirmation and rejection of PPP are both acceptable in empirical research using a particular set of time series data, though different test results give rise to rather different policy implications. It is understandable that, relative to the ADF test, the KPSS test is less likely to reject PPP.

2.1.4 *Panel unit root tests*

Often in an empirical study, there is more than one time series to be examined. These time series are the same kind of data, such as the real exchange rate, current account balance or dividend payout, but they are for a group of economies or companies. These time series probably have the same length with the same start date and end date, or can be adapted without losing general properties. Under such circumstances, a test on pooled cross-section time series data, or panel data, can be carried out. Panel unit root tests provide an overall aggregate statistic to examine whether there exists a unit root in the pooled cross-section time series data and to judge the time series property of the data accordingly. This, on the one hand, can avoid obtaining contradictory results in individual time series to which no satisfactory explanations can be offered. On the other hand, good asymptotic properties can be reached with relatively small samples in individual time series, which are otherwise too small to be estimated effectively. In the procedure developed by Levin and Lin (1992, 1993), when the disturbances are independent identical distribution (i.i.d.), the unit root t-statistic converges to the normal distribution; when fixed effects or serial correlation is specified for the disturbances, a straightforward transformation of the t-statistic converges to the normal distribution too. Therefore, their unit root t-statistic converges to the normal distribution under various assumptions about disturbances. Due to the presence of a unit root, the convergence is achieved more quickly as the number of time periods grows than as the number of individuals grows. It is claimed that the panel framework provides remarkable improvements in statistical power compared to performing a separate unit root for each individual time series. Monte Carlo simulations indicate that good results can be achieved in relatively small samples with 10 individual time series and 25 observations in each time series. Im *et al.* (1995) developed a $\bar{t}$ (t bar) statistic based on the average of the ADF t-statistics for panel data. It is shown that under certain conditions, the $\bar{t}$-statistic has a standard normal distribution for a finite number of individual time series observations, so long as the number of cross-sections is sufficiently large. Commenting on and summarising the Levin and Lin (1992, 1993) and Im *et al.* (1995) procedures, Maddala and Wu (1999) argue that the Levin and Lin test is too restrictive to be of interest in practice. While the test of Im *et al.* (1995) relaxes Levin and Lin's assumptions, it presents test results which merely summarise the evidence from a number of independent tests of the sample hypothesis. They subsequently suggest the Fisher test as a panel data unit root test and claim that the Fisher test with bootstrap-based critical values is the preferred choice.

2.2   Cointegration

Cointegration is one of the most important developments in time series econometrics in the last quarter-century. A group of non-stationary $I(1)$ time series is said to have cointegration relationships if a certain linear combination of these time series is stationary. There are two major approaches to testing for cointegration, the Engle–Granger two-step method (Engle and Granger 1987) and the Johansen procedure (Johansen 1988, 1991; Johansen and Juselius 1990). In addition, procedures for panel cointegration (Kao and Chiang 1998; Moon and Phillips 1999; Pedroni 1999) have been recently developed, in the same spirit of panel unit roots and to address similar issues found in unit root tests. Since most panel cointegration tests employ the same estimation methods of, or make minor adjustments to, the asymptotic theory of non-stationary panel data, they are not to be discussed in this chapter. The Engle–Granger method involves first the running regression of one variable on another, and second checking whether the regression residual from the first step is stationary using, say, an ADF test. In this sense, the Engle–Granger method is largely the unit root test and will not be deliberated either. This chapter only presents the Johansen procedure which is to test the restrictions imposed by cointegration on a vector autoregression (VAR) model:

$$\mathbf{y}_t = \boldsymbol{\mu} + \mathbf{A}_1 \mathbf{y}_{t-1} + \cdots + \mathbf{A}_p \mathbf{y}_{t-p} + \boldsymbol{\varepsilon}_t \qquad (10)$$

where $\mathbf{y}_t$ is a k-dimension vector of variables which are assumed to be $I(1)$ series (but can also be $I(0)$), $\mathbf{A}_i, i = 1, \ldots, p$ is the coefficient matrix, and $\mathbf{\varepsilon}_t$ is a k-dimension vector of residuals. Subtracting $\mathbf{y}_{t-1}$ from both sides of equation (10) yields:

$$\Delta \mathbf{y}_t = \mathbf{\mu} + \mathbf{\Pi} \mathbf{y}_{t-1} + \mathbf{\Gamma}_1 \Delta \mathbf{y}_{t-1} + \cdots + \mathbf{\Gamma}_{p-1} \Delta \mathbf{y}_{t-p+1} + \mathbf{\varepsilon}_t \qquad (11)$$

where

$$\mathbf{\Pi} = \sum_{i=1}^{p} \mathbf{A}_i - \mathbf{I}$$

and

$$\mathbf{\Gamma}_i = - \sum_{j=i+1}^{p} \mathbf{A}_j$$

We can observe from equation (11) that only one term in the equation, $\mathbf{\Pi} \mathbf{y}_{t-1}$, is in levels, cointegration relations depend crucially on the property of matrix $\mathbf{\Pi}$. It is clear that $\mathbf{\Pi} \mathbf{y}_{t-1}$ must be either $I(0)$ or zero except that $\mathbf{y}_t$ is already stationary. There are three situations:

1. $\mathbf{\Pi} = \mathbf{\alpha} \mathbf{\beta}'$ has a reduced rank $0 < r < k$;
2. $\mathbf{\Pi} = \mathbf{\alpha} \mathbf{\beta}'$ has a rank of zero; and
3. $\mathbf{\Pi} = \mathbf{\alpha} \mathbf{\beta}'$ has a full rank.

Under situation (1), $\mathbf{\alpha}$ and $\mathbf{\beta}$ are both $k \times r$ matrices and have a rank of r. There are r cointegration vectors $\mathbf{\beta}' \mathbf{y}_t$ which are stationary $I(0)$ series. It is equivalent to having r common trends among $\mathbf{y}_t$. The stationarity of $\mathbf{\beta}' \mathbf{y}_t$ implies a long-run relationship among $\mathbf{y}_t$ or a subset of $\mathbf{y}_t$ – the variables in the cointegration vectors will not depart from each other over time. $\mathbf{\beta}' \mathbf{y}_t$ are also error correction terms, in that, departure of individual variables in the cointegration vectors from the equilibrium will be subsequently reversed back to the equilibrium – a dynamic adjustment process called error correction mechanism (ECM). Equation (11) is therefore called VAR with ECM. Under situation (2), there is no cointegration relation among $\mathbf{y}_t$ and the variables in levels do not enter equation (11) which simply becomes a VAR without ECM. The variables in levels are already stationary under situation (3).

Depending on whether $\mathbf{y}_t$ and/or the cointegration vectors have an intercept and/or deterministic trend, there are five models in practice: (a) there are no deterministic trends in $\mathbf{y}_t$ and no intercepts in the cointegration vectors; (b) there is no deterministic trend in $\mathbf{y}_t$ but there are intercepts in the cointegration vectors; (c) there are deterministic trends in $\mathbf{y}_t$ and intercepts in the cointegration vectors; (d) there are deterministic trends in $\mathbf{y}_t$ and in the cointegration vectors; (e) there are quadratic trends in $\mathbf{y}_t$ and deterministic trends in the cointegration vectors. For details of these specifications, see Johansen and Juselius (1990), and for the critical values of test statistics see Osterwald-Lenum (1992). The Johansen test is a kind of principal component analysis where eigenvalues of $\mathbf{\Pi}$ are calculated through a maximisation procedure. Then, the five specifications or hypotheses are tested using the maximum eigenvalue statistic and the trace statistic which often convey contradictory messages. To test the hypothesis that there are r cointegration vectors against the alternative of $(r + 1)$ cointegration vectors, there is the following maximum eigenvalue statistic:

$$\lambda_{\max} = -T \ln(1 - \hat{\lambda}_{r+1}) \tag{12}$$

where $\hat{\lambda}_r$ is the eigenvalue corresponding to r cointegration vectors and T is the number of observations. The trace statistic is calculated as:

$$\lambda_{\text{trace}} = -T \sum_{i=r+1}^{k} \ln(1 - \hat{\lambda}_i) \tag{13}$$

Indeed, the trace statistic for the existence of r cointegration vectors is the sum of the maximum eigenvalue statistics from zero up to r cointegration vectors.

2.3   Common trends and common cycles

It should be noted that cointegration is not exactly the same as common trend analysis. While cointegration implies common trends, it also requires non-existence of uncommon trends. A group of time series variables can share one or more common trends but the variables are not cointegrated because, for example, one of the variables, y_{2t}, possesses, in addition to the common trends, a trend which is unique to itself and uncommon to others. Under such circumstances, the cointegration vector $\boldsymbol{\beta}'\mathbf{y}_t$ in equation (11) will exclude y_{2t} and it appears that y_{2t} does not share common trends with other variables in $\mathbf{y}_t$. Consider the following k-variable system:

$$\begin{aligned}
y_{1t} &= a_{11}T_{1t} + \cdots + a_{1r}T_{rt} + \tau_{1t} + c_{1t} + \varepsilon_{1t} \\
y_{2t} &= a_{21}T_{1t} + \cdots + a_{2r}T_{rt} + \tau_{2t} + c_{2t} + \varepsilon_{2t} \\
&\vdots \\
y_{kt} &= a_{k1}T_{1t} + \cdots + a_{kr}T_{rt} + \tau_{kt} + c_{kt} + \varepsilon_{kt}
\end{aligned} \tag{14}$$

where $T_{it}, i = 1, \ldots, r$ is the ith common trend, $\tau_{jt}, j = 1, \ldots, k$ is the unique trend in y_{jt}, and $c_{jt}, j = 1, \ldots, k$ is the cycle or stationary component in y_{jt}. If there are no unique trends, that is, $\tau_{jt} = 0, j = 1, \ldots, k$, then from linear algebra we know that a certain linear combination of $y_{jt}, j = 1, \ldots, k$ is zero when $r < k$. So there are only cycles or stationary components, $c_{jt}, j = 1, \ldots, k$, left in the linear combination of $y_{jt}, j = 1, \ldots, k$, which exhibits no trends. This is exactly the idea of cointegration discussed above. When there is unique trend in, for example, y_{2t} (i.e. $\tau_{2t} \neq 0; \tau_{jt} = 0, j \neq 2$), y_{2t} will not be cointegrated with any other variables in the system as any linear combination involving y_{2t} will be non-stationary, though y_{2t} does share common trends with the rest of the variables. It is clear that if y_{2t} does join other variables in $\boldsymbol{\beta}'\mathbf{y}_t$, it must contain no unique trend. For convenience, common trends are treated the same as cointegration in this chapter. That is, unique trends are excluded from analysis.

In the following, we extend cointegration and common trend analysis to the case of cycles. It is said (Engle and Kozicki 1993; Vahid and Engle 1993; Engle and Issler 1995) there are common cycles (in the same spirit, uncommon cycles are excluded from analysis) among $\mathbf{y}_t$ in equation (10) if there exists a vector $\tilde{\boldsymbol{\beta}}$ such that:

$$\tilde{\boldsymbol{\beta}}'\mathbf{y}_t = \tilde{\boldsymbol{\beta}}'\boldsymbol{\varepsilon}_t \tag{15}$$

That is, a combination of the time series in $\mathbf{y}_t$ exhibits no cyclical movement or fluctuation. Common trends and common cycles are two major common factors driving economic and financial variables to move and develop in a related way.[3] It is therefore helpful to inspect them together in a unified dynamic system.

According to the Wold representation theorem, time series or a vector of time series can be expressed as an infinite moving average process:

$$\Delta \mathbf{y}_t = \mathbf{C}(\mathbf{L})\boldsymbol{\varepsilon}_t, \quad \mathbf{C}(\mathbf{L}) = \mathbf{I} + \mathbf{C}_1\mathbf{L} + \mathbf{C}_2\mathbf{L}^2 + \cdots \tag{16}$$

$\mathbf{C}(\mathbf{L})$ can be decomposed as $\mathbf{C}(1) + (1-L)\mathbf{C}^*(\mathbf{L})$, therefore:

$$\Delta \mathbf{y}_t = \mathbf{C}(1)\boldsymbol{\varepsilon}_t + (1-L)\mathbf{C}^*(\mathbf{L})\boldsymbol{\varepsilon}_t, \quad \mathbf{C}_i^* = \sum_{j>i} -\mathbf{C}_j, \quad \mathbf{C}_0^* = \mathbf{I} - \mathbf{C}(1) \tag{17}$$

Taking the summation to get the variables in levels:

$$\mathbf{y}_t = \mathbf{C}(1)\sum_{i=0}^{\infty} \boldsymbol{\varepsilon}_{t-i} + \mathbf{C}^*(\mathbf{L})\varepsilon_t \tag{18}$$

Equation (18) is the Stock and Watson (1988) multivariate generalisation of the Beveridge and Nelson (1981) trend-cycle decomposition and is referred to as the BNSW decomposition. Common trends in the sense of cointegration require:

$$\boldsymbol{\beta}'\mathbf{C}(1) = 0 \tag{19}$$

and common cycles require:

$$\tilde{\boldsymbol{\beta}}'\mathbf{C}^*(\mathbf{L}) = 0 \tag{20}$$

Equation (18) can be written as the sum of two components of trends and cycles:

$$\mathbf{y}_t = \mathbf{T}_t + \mathbf{C}_t \tag{21}$$

When the sum of the rank of $\boldsymbol{\beta}$, r, and the rank of $\tilde{\boldsymbol{\beta}}$, s, is equal to k, the stack of $\boldsymbol{\beta}$ and $\tilde{\boldsymbol{\beta}}$ is a $k \times k$ full rank matrix:

$$\mathbf{B} = \begin{bmatrix} \boldsymbol{\beta} & \tilde{\boldsymbol{\beta}} \end{bmatrix} \tag{22}$$

and trends and cycles can be exclusively expressed in the common factor coefficient vectors, $\boldsymbol{\beta}$ and $\tilde{\boldsymbol{\beta}}$, and their combinations. According to equations (19) and (20):

$$\begin{bmatrix} \boldsymbol{\beta} & \tilde{\boldsymbol{\beta}} \end{bmatrix}' \mathbf{y}_t = \begin{bmatrix} \boldsymbol{\beta}' \mathbf{y}_t \\ \tilde{\boldsymbol{\beta}}' \mathbf{y}_t \end{bmatrix} = \begin{bmatrix} \boldsymbol{\beta}' \mathbf{C}^*(\mathbf{L}) \boldsymbol{\varepsilon}_t \\ \tilde{\boldsymbol{\beta}}' \mathbf{C}(1) \displaystyle\sum_{i=0}^{\infty} \boldsymbol{\varepsilon}_{t-i} \end{bmatrix}$$

So

$$\mathbf{y}_t = \begin{bmatrix} \boldsymbol{\beta}' \\ \tilde{\boldsymbol{\beta}}' \end{bmatrix}^{-1} \begin{bmatrix} \boldsymbol{\beta}' \mathbf{C}^*(\mathbf{L}) \boldsymbol{\varepsilon}_t \\ \tilde{\boldsymbol{\beta}}' \mathbf{C}(1) \displaystyle\sum_{i=0}^{\infty} \boldsymbol{\varepsilon}_{t-i} \end{bmatrix} \tag{23}$$

Defining $\mathbf{B}^{-1} = \begin{bmatrix} \boldsymbol{\beta}^{-1} & \tilde{\boldsymbol{\beta}}^{-1} \end{bmatrix}$ and refer to equation (18), we have:[4]

$$\mathbf{y}_t = \begin{bmatrix} \boldsymbol{\beta}^{-1} & \tilde{\boldsymbol{\beta}}^{-1} \end{bmatrix} \begin{bmatrix} \boldsymbol{\beta}' \boldsymbol{\beta}^*(\mathbf{L}) \boldsymbol{\varepsilon}_t \\ \tilde{\boldsymbol{\beta}}' \mathbf{C}(1) \displaystyle\sum_{i=0}^{\infty} \boldsymbol{\varepsilon}_{t-i} \end{bmatrix}$$

$$= \boldsymbol{\beta}^{-1} \boldsymbol{\beta}' \mathbf{C}^*(\mathbf{L}) \boldsymbol{\varepsilon}_t + \tilde{\boldsymbol{\beta}}^{-1} \tilde{\boldsymbol{\beta}}' \mathbf{C}(1) \sum_{i=0}^{\infty} \boldsymbol{\varepsilon}_{t-i}$$

$$= \boldsymbol{\beta}^{-1} \boldsymbol{\beta}' \mathbf{y}_t + \tilde{\boldsymbol{\beta}}^{-1} \tilde{\boldsymbol{\beta}}' \mathbf{y}_t = \mathbf{C}_t + \mathbf{T}_t \tag{24}$$

Therefore, we get $\mathbf{C}_t = \boldsymbol{\beta}^{-1} \boldsymbol{\beta}' \mathbf{y}_t$ and $\mathbf{T}_t = \tilde{\boldsymbol{\beta}}^{-1} \tilde{\boldsymbol{\beta}}' \mathbf{y}_t$, exclusively expressed in the common factor coefficient vectors, $\boldsymbol{\beta}$ and $\tilde{\boldsymbol{\beta}}$, and their combinations.

2.4 Examples and cases

It is probably not worthwhile demonstrating any unit root test examples individually nowadays since these tests have been made straightforwardly simple. Nevertheless, unit root tests are still routine procedures prior to cointegration analysis, that is, studies of cointegration will almost inevitably involve unit root tests. Accordingly, one case on cointegration and one on common cycles, which largely cover the topics of this chapter, are presented in the following.

Example 1

This is a case on dynamic links and interactions between American Depository Receipts (ADRs) and their underlying foreign stocks by Kim *et al.* (2000). ADRs are certificates issued by US banks which represent indirect ownership of a certain number of shares in a specific foreign firm. Shares are held on deposit in the firm's home bank. ADRs are traded in US dollars and investors receive dividends in US dollars too. Therefore, returns on ADRs reflect the domestic returns on the stock as well as the exchange rate effect. ADRs have become popular in the US due to their diversification benefits, especially when US investors have little knowledge in foreign countries' business and political systems and, risks associated with investing in foreign securities may thus be overestimated.

In addition to the factors of underlying foreign stocks and the exchange rate, the paper has also considered the influence of the US stock market on ADR returns. To this end, they use the cointegration approach and other models to examine the effect on ADRs of the three factors. Their results show that the price of the underlying stock is most important, whereas the exchange rate and the US market also have an impact on ADR prices. We only present results related to cointegration analysis of 21 British firms. The data set used in the paper is daily closing prices from 4 January 1988 to 31 December 1991.

The first thing to do prior to cointegration tests is almost a routine check on whether there is a unit root in the time series data, as we require $I(1)$ series to carry out cointegration analysis. The paper adopts the ADF test to examine the existence of a unit root, with the critical values being taken from Davidson and Mackinnon (1993), obtained from a much larger set of simulations than those tabulated by Dickey and Fuller. The lag length in the ADF test is chosen such that the Q-statistic at 36 lags indicates no serial correlation in the residuals. The lag length can also be chosen by using the Akaike information criterion (AIC) or the Schwarz criterion (SC), or more ideally, a combination of the Q-statistic and one of the AIC or the SC which, though, may produce non-conciliatory recommendations. It can be seen from Table 2.1 that all the series, except series 8 and 19 (interestingly both ADRs and underlying stocks), have a unit root in levels and no unit root in the first difference. Although the null hypothesis of a unit root is rejected for series 8 and 19 in levels, the rejection is at a rather low 10 per cent significance level. So, all the series are treated as $I(0)$ and cointegration analysis can be carried out for all of them. In Table 2.2, the exchange rate and one of the US stock market indices, S&P 500, are also confirmed to be $I(1)$ series, and can be included in cointegration analysis as well.

The results of cointegration analysis between ADRs, corresponding foreign stocks, the exchange rate and the S&P 500 index are reported in Table 2.3. The lag length k is chosen by Sims' likelihood ratio test. Both trace and eigenvalue test statistics indicate that for each of 21 groups, there exists at least one cointegrating relationship among the variables. Nine groups have at least two and three groups have at least three cointegrating relationships. Each group's cointegrating vector is calculated and incorporated in the VAR to form a VAR–ECM model. Based

Table 2.1 ADF unit root tests – ADRs and underlying foreign stocks, UK

Firm	ADR		Underlying	
	Level	First difference	Level	First difference
1	−2.559	−35.842***	−2.461	−22.132***
2	−1.245	−13.821***	−1.725	−19.753***
3	−1.652	−14.873***	−1.823	−12.694***
4	−2.235	−15.985***	−1.927	−13.346***
5	−1.985	−26.879***	−1.969	−28.566***
6	−2.237	−27.522***	−1.878	−25.997***
7	−2.334	−20.464***	−1.200	−23.489***
8	−2.652*	−30.435***	−2.800*	−29.833***
9	−1.287	−10.156***	−2.382	−14.489***
10	−1.823	−26.372***	−1.014	−21.788***
11	−1.021	−27.825***	−1.087	−19.482***
12	−1.934	−29.225***	−2.425	−27.125***
13	−2.324	−13.223***	−1.894	−12.854***
14	−1.997	−17.325***	−1.823	−16.478***
15	−1.333	−11.528***	−1.458	−37.311***
16	−1.223	−10.285***	−1.253	−18.244***
17	−1.110	−16.742***	−2.182	−33.245***
18	−1.559	−14.522***	−1.285	−17.354***
19	−2.678*	−22.485***	−2.677*	−15.660***
20	−1.546	−14.266***	−1.024	−14.266***
21	−2.364	−22.333***	−1.625	−24.757***

Source: Asymptotic critical values are from Davidson and Mackinnon (1993). Lag length k is chosen such that the Q-statistic at 36 lags indicates absence of autocorrelation in the residuals. Estimation period is 4 January 1988–31 December 1991.

Notes
  * Significant at the 10% level.
 ** Significant at the 5% level.
*** Significant at the 1% level.

Table 2.2 ADF unit root tests – the exchange rate and the S&P 500 index

	Level	First difference
£ via-à-vis $	−1.625	−19.124***
S&P 500 index	−2.115	−20.254***

Source: Asymptotic critical values are from Davidson and Mackinnon (1993). Lag length k is chosen such that the Q-statistic at 36 lags indicates absence of autocorrelation in the residuals. Estimation period is 4 January 1988–31 December 1991.

Note
  * Significant at the 10% level.
 ** Significant at the 5% level.
*** Significant at the 1% level.

Table 2.3 Johansen multivariate cointegration tests – United Kingdom

Firm	Trace				λ_{max}			
	$r = 0$	$r \leq 1$	$r \leq 2$	$r \leq 3$	$r = 0$	$r \leq 1$	$r \leq 2$	$r \leq 3$
1	91.22***	21.28	2.95	1.04	70.11***	10.09	1.89	1.04
2	52.18***	12.45	6.06	1.25	36.37***	10.65	4.75	1.25
3	68.02***	20.24	5.79	0.50	84.67***	12.34	5.00	0.50
4	105.24***	28.45*	7.64	1.25	96.77***	19.65*	6.75	1.25
5	45.33*	11.02	1.24	0.37	39.32***	9.88	1.05	0.37
6	163.26***	32.84**	9.75	3.94	141.21***	27.87***	13.25**	3.94
7	85.24***	19.45	2.25	1.00	66.47***	10.65	1.75	1.00
8	150.33***	30.02*	8.24	3.54	120.32***	20.78*	6.45	3.54
9	49.23***	12.02	1.29	0.98	29.32**	9.78	9.24	0.98
10	50.24**	13.45	1.54	1.08	46.37***	10.65	3.25	1.08
11	190.33***	38.02***	18.24***	3.99	145.31***	28.88**	11.48	3.99
12	96.96***	21.84	3.00	1.52	72.50***	12.09	2.69	1.52
13	150.24***	30.00*	7.34	3.24	120.22***	20.74*	5.45	3.24
14	199.43***	42.02***	19.24***	4.57	150.32***	38.99***	18.45***	4.57
15	153.33***	31.25**	8.66	3.25	125.43***	21.27**	5.75	3.25
16	81.43***	21.34	5.24	2.08	52.45***	17.24	3.78	2.08
17	210.24***	68.24***	21.78***	4.02	139.32***	34.28***	16.27**	4.02
18	62.96***	13.11	1.75	0.99	42.11***	10.09	1.29	0.99
19	49.24**	9.92	1.24	0.61	27.88**	8.45	1.05	0.61
20	120.33***	24.91	6.24	2.01	84.56***	15.74	3.45	2.01
21	173.86***	33.24**	8.03	4.06	121.54***	33.34***	10.49	4.06

Source: The cointegration equation is based on four variables: (1) British ADRs, (2) British underlying shares, (3) British pound spot exchange rates and (4) the S&P 500 index cash prices. Estimation period is 4 January 1988–31 December 1991.

Notes
* Significant at the 10% level.
** Significant at the 5% level.
*** Significant at the 1% level.

on the estimated VAR–ECM model, the paper has further performed variance decomposition and impulse response analysis which are beyond the reach of this chapter.[5] While cointegration analysis indicates a dynamic adjustment process and long-run equilibrium relationship among ADRs and the three factors, results from variance decomposition and impulse response suggest that the largest effect on ADRs is due to shocks in their underlying stocks. Nevertheless, the exchange rate also has a role and that role is growing in recent years. The effect of the US stock market has been found but the effect is small. More likely, the last link might be superficial and due to a common factor driving both the US and foreign markets or the US stock market and the foreign exchange market.

Example 2

This is an example mainly on common cycles, but also covers common trends, among annual sectoral per-capita real GNP of the US economy 1947–1989, from a paper entitled 'Estimating common sectoral cycles' by Engle and Issler (1995). The sectors examined are Agriculture, forestry and fisheries, Mining, Manufacturing, Construction, Wholesale and retail, Transportation and public utilities, Finance, insurance and real estate, and Services.

The paper does not check for unit roots itself; instead it cites the results of Durlauf (1989) that the sectoral GNP data are $I(1)$ processes. The first set of empirical results is on cointegration or common trends, and the second set of results is on common cycles. Table 2.4 reports the cointegration results which show that there are two cointegration vectors, judged by both the trace and maximum eigenvalue test statistics, adopting the model with unrestricted intercept and a linear time trend. The trace statistic also points to a third cointegration relation at a low significance level. The paper then sets up a VAR–ECM model of two cointegration vectors to investigate the dynamics among the sectors.

The common cycle test is based on canonical correlation[6] and the results are reported in Table 2.5. They are interpreted in this way: the number of common

Table 2.4 Cointegration results – Johansen's approach (1988)

No. of CI vectors	λ_{max}	5% critical value	Trace	5% critical value
At most 7	1.9	3.7	1.9	3.7
At most 6	10.5	16.9	12.4	18.2
At most 5	15.5	23.8	27.6	34.5
At most 4	20.3	30.3	47.9	54.6
At most 3	25.3	36.4	73.2	77.7
At most 2	32.9	42.5	106.1**	104.9
At most 1	68.4***	48.4	174.5***	136.6
At most 0	108.4***	54.2	282.8***	170.8

Notes
  * Significant at the 10% level.
 ** Significant at the 5% level.
*** Significant at the 1% level.

Table 2.5 Common cycle results

No. of common cycles	Squared canonical correlation ρ_i^2	Pr > F
8 ($\rho_i^2 = 0, i = 1, \ldots, 8$)	0.9674	0.0001
7 ($\rho_i^2 = 0, i = 1, \ldots, 7$)	0.8949	0.0113
6 ($\rho_i^2 = 0, i = 1, \ldots, 6$)	0.7464	0.4198
5 ($\rho_i^2 = 0, i = 1, \ldots, 5$)	0.5855	0.7237
4 ($\rho_i^2 = 0, i = 1, \ldots, 4$)	0.5130	0.7842
3 ($\rho_i^2 = 0, i = 1, \ldots, 3$)	0.4367	0.8088
2 ($\rho_i^2 = 0, i = 1, \ldots, 2$)	0.3876	0.7922
1 ($\rho_i^2 = 0$)	0.2775	0.7848

cycle relations is the number of zero canonical correlations. Since the test statistic (2nd column) rejects that five canonical correlations are zero and cannot reject that six or more canonical correlations are zero, the number of common cycle relations is decided to be six. To find a larger number of common factor relations must be rather confusing. Adeptly, the paper suggests that very similar cyclical behaviour for sectors be observed without going into the details of these common cycle vector coefficients.

Because the sum of the number of cointegration or common trend relations and the number of common cycle relations is eight – the number of sectors or variables in the VAR, trends and cycles can be expressed exclusively in the common factor coefficient vectors and their combinations. Table 2.5 presents these vectors – six of them are common cycle coefficient vectors and two of them common trend coefficient vectors.

2.5   Empirical literature

Research on unit roots and tests for stationarity is one of the frontiers in contemporary time series econometrics. The distinction between stationary and non-stationary time series data can reflect, explicitly or implicitly, the economic or financial characteristics and attributes of the data. For example, if the current state or value of a variable is derived through accumulation of all previous increases (decreases as negative increases) in its value, then this variable is almost certainly non-stationary. If a variable is a relative measure, for example, the growth rate in GDP, or the rate of return on a stock, which has nothing to do with its history, then it is more likely to be stationary, though non-stationarity cannot be ruled out when there is non-trivial change in the rate (acceleration or deceleration). For some other relative measures, such as dividend yields (dividend/price), the proportion of public sector borrowing requirement in GDP (PSBR/GDP), or asset turnover (sales/asset value), it is an empirical matter whether the time series data are stationary or not. Indeed, stationarity of this type of relative measures amounts to cointegration, with the cointegration vector being restricted to [1, −1], between the two variables involved in the construction of the measure (when logarithms are taken). So, we derive the concept of cointegration, another frontier in time series econometrics, in a very natural way, closely related to real world phenomena. Extending this relative measure to cross-sections, for example, data of different entities, we have cointegration in general forms, to examine whether these entities progress in pace or proportionally in the long run. As a result, tests for unit roots and cointegration infer the attributes of economic and financial variables and their relationships reflected by the characteristics of time series data. To a lesser significant extent, there is research in common cycles that two or more variables, which are stationary, move in a rather similar way in the short term.

Much research on the subjects focuses on both economic analysis and financial markets, in a variety of application areas. So let us start with the interest rate and the exchange rate which are to the common interest of most economic and financial variables. Examining well-known international parity conditions of covered interest parity (CIP), uncovered interest parity (UIP), the forward rate hypothesis (FRH), and the international Fisher effect (IFE), Turtle and Abeysekera (1996) adopt cointegration procedures to test the validity of these hypotheses implied by the cointegration relationship between spot rates, forward rates, interest rates and inflation rates using monthly data from January 1975 to August 1990 for Canada, Germany, Japan and the UK against the US. They claim that the cointegration test results generally support the relationships considered. In a more focused study, MacDonald and Nagayasu (2000) investigate the long-run relationship between real exchange rates and real interest rate differentials with a panel data set consisting of 14 industrialised countries, over the recent floating period. Similar to a few of other empirical studies with panel data, the procedure of panel unit root and cointegration tests tends to favour stationarity with which the paper finds evidence of statistically significant long-run relationships between real exchange rates and real interest rate differentials. Likewise, Wu and Fountas (2000) suggest bilateral real interest rate convergence between the US and the rest of the G7 countries, and Felmingham *et al.* (2000) find interdependence between the Australian short-term real interest rates and those of the US, Japan, the UK, Canada, Germany and New Zealand during 1970 and 1997, after accommodating regime shifts in the time series. Fountas and Wu (1999) show similar findings of real interest rate convergence among European monetary mechanism countries for the period of 1979–1993. Chiang and Kim (2000) present a set of empirical results for Eurocurrency market rates. They find that the domestic short-term interest rate is cointegrated with longer term interest rates of a particular country; and the domestic short-term interest rate is also cointegrated with the comparable foreign short-term interest rate adjusted for the foreign exchange forward premium/discount. They consequently set up an error correction model including both cointegration vectors, and claim that the model shows improvements in explaining short-term interest rate movements. Extending research in foreign exchange rates to a non-standard setting, Siddiki (2000) examines the determinants of black market exchange rates in India using annual data from 1955 to 1994 in the framework of unit root and cointegration analysis. The paper confirms that the import capacity of official foreign exchange reserves and restrictions on international trade are two important determinants of black market rates in India. It finds that black market rates are negatively affected by a low level of official foreign exchange reserves and positively affected by a high level of trade restrictions, as well as interest rate policies. Of more practical orientation is a study by Darrat *et al.* (1998) on the possible link between the mortgage loan rate and the deposit rate, and the question of which rate leads the other. While the deposit-cost mark-up theory suggests that the cost of attracting funds (deposit rates) determines prices (mortgage loan rates), mortgage loan rates may induce changes in deposit interest rates via a mechanism of the reverse chain of events. The authors employ cointegration and Granger causality tests to empirically examine these alternative hypotheses, using monthly data over the period 1970–1994. The results appear to accommodate both hypotheses, that there exists a bidirectional causality between mortgage loan rates and deposit interest rates in an error correction model where the two types of rates exhibit a cointegration relationship. Many recent studies of the kind can be found, for example, in Toma (1999), Wright (2000), Cheng (1999), Pesaran *et al.* (2000), and Koustas and Serletis (1999).

Research on long-run relationships in stock markets is controversial in that it constitutes a contest to market efficiency. Adopting a pragmatic stance in empirical analysis, Harasty and Roulet (2000) employ the Engle–Granger two-step method for cointegration analysis and error correction modelling of stock market movements in 17 countries. They present in- and out-of-sample tests of the model's ability to forecast future stock market returns, and their results, it is claimed, indicate that the error correction model does have predictive power and can thus be a useful tool in the investment decision process. A long-run cointegration relationship has also been found to exist in Eastern European stock markets between 1995 and 1997 by Jochum *et al.* (1999). They report that the cointegration relationship has disappeared after the 1997 stock market crisis. With a total sample period of three years and the post-crisis sub-period of only one year, these results can hardly have helpful implications, though the problem is mainly due to the availability of data. Olienyk *et al.* (1999) attempt to avoid the problems of non-synchronous trading, fluctuations in foreign exchange rates, non-liquidity, trading restrictions and index replication by using World equity benchmark shares (WEBS) to effectively represent the world's stock markets. They observe that a long-run relationship exists among the 18 market indices, as well as between individual closed-end country funds and their own country's WEBS. They further find that there exists short-term Granger causality between these series, implying market inefficiencies and short-term arbitrage opportunities. In an effort to explain market efficiency in the context of cointegration, Hassapis *et al.* (1999) extend the work of Dwyer and Wallace (1992) through investigating the linkages among international commodity markets in the long run and the short term. Efficiency in these markets requires that the corresponding real exchange rates be martingales with respect to any information set available in the public domain. In a VAR consisting only of real exchange rates, it is shown that the necessary and sufficient conditions for joint efficiency of all the markets under consideration amount to the VAR being of order one (Markovness) and non-cointegrated. On the contrary, in a VAR extended by other potentially 'relevant' variables, such as the corresponding real interest rates, non-cointegration and Markovness are only sufficient conditions for the same commodity markets to be characterised as jointly efficient.

In labour market studies, the relationships between wage costs and employment have been subject to extensive scrutiny for many decades. The new techniques of unit root tests and cointegration offer an additional dimension to the research in terms of the long-run characteristics of wages and employment and the long-run relationship between wages and employment. In this framework, Bender and Theodossiou (1999) investigate the relationship between employment and real wages for 10 countries since 1950. Their results suggest that there is little evidence of cointegration between real wages and employment and consequently reject the neoclassical hypothesis of a long-run relationship between these two important variables. Including more variables in the analysis of the Mexican labour market, Lopez (1999) finds cointegration relationships between employment and output, and among nominal wages, minimum wages, the price index and labour productivity. The results do not directly contradict those of Bender and Theodossiou (1999) but they offer explanations to the dynamic adjustment of employment and wages to a set of macroeconomic variables. Similarly, Carstensen and Hansen (2000), using a structural VAR incorporating cointegration, find two common trends, which push unemployment, in the West German labour market.

Various other recent application examples cover the examination of the Fisher effect by Koustas and Serletis (1999) in Belgium, Canada, Denmark, France, Germany, Greece, Ireland, Japan, the Netherlands, the UK and the US with results generally rejecting the Fisher hypothesis, and by Malliaropulos (2000) for the US who supports the hypothesis; interactions between the stock market and macroeconomic variables by Choi *et al.* (1999) who suggest that stock markets help predict industrial production in the US, UK, Japan and Canada out of the G7, and by Nasseh and Strauss (2000) where not only domestic, but also international, macroeconomic variables enter the cointegration vectors to share long-run relationships with stock prices; long-run relationships between real estate as represented by REITs, and the bond market and stock market by Glascock *et al.* (2000); and joint efficiency of the US stock market and foreign exchange markets by Rapp *et al.* (1999). It requires a very long list indeed to cover all the studies in these areas.

Questions and problems

1 Discuss the concept of stationarity and non-stationarity in relation to the characteristics of financial variables, for example, prices and returns are the accumulation of income (dividends) over time, so are their statistical properties.
2 Describe a unit root process and show that it does not have a constant limited variance.
3 Discuss the cointegration relationship in econometrics and the comovement of certain non-stationary financial and economic variables, for example, dividends

and prices, inflation and nominal interest rates, and industrial production and stock market returns.

4 What are the features of common cycles in contrast to common trends and cointegration?

5 Discuss the common cycle relationship in econometrics and the comovement of certain stationary variables in economics and finance.

6 Discuss in what circumstances cointegration implies market inefficiency and in what circumstances cointegration means market efficiency.

7 Collect data from Datastream to test for unit roots in the following time series:

a GDP of the UK, US, Japan, China, Russia and Brazil in logarithms;
b total return series of IBM, Microsoft, Sage, Motorola, Intel, Vodafone and Telefonica in logarithms;
c nominal interests in selected countries.

What do you find of their characteristics?

8 Test for unit roots in the above time series in log differences. What do you find of their characteristics?

9 Collect data from Datastream to test for cointegration between the following pairs:

a the sterling *vis-à-vis* US$ exchange rates, spot and 30 days forward;
b Tesco and Sainbury's share prices;
c UK underlying RPI and the Bank of England base rate.

Discuss your findings.

Notes

1 Readers familiar with difference equations, deterministic and/or stochastic, would understand this easily. Equation (6) also has a pole at $p = \infty$, which is not as important in relation to the topic.

2 Precisely, it is the spectrum obtained from letting Δy_t pass a rectangular window of size M.

3 Other common factors include regime shifts, see, for example, co-break in Hendry and Mizon (1998).

4 Notice β^{-1} is not the inverse matrix of β (such inverse matrix does not exist), it is simply the first r columns of $\mathbf{B}^{-1} = \begin{bmatrix} \beta' \\ \tilde{\beta}' \end{bmatrix}^{-1}$, similarly $\tilde{\beta}^{-1}$ is the last s columns of $\mathbf{B}^{-1}$.

5 We can introduce briefly the ideas of variance decomposition and impulse response here. Variance decomposition is to inspect the contributions to one sector's variance from all other sectors, including itself, so the relative importance of these sectors can be evaluated. Impulse response analysis is to examine the impact of a unit shock in one sector on the other; similar to variance decomposition, the influence of one sector on the other and the relative importance of all the sectors to an individual sector can be evaluated. Both impulse response and variance decomposition, especially the former, are usually carried out over a long time horizon; and impulse response is normally presented in the form of visual graphs.

6 A technique similar to, if at all appropriate, Johansen's multivariate cointegration analysis is its stationary counterpart. The technique is not widely applied as more than one

common cycle relation, similar to more than one cointegration relation, is difficult to be conferred a meaningful economic interpretation. If feasible, pairwise analysis will usually be applied.

References

Bender, K. A. and Theodossiou, I. (1999), International comparisons of the real wage–employment relationship, *Journal of Post-Keynesian Economics*, 21, 621–637.

Beveridge, S. and Nelson, C. R. (1981), A new approach to decomposition of economic time series into permanent and transitory components with particular attention to measurement of the 'business cycles', *Journal of Monetary Economics*, 7, 151–174.

Carstensen, K. and Hansen, G. (2000), Cointegration and common trends on the West German labour market, *Empirical Economics*, 25, 475–493.

Cheng, B. S. (1999), Beyond the purchasing power parity: testing for cointegration and causality between exchange rates, prices, and interest rates, *Journal of International Money and Finance*, 18, 911–924.

Chiang, T. C. and Kim, D. (2000), Short-term Eurocurrency rate behavior and specifications of cointegrating processes, *International Review of Economics and Finance*, 9, 157–179.

Choi, J. J., Hauser, S. and Kopecky, K. J. (1999), Does the stock market predict real activity? Time series evidence from the G-7 countries, *Journal of Banking and Finance*, 23, 1771–1792.

Darrat, A. F., Dickens, R. N. and Glascock, J. L. (1998), Mortgage loan rates and deposit costs: are they reliably linked? *Journal of Real Estate Finance and Economics*, 16, 27–42.

Davidson, R. and Mackinnon, J. G. (1993), *Estimation and Inference in Econometrics*, Oxford University Press, England.

Dickey, D. A. and Fuller, W. A. (1979), Distribution of the estimators for autoregressive time series with a unit root, *Journal of the American Statistical Association*, 74, 427–431.

Dickey, D. A. and Fuller, W. A. (1981), The likelihood ratio statistics for autoregressive time series with a unit root, *Econometrica*, 49, 1057–1072.

Durlauf, S. N. (1989), Output persistence, economic structure, and the choice of stabilisation policy, *Brookings Papers in Economic Activity*, 2, 69–136.

Dwyer, G. P. Jr. and Wallace, M. S. (1992), Cointegration and market efficiency, *Journal of International Money and Finance*, 11, 318–327.

Engle, R. F. and Granger, C. W. J. (1987), Co-integration and error correction: Representation, estimation, and testing, *Econometrica*, 55, 251–267.

Engle, R. F. and Issler, J. V. (1995), Estimating common sectoral cycles, *Journal of Monetary Economics*, 35, 83–113.

Engle, R. F. and Kozicki, S. (1993), Testing for common features, *Journal of Business and Economic Statistics*, 11, 369–395.

Felmingham, B., Qing, Z. and Healy, T. (2000), The interdependence of Australian and foreign real interest rates, *Economic Record*, 76, 163–171.

Fountas, S. and Wu, J. L. (1999), Testing for real interest rate convergence in European countries, *Scottish Journal of Political Economy*, 46, 158–174.

Glascock, J. L., Lu, C. and So, R. W. (2000), Further evidence on the integration of REIT, bond, and stock returns, *Journal of Real Estate Finance and Economics*, 20, 177–194.

Harasty, H. and Roulet, J. (2000), Modelling stock market returns, *Journal of Portfolio Management*, 26(2), 33–46.

Hassapis, C., Kalyvitis, S. C. and Pittis, N. (1999), Cointegration and joint efficiency of international commodity markets, *Quarterly Review of Economics and Finance*, 39, 213–231.

Hendry, D. F. and Mizon, G. E. (1998), Exogeneity, causality, and co-breaking in economic policy analysis of a small econometric model of money in the UK, *Empirical Economics*, 23, 267–294.

Im, K. S., Pesaran, M. H. and Shin, Y. (1995), Testing for unit roots in heterogeneous panels, *University of Cambridge, Department of Applied Economics Working Paper, Amalgamated Series*: 95-26.

Jochum, C., Kirchgassner, G. and Platek, M. (1999), A long-run relationship between Eastern European stock markets? Cointegration and the 1997/98 crisis in emerging markets, *Weltwirtschaftliches Archiv – Review of World Economics*, 135, 454–479.

Johansen, S. (1988), Statistical analysis of cointegration vectors, *Journal of Economic Dynamics and Control*, 12, 231–254.

Johansen, S. (1991), Estimation and hypothesis testing of cointegration vectors in Gaussian vector autoregressive models, *Econometrica*, 59, 1551–1580.

Johansen, S. and Juselius, K. (1990), Maximum likelihood estimation and inference on cointegration – with applications to the demand for money, *Oxford Bulletin of Economics and Statistics*, 52, 169–210.

Kao, C. and Chiang, M. H. (1998), On the estimation and inference of a cointegrated regression in panel data, *Centre for Policy Research Working Paper, Syracuse University*.

Kim, M., Szakmary, A. C. and Mathur, I. (2000), Price transmission dynamics between ADRs and their underlying foreign securities, *Journal of Banking and Finance*, 24, 1359–1382.

Koustas, Z. and Serletis, A. (1999), On the Fisher effect, *Journal of Monetary Economics*, 44, 105–130.

Kwiatkowski, D., Phillips, P. C. B., Schmidt, P. and Shin, Y. (1992), Testing the null hypothesis of stationarity against the alternative of a unit root: How sure are we that economic time series have a unit root? *Journal of Econometrics*, 54, 159–178.

Levin, A. and Lin, C. F. (1992), Unit root tests in panel data: Asymptotic and finite sample properties, *University of California, San Diego Department of Economics Working Paper*: 92-23.

Levin, A. and Lin, C. F. (1993), Unit root tests in panel data: New results, *University of California, San Diego Department of Economics Working Paper*: 93-56.

Lopez, G. J. (1999), The macroeconomics of employment and wages in Mexico, *Labour*, 13, 859–878.

MacDonald, R. and Nagayasu, J. (2000), The long-run relationship between real exchange rates and real interest rate differentials: A panel study, *IMF Staff Papers*, 47, 116–128.

Maddala, G. S. and Wu, S. (1999), A comparative study of unit root tests with panel data and a new simple test, *Oxford Bulletin of Economics and Statistics*, 61(0) (Special issue), 631–652.

Malliaropulos, D. (2000), A note on nonstationarity, structural breaks, and the Fisher effect, *Journal of Banking and Finance*, 24, 695–707.

Moon, H. R. and Phillips, P. C. B. (1999), Maximum likelihood estimation in panels with incidental trends, *Oxford Bulletin of Economics and Statistics*, 60(0) (Special issue), 711–747.

Nasseh, A. and Strauss, J. (2000), Stock prices and domestic and international macroeconomic activity: A cointegration approach, *Quarterly Review of Economics and Finance*, 40, 229–245.

Olienyk, J. P., Schwebach, R. G. and Zumwalt, J. K. (1999), WEBS, SPDRs, and country funds: An analysis of international cointegration, *Journal of Multinational Financial Management*, 9, 217–232.

Osterwald-Lenum, M. (1992), A note with quantiles of the asymptotic distribution of the maximum likelihood cointegration rank test statistics, *Oxford Bulletin of Economics and Statistics*, 54, 461–472.

Pedroni, P. (1999), Critical values for cointegration tests in heterogeneous panels with multiple regressors, *Oxford Bulletin of Economics and Statistics*, 61(0) (Special issue), 653–670.

Pesaran, M. H., Shin, Y. and Smith, R. J. (2000), Structural analysis of vector error correction models with exogenous I(1) variables, *Journal of Econometrics*, 97, 293–343.

Phillips, P. C. B. and Perron, P. (1988), Testing for a unit root in time series regression, *Biometrika*, 75, 335–346.

Rapp, T. A., Parker, M. E. and Phillips, M. D. (1999), An empirical investigation of the joint efficiency of the U.S. stock and foreign exchange markets, *Journal of Economics*, 25, 63–71.

Siddiki, J. U. (2000), Black market exchange rates in India: An empirical analysis, *Empirical Economics*, 25, 297–313.

Stock, J. H. and Watson, M. W. (1988), Testing for common trends, *Journal of the American Statistical Association*, 83, 1097–1107.

Toma, M. (1999), A positive model of reserve requirements and interest on reserves: A clearinghouse interpretation of the Federal Reserve System, *Southern Economic Journal*, 66, 101–116.

Turtle, H. J. and Abeysekera, S. P. (1996), An empirical examination of long run relationships in international markets, *Journal of Multinational Financial Management*, 6, 109–134.

Vahid, F. and Engle, R. F. (1993), Common trends and common cycles, *Journal of Applied Econometrics*, 8, 341–360.

Wright, G. (2000), Spot and period rates in the wet bulk shipping market: Testing for long-run parity, *Journal of Transport Economics and Policy*, 34, 291–300.

Wu, J. L. and Fountas, S. (2000), Real interest rate parity under regime shifts and implications for monetary policy, *The Manchester School of Economic and Social Studies*, 68, 685–700.

3 Time-varying volatility models – GARCH and stochastic volatility

Time-varying volatility models have been popular since the early 1990s in empirical research in finance, following an influential paper 'Generalized Autoregressive Conditional Heteroskedasticity' by Bollerslev (1986). Models of this type are well known as generalised autoregressive conditional heteroscedasticity (GARCH) in the time series econometrics literature. Time-varying volatility has been observed and documented in as early as 1982 (Engle 1982) and was initially concerned with an economic phenomenon – time-varying and autoregressive variance of inflation. Nevertheless, it was data availability and strong empirical research interest in finance, motivated by exploring any kind of market inefficiency, that encouraged the application and facilitated the development of these models and their variations. For instance, the GARCH in mean model is related to asset pricing with time-varying risk instead of constant risk in traditional models such as the CAPM. An exponential GARCH (EGARCH) model addresses asymmetry in volatility patterns which are well observed in corporate finance and financial markets and can sometimes be attributed to leverage effects. GARCH with t-distribution reflects fat tails found in many types of financial time series data where the assumption of conditional normality is violated. Finally, multivariate GARCH models are helpful tools for investigating volatility transmissions and patterns between two or more financial markets.

Although GARCH family models have time-varying variance, the variance is not stochastic. Therefore, GARCH is not exactly the ARMA equivalent in the second moment. Stochastic volatility, as discussed in Section 3.3 is not only time varying, but also stochastic, and is probably the closest equivalent to an AR or ARMA process in the second moment.

3.1 ARCH and GARCH and their variations

3.1.1 ARCH and GARCH models

A stochastic process is called autoregressive conditional heteroscedasticity (ARCH) if its time-varying conditional variance is heteroscedastic with autoregression

$$y_t = \varepsilon_t, \quad \varepsilon_t \sim N(0, \sigma_t^2) \tag{1a}$$

$$\sigma_t^2 = \alpha_0 + \alpha_1 \varepsilon_{t-1}^2 + \cdots + \alpha_q \varepsilon_{t-q}^2 \tag{1b}$$

Equation (1a) is the mean equation where regressors can generally be added to the right-hand side along side ε_t. Equation (1b) is the variance equation, which is an ARCH(q) process where autoregression in its squared residuals has an order of q, or has q lags.

A stochastic process is called GARCH if its time-varying conditional variance is heteroscedastic with both autoregression and moving average.

$$y_t = \varepsilon_t, \quad \varepsilon_t \sim N(0, \sigma_t^2) \tag{2a}$$

$$\sigma_t^2 = \alpha_0 + \alpha_1 \varepsilon_{t-1}^2 + \cdots + \alpha_q \varepsilon_{t-q}^2 + \beta_1 \sigma_{t-1}^2 + \cdots + \beta_p \sigma_p^2$$

$$= \alpha_0 + \sum_{i=1}^{q} \alpha_i \varepsilon_{t-i}^2 + \sum_{j=1}^{p} \beta_j \sigma_{t-j}^2 \tag{2b}$$

Equation (2) is a GARCH (p, q) process where autoregression in its squared residuals has an order of q, and the moving average component has an order of p.

One of the advantages of GARCH over ARCH is parsimonious, that is, fewer lags are required to capture the property of time-varying variance in GARCH. In empirical applications a GARCH (1, 1) model is widely adopted. While in ARCH, for example, a lag length of five for daily data may still not be long enough. We demonstrate this with a GARCH (1, 1) model. Extending the variance process backwards yields:

$$\sigma_t^2 = \alpha_0 + \alpha_1 \varepsilon_{t-1}^2 + \beta_1 \sigma_{t-1}^2$$

$$= \alpha_0 + \alpha_1 \varepsilon_{t-1}^2 + \beta_1 \left(\alpha_0 + \alpha_1 \varepsilon_{t-2}^2 + \beta_1 \sigma_{t-2}^2 \right)$$

$$\vdots$$

$$= \frac{\alpha_0}{1 - \beta_1} + \alpha_1 \sum_{n=1}^{\infty} \beta_1^{n-1} \varepsilon_{t-n}^2 \tag{3}$$

Indeed, only the first few terms would have noteworthy influence since $\beta_1^n {}_{n \to \infty} \to 0$. This shows how a higher order ARCH specification can be approximated by a GARCH (1, 1) process.

Similar to ARMA models, there are conditions for stationarity to be met. As the name of the model suggests, the variances specified above are conditional. The unconditional variance of GARCH would be of interest with respect to the property of the model. Applying the expectations operator to both sides of equation (2b), we have:

$$E(\sigma_t^2) = \alpha_0 + \sum_{i=1}^{q} \alpha_i E(\varepsilon_{t-1}^2) + \sum_{j=1}^{p} \beta_j E(\sigma_{t-j}^2)$$

Noting $E(\sigma_t^2) = E(\varepsilon_{t-i}^2) = E(\sigma_{t-j}^2)$ is the unconditional variance of the residual, which is solved as:

$$\sigma^2 = E(\sigma_t^2) = \frac{\alpha_0}{1 - \sum_{i=1}^{q} \alpha_i + \sum_{j=1}^{p} \beta_j}$$

It is clear that for the process to possess a finite variance, the following condition must be met:

$$\sum_{i=1}^{q} \alpha_i + \sum_{j=1}^{p} \beta_j < 1 \tag{4}$$

In commonly used GARCH (1, 1) models, the condition is simply $\alpha_1 + \beta_1 < 1$. Many financial time series have persistent volatility, that is, the sum of α_i and β_j is close to being unity. A unity sum of α_i and β_j leads to the so-called integrated GARCH (IGARCH) as the process is not covariance stationary. Nevertheless, this does not pose as serious a problem as it appears. According to Nelson (1990), Bougerol and Picard (1992) and Lumsdaine (1991), even if a GARCH (IGARCH) model is not covariance stationary, it is strictly stationary or ergodic, and the standard asymptotically based inference procedures are generally valid. See Chapter 1 of this book for various definitions of stationarity and ergodicity.

3.1.2   Variations of the ARCH/GARCH model

Variations are necessary to adapt the standard GARCH model to the needs arising from examining the time series properties of specific issues in finance and economics. Here we present the model relating the return on a security to its time-varying volatility or risk – ARCH-in-Mean (ARCH-M), and the models of asymmetry – EGARCH and threshold GARCH (TGARCH).

The ARCH-M model

When the conditional variance enters the mean equation for an ARCH process, the ARCH-M model is derived:

$$y_t = \lambda_1 x_1 + \cdots + \lambda_m x_m + \varphi \sigma_t^2 + \varepsilon_t, \quad \varepsilon_t \sim N(0, \sigma_t^2) \tag{5a}$$

$$\sigma_t^2 = \alpha_0 + \alpha_1 \varepsilon_{t-1}^2 + \cdots + \alpha_q \varepsilon_{t-q}^2 \tag{5b}$$

where $x_k, k = 1, \ldots, m$ are exogenous variables which could include lagged y_t. In the sense of asset pricing, if y_t is the return on an asset of a firm, then $x_k, k = 1, \ldots, m$ would generally include the return on the market and possibly other explanatory variables such as the price earnings ratio and the size. The parameter φ captures the sensitivity of the return to the time-varying volatility, or in other words, links the return to a *time-varying risk premium*. The ARCH-M model is generalised from the standard ARCH by Engle *et al.* (1987) and can be further generalised so that the conditional variance is GARCH instead of ARCH, and that the conditional standard deviation, instead of the conditional variance, enters the mean equation.

The EGARCH model

This model captures asymmetric responses of the time-varying variance to shocks and, at the same time, ensures that the variance is always positive. It was developed by Nelson (1991) with the following specification:

$$\ln(\sigma_t^2) = \alpha_0 + \beta \ln(\sigma_{t-1}^2) + \alpha \left\{ \left| \frac{\varepsilon_{t-1}}{\sigma_{t-1}} \right| - \sqrt{\frac{2}{\pi}} \right\} - \gamma \frac{\varepsilon_{t-1}}{\sigma_{t-1}} \tag{6}$$

where γ is the asymmetric response parameter or leverage parameter. The sign of γ is expected to be positive in most empirical cases so that a negative shock increases future volatility or uncertainty while a positive shock eases the effect on future uncertainty. This is in contrast to the standard GARCH model where shocks of the same magnitude, positive or negative, have the same effect on future volatility. In macroeconomic analysis, financial markets and corporate finance, a negative shock usually implies bad news, leading to a more uncertain future. Consequently, for example, shareholders would require a higher expected return to compensate for bearing increased risk in their investment. A statistical asymmetry is, under various circumstances, also a reflection of the real world asymmetry, arising from the nature, process or organisation of economic and business activity, for example, the change in financial leverage is asymmetric to shocks to the share price of a firm.

Equation (6) is, exactly speaking, an EGARCH (1, 1) model. Higher order EGARCH models can be specified in a similar way, for example, EGARCH (p, q) is as follows:

$$\ln(\sigma_t^2) = \alpha_0 + \sum_{j=1}^{p} \beta_j \ln(\alpha_{t-j}^2) + \sum_{i=1}^{q} \left\{ \alpha_i \left(\left| \frac{\varepsilon_{t-i}}{\sigma_{t-i}} \right| - \sqrt{\frac{2}{\pi}} \right) - \gamma_i \frac{\varepsilon_{t-i}}{\sigma_{t-i}} \right\} \tag{7}$$

The threshold GARCH model

It is also known as the GJR model, named after Glosten, Jagannathan and Runkle (1993). Despite the advantages EGARCH appears to enjoy, the empirical estimation of the model is technically difficult as it involves highly non-linear algorithms. In contrast, the GJR model is much simpler than, though not as elegant as, EGARCH. A general GJR model is specified as follows:

$$\sigma_t^2 = \alpha_0 + \sum_{i=1}^{q} \left\{ \alpha_i \varepsilon_{t-i}^2 + \delta_i \varepsilon_{t-i}^2 \right\} + \sum_{j=1}^{p} \beta_j \sigma_{t-j}^2 \tag{8}$$

where $\delta_i = 0$ if $\varepsilon_{t-i} > 0$. So, γ_i catches asymmetry in the response of volatility to shocks in a way that imposes a prior belief that for a positive shock and a negative shock of the same magnitude, future volatility is always higher, or at least the same, when the sign of the shock is negative. This may make sense under many circumstances but may not be universally valid. An alternative to the GJR specification is:

$$\sigma_t^2 = \alpha_0 + \sum_{i=1}^{q} \left\{ \alpha_i^+ \varepsilon_{t-i}^2 + \alpha_i^- \varepsilon_{t-i}^2 \right\} + \sum_{j=1}^{p} \beta_j \sigma_{t-j}^2 \tag{9}$$

where $\alpha_i^+ = 0$ if $\varepsilon_{t-i} < 0$, and α_i^- if $\varepsilon_{t-i} > 0$. In such a case, whether a positive shock or a negative shock of the same magnitude will have a larger effect on volatility will be subject to empirical examination.

3.2   Multivariate GARCH

We restrict our analysis to bivariate models as a multivariate GARCH with more than two variables would be extremely difficult to estimate technically and convey meaningful messages theoretically. A bivariate GARCH model expressed in matrices takes the form:

$$\mathbf{y}_t = \boldsymbol{\varepsilon}_t \tag{10a}$$

$$\boldsymbol{\varepsilon}_t | \Omega_{t-1} \sim N(0, \mathbf{H}_t) \tag{10b}$$

where vectors $\mathbf{y}_t = [y_{1,t} \ \ y_{2,t}]'$ and $\boldsymbol{\varepsilon}_t = [\varepsilon_{1,t} \ \ \varepsilon_{2,t}]'$ and

$$\mathbf{H}_t = \begin{bmatrix} h_{11t} & h_{12t} \\ h_{21t} & h_{22t} \end{bmatrix}$$

is the covariance matrix which can be designed in a number of ways. Commonly used specifications of the covariance include constant correlation, VECH (full parameterisation), and BEKK (positive definite parameterisation) named after Baba, Engle, Kraft and Kroner (1990). We now introduce them in turn.

3.2.1   Constant correlation

A constant correlation means that:

$$\frac{h_{12t}}{\sqrt{h_{11t} h_{22t}}} = \rho$$

is constant over time or it is not a function of time. Therefore, h_{12t} is determined as:

$$h_{12t} = \rho \sqrt{h_{11t} h_{22t}} \tag{11}$$

An obvious advantage of the constant correlation specification is simplicity. Nonetheless, it can only establish a link between the two uncertainties, failing to tell the directions of volatility spillovers between the two sources of uncertainty.

3.2.2   Full parameterisation

The full parameterisation, or VECH, converts the covariance matrix to a vector of variance and covariance. As $\sigma_{ij} = \sigma_{ji}$, the dimension of the vector converted from an $m \times m$ matrix is $m(m+1)/2$. Thus, in a bivariate GARCH process, the dimension of the variance/covariance vector is three. With a trivariate GARCH, the dimension of the vector is six, that is, there are six equations to describe the time-varying variance/covariance. Therefore, it is unlikely to be feasible when more than two variables are involved in a system. The VECH specification is presented as:

$$\text{vech}(\mathbf{H}_t) = \text{vech}(\mathbf{A}_0) + \sum_{i=1}^{q} \mathbf{A}_i \text{vech}(\boldsymbol{\varepsilon}_{t-i}\boldsymbol{\varepsilon}'_{t-i}) + \sum_{j=1}^{p} \mathbf{B}_j \text{vech}(\mathbf{H}_{t-j}) \quad (12)$$

where $\mathbf{H}_t$, $\mathbf{A}_0$, $\mathbf{A}_i$, $\mathbf{B}_j$ and $\boldsymbol{\varepsilon}_t\boldsymbol{\varepsilon}'_t$ are matrices in their conventional form, and vech $(\cdot)$ means the procedure of conversion of a matrix into a vector, as described above. For $p = q = 1$, equation (12) can be written explicitly as:

$$\mathbf{H}_t = \begin{bmatrix} h_{11,t} \\ h_{12,t} \\ h_{22,t} \end{bmatrix} = \begin{bmatrix} \alpha_{11,0} \\ \alpha_{12,0} \\ \alpha_{22,0} \end{bmatrix} + \begin{bmatrix} \alpha_{11,1} & \alpha_{12,1} & \alpha_{13,1} \\ \alpha_{21,1} & \alpha_{22,1} & \alpha_{23,1} \\ \alpha_{31,1} & \alpha_{32,1} & \alpha_{33,1} \end{bmatrix} \begin{bmatrix} \varepsilon_{1,t-1}^2 \\ \varepsilon_{1,t-1}\varepsilon_{2,t-1} \\ \varepsilon_{2,t-1}^2 \end{bmatrix}$$

$$+ \begin{bmatrix} \beta_{11,1} & \beta_{12,1} & \beta_{13,1} \\ \beta_{21,1} & \beta_{22,1} & \beta_{23,1} \\ \beta_{31,1} & \beta_{32,1} & \beta_{33,1} \end{bmatrix} \begin{bmatrix} h_{11,t-1} \\ h_{12,t-1} \\ h_{22,t-1} \end{bmatrix} \quad (13)$$

So, the simplest multivariate model has 21 parameters to estimate.

3.2.3   Positive definite parameterisation

It is also known as BEKK, suggested by Baba, Engle, Kraft and Kroner (1990). In fact, it is the most natural way to deal with multivariate matrix operations. The BEKK specification takes the following form:

$$\mathbf{H}_t = \mathbf{A}_0'\mathbf{A}_0 + \mathbf{A}_i'\boldsymbol{\varepsilon}_{t-i}\boldsymbol{\varepsilon}'_{t-i}\mathbf{A}_i + \mathbf{B}_j'\mathbf{H}_{t-j}\mathbf{B}_j \quad (14)$$

where $\mathbf{A}_0$ is a symmetric $(N \times N)$ parameter matrix, and $\mathbf{A}_i$ and $\mathbf{B}_j$ are unrestricted $(N \times N)$ parameter matrices. The important feature of this specification is that it builds in sufficient generality, allowing the conditional variances and covariances of the time series to influence each other, and at the same time, does not require the estimation of a large number of parameters. For $p = q = 1$ in a bivariate GARCH process, equation (14) has only 11 parameters compared with 21 parameters in the VECH representation. Even more importantly, the BEKK process guarantees that the covariance matrices are positive definite under very weak conditions; and it can be shown that given certain non-linear restrictions on $\mathbf{A}_i$ and $\mathbf{B}_j$, equation (14) and the VECH representation are equivalent (Engle and Kroner 1995). In the bivariate system with $p = q = 1$, equation (14) becomes:

$$
\begin{bmatrix} h_{11,t} & h_{12,t} \\ h_{21,t} & h_{22,t} \end{bmatrix} = \begin{bmatrix} \alpha_{11,0} & \alpha_{12,0} \\ \alpha_{21,0} & \alpha_{22,0} \end{bmatrix}
$$

$$
+ \begin{bmatrix} \alpha_{11,1} & \alpha_{12,1} \\ \alpha_{21,1} & \alpha_{22,1} \end{bmatrix} \begin{bmatrix} \varepsilon_{1,t-1}^2 & \varepsilon_{1,t-1}\varepsilon_{2,t-1} \\ \varepsilon_{1,t-1}\varepsilon_{2,t-1} & \varepsilon_{2,t-1}^2 \end{bmatrix} \begin{bmatrix} \alpha_{11,1} & \alpha_{12,1} \\ \alpha_{21,1} & \alpha_{22,1} \end{bmatrix}
$$

$$
+ \begin{bmatrix} \beta_{11,1} & \beta_{12,1} \\ \beta_{21,1} & \beta_{22,1} \end{bmatrix} \begin{bmatrix} h_{11,t-1} & h_{12,t-1} \\ h_{21,t-1} & h_{22,t-1} \end{bmatrix} \begin{bmatrix} \beta_{11,1} & \beta_{12,1} \\ \beta_{21,1} & \beta_{22,1} \end{bmatrix} \tag{15}
$$

We can examine the sources of uncertainty and, moreover, assess the effect of signs of shocks with equation (15). Writing the variances and covariance explicitly:

$$
h_{11,t} = \alpha_{11,0} + (\alpha_{11,1}^2 \varepsilon_{1,t-1}^2 + 2\alpha_{11,1}\alpha_{21,1}\varepsilon_{1,t-1}\varepsilon_{2,t-1} + \alpha_{21,1}^2 \varepsilon_{2,t-1}^2)
$$

$$
+ (\beta_{11,1}^2 h_{11,t-1} + 2\beta_{11,1}\beta_{21,1} h_{12,t-1} + \beta_{21,1}^2 h_{22,t-1}) \tag{16a}
$$

$$
h_{12,t} = h_{21,t} = \alpha_{12,0} + [\alpha_{11,1}\alpha_{12,1}\varepsilon_{1,t-1}^2 + (\alpha_{12,1}\alpha_{21,1}
$$

$$
+ \alpha_{11,1}\alpha_{22,1})\varepsilon_{1,t-1}\varepsilon_{2,t-1} + \alpha_{21,1}\alpha_{22,1}\varepsilon_{2,t-1}^2]
$$

$$
+ [\beta_{11,1}\beta_{21,1} h_{11,t-1} + (\beta_{12,1}\beta_{21,1} + \beta_{11,1}\beta_{22,1}) h_{12,t-1}
$$

$$
+ \beta_{21,1}\beta_{22,1} h_{22,t-1}] \tag{16b}
$$

$$
h_{22,t} = \alpha_{22,0} + (\alpha_{12,1}^2 \varepsilon_{1,t-1}^2 + 2\alpha_{12,1}\alpha_{22,1}\varepsilon_{1,t-1}\varepsilon_{2,t-1} + \alpha_{22,1}^2 \varepsilon_{2,t-1}^2)
$$

$$
+ (\beta_{12,1}^2 h_{11,t-1} + 2\beta_{12,1}\beta_{22,1} h_{12,t-1} + \beta_{22,1}^2 h_{22,t-1}) \tag{16c}
$$

Looking at the diagonal elements in the above matrix, that is, $h_{11,t}$ and $h_{22,t}$, we can assess the impact of the shock in one series on the uncertainty or volatility of the other, and the impact could be asymmetric or only be one way effective. In particular, one might also be interested in assessing the effect of the signs of shocks in the two series. To this end the diagonal elements representing the previous shocks can be rearranged as follows:

$$
\alpha_{11,1}^2 \varepsilon_{1,t-1}^2 + 2\alpha_{11,1}\alpha_{21,1}\varepsilon_{1,t-1}\varepsilon_{2,t-1} + \alpha_{21,1}^2 \varepsilon_{2,t-1}^2
$$

$$
= (\alpha_{11,1}\varepsilon_{1,t-1} + \alpha_{21,1}\varepsilon_{2,t-1})^2 \tag{17a}
$$

$$
\alpha_{12,1}^2 \varepsilon_{1,t-1}^2 + 2\alpha_{12,1}\alpha_{22,1}\varepsilon_{1,t-1}\varepsilon_{2,t-1} + \alpha_{22,1}^2 \varepsilon_{2,t-1}^2
$$

$$
= (\alpha_{12,1}\varepsilon_{1,t-1} + \alpha_{22,1}\varepsilon_{2,t-1})^2 \tag{17b}
$$

It is clear that $\alpha_{11,1}$ and $\alpha_{22,1}$ represent the effect of the shock on the future uncertainty of the same time series and $\alpha_{21,1}$ and $\alpha_{12,1}$ represent the cross effect, that is, the effect of the shock of the second series on the future uncertainty of the first series, and vice versa. The interesting point is that, if $\alpha_{11,1}$ and $\alpha_{21,1}$ have different signs, then the shocks with different signs in the two time series tend to increase the future uncertainty in the first time series. Similarly, if $\alpha_{12,1}$ and $\alpha_{22,1}$ have different signs, the future uncertainty of the second time series might increase if the two shocks have different signs. It seems that this model specification is appropriately fitted to investigate volatility spillovers between two financial markets.

The positive definite specification of the covariance extends the univariate GARCH model naturally, for example, a BEKK–GARCH (1, 1) model can reduce to a GARCH (1, 1) when the dimension of the covariance matrix becomes one. Therefore, it is of interest to make inquiry into the conditions for covariance stationarity in the general matrix form. For this purpose, we need to vectorise the BEKK representation, that is, to arrange the elements of each of the matrices into a vector. Due to the special and elegant design of the BEKK covariance, the vectorisation can be neatly and orderly derived, using one of the properties of vectorisation, that is, vech(ABC) = $[C' \otimes A]$vech(B), where $\otimes$ is the Kroneker product. In this case, the innovation matrix

$$
\boldsymbol{\varepsilon}_{t-1}\boldsymbol{\varepsilon}'_{t-1} =
\begin{bmatrix}
\varepsilon^2_{1,t-1} & \varepsilon_{1,t-1}\varepsilon_{2,t-1} \\
\varepsilon_{2,t-1}\varepsilon_{1,t-1} & \varepsilon^2_2
\end{bmatrix}
$$

and the covariance matrix

$$
\mathbf{H}_{t-1} =
\begin{bmatrix}
h_{1,t-1} & h^{1/2}_{1,t-1}h^{1/2}_{2,t-1} \\
h^{1/2}_{2,t-1}h^{1/2}_{1,t-1} & h_{2,t-1}
\end{bmatrix}
$$

are represented by B; and the fact that the parameter matrices $\mathbf{A}'$ and $\mathbf{A}$ and $\mathbf{B}'$ and $\mathbf{B}$ have already been transposed to each other further simplifies the transformation. For more details on these operations refer to Judge *et al.* (1988) and Engle and Kroner (1995). The vectorised $\mathbf{H}_t$ is derived as:

$$
\text{vech}(\mathbf{H}_t) = (A_0 \otimes A_0)'\text{vech}(\mathbf{I}) + (A_i \otimes A_i)'\text{vech}(\boldsymbol{\varepsilon}_t - 1\boldsymbol{\varepsilon}'_{t-1})
$$
$$
+ (\mathbf{B}_j \otimes \mathbf{B}_j)'\text{vech}(\mathbf{H}_{t-1}) \tag{18}
$$

the unconditional covariance is:

$$
E(\mathbf{H}_t) = [\mathbf{I} - (\mathbf{A}_i \otimes \mathbf{A}_i)' - (\mathbf{B}_j \otimes \mathbf{B}_j)']^{-1}\text{vech}(\mathbf{A}'_0 \otimes \mathbf{A}_0) \tag{19}
$$

and the conditions for covariance stationarity is:

$$
\text{mod}\lfloor(\mathbf{A_i} \otimes \mathbf{A}_i)' + (\mathbf{B}_j \otimes \mathbf{B}_j)'\rfloor < 1 \tag{20}
$$

That is, for ε_t to be covariance stationary, all the eigenvalues of $(\mathbf{A}_i \otimes \mathbf{A}_i)' + (\mathbf{B}_j \otimes \mathbf{B}_j)'$ are required to be less than one in modules. There are altogether four eigenvalues for a bivariate GARCH process as the Kroneker product of two (2×2) matrices produces a (4×4) matrix. These eigenvalues would be complex numbers in general. When the dimension of the covariance is one, equation (20) reduces to equation (4) for the univariate case.[1]

3.3 Stochastic volatility

ARCH/GARCH processes are not really stochastic, rather they are deterministic and the conditional variance possesses no unknown innovations at the time. ARCH and GARCH are not exactly the second moment equivalent to AR and ARMA processes in the mean. Stochastic volatility, as favoured by Harvey *et al.* (1994), Ruiz (1994), Andersen and Lund (1997) and others, is probably the closest equivalent to an AR or ARMA process in describing the dynamics of variance/covariance. Let us look at a simple case:

$$y_t = \sigma_t \varepsilon_t$$

$$\varepsilon_t \sim N(0, \sigma_\varepsilon^2) \tag{21}$$

$$h_t = \ln \sigma_t^2 \sim \text{ARMA}(q, p)$$

The logarithm of the variance in a stochastic volatility model, $h_t = \ln \sigma_t^2$, behaves exactly as a stochastic process in the mean, such as random walks or AR or ARMA processes. For example, if h_t is modelled as an AR(1) process, then:

$$h_t = \alpha + \rho h_{t-1} + v_t, \quad v_t \sim N(0, \sigma_v^2) \tag{22}$$

Alternatively when h_t is modelled as an ARMA(1, 1) process:

$$h_t = \alpha + \rho h_{t-1} + v_t + \theta v_{t-1}, \quad v_t \sim N(0, \sigma_v^2) \tag{23}$$

When the stochastic part of volatility, v_t, does not exist (i.e. $\sigma_v^2 = 0$), equation (22) does not reduce to ARCH (1) but to GARCH (1,0). So the difference in modelling variance is substantial between GARCH and stochastic volatility approaches. To estimate stochastic volatility models, expressing equation (21) as:

$$g_t = h_t + \kappa_t \tag{24}$$

where $g_t = \ln(y_t^2)$ and $\kappa_t = \ln(\varepsilon_t^2)$. We can see that h_t becomes part, or a component, of the (transformed) time series, in contrast to traditional statistical models where the variance expresses the distribution of variables in a different way. As the time series now has more than one component, neither is readily observable, so the components are often referred to as unobserved components. These components together form the whole system and individually describe the state of the system from certain perspectives, so they can be referred to as state variables as well. Such a specification poses problems as well as advantages: decomposition

into components can be arbitrary and estimation can be complicated and sometimes difficult. Nevertheless, the state variables and their dynamic evolution and
interaction may reveal the fundamental characteristics and dynamics of the system or the original time series more effectively, or provide more insights into the
working of the system. Models of this type are usually estimated in the state space,
often accompanied by the use of Kalman filters. See Chapter 8 for details of the
state space representation and the Kalman filter.

3.4   Examples and cases

When the time comes to implement an empirical study, the problem may never
be exactly the same as illustrated in the text. This is hopefully what a researcher
expects to encounter rather than attempting to avoid if s/he imagines new discov-
eries in her/his study or would like to differentiate her/his study from others. This
section provides such examples.

Example 1

This is an example incorporating macroeconomic variables into the conditional
variance equation for stock returns by Hasan and Francis (1998), entitled 'Macroeconomic factors and the asymmetric predictability of conditional variances'. The
paper includes the default premium, dividend yield and the term premium as state
variables in the conditional variance equation, though its main purpose is to investigate the predictability of the volatilities of large v. small firms. The paper shows
that volatility surprises of small (large) firms are important in predicting the conditional variance of large (small) firms, and this predictive ability is still present when
the equation of conditional variance includes the above-mentioned state variables.

The paper uses monthly returns of all NYSE and AMEX common stocks with
available year-end market value information gathered from the Center for Research
in Security Prices (CRSP) monthly master tape from 1926 to 1988. All stocks in
the sample are equally divided into twenty size-based portfolios, S1 (smallest) to
S20 (largest), according to the market value of equity at the end of the prior year.
Monthly excess returns on each of the portfolios are obtained by averaging returns
across all the stocks included in the portfolio. Their specification is as follows:

$$R_{i,t} = \alpha_{i,t} + \beta_i R_{i,t-1} + \mu_{i,1} \text{JAN}_t + \gamma_i R_{j,t-1} + e_{i,t} \tag{25a}$$

$$h_{i,t} = \delta_{i,0} + \alpha_i e_{i,t-1}^2 + \theta_i h_{i,t-1} + \delta_{i1} \text{JAN}_t + \varphi_j e_{j,t-1}^2 + \sum \omega_k Z_{k,t-1} \tag{25b}$$

The mean equation follows an AR(1) process. JAN_t is the dummy which is equal to
one when in January and zero otherwise. $Z_{k,t}$ ($k = 1, 2, 3$) are the state variables of
default premium (DEF), dividend yield (DYLD) and the term premium (TERM)
respectively. These state variables are those used by Fama and French (1989)
and Chen (1991). The effect of return and volatility spillovers across portfolios
is through the inclusion of lagged returns on portfolio j in the mean equation

for portfolio i, and the inclusion of lagged squared errors for portfolio j in the conditional variance equation of portfolio i. Squared errors for portfolio j are obtained through estimating a basic GARCH model whose conditional variance is a standard GARCH $(1, 1)$ plus the January dummy. Therefore, the model is univariate rather than bivariate in nature.

The paper then estimates the model for two portfolios, the small stock portfolio and the large stock portfolio. Volatility spillovers across these two portfolios are examined. The major findings are that while return spillovers are from the small stock portfolio to the large stock portfolio only, volatility spillovers are bidirectional, though the effect of the small stock portfolio on the large stock portfolio is greater than vice versa. Only the main results are presented in Tables 3.1 and 3.2. Model (1) does not include the state variables, Models (2)–(4) include one of the state variables each, and Model (5) incorporates all the state variables. As there is not much difference in the mean equation results, only the results from Model (5) are provided.

Example 2

This is an example of the bivariate GARCH model applied to the foreign exchange market by Wang and Wang (2001). In this study, the daily spot and forward foreign exchange rates of the British pound, German mark, French franc and Canadian dollar against the US dollar are used. All of the data sets start from 2 January 1976 and end on 31 December 1990; so there are 3,758 observations in each series. These long period high-frequency time series data enable us to observe a very

Table 3.1 Small stock portfolio

Mean equation							
μ_0		$R_{1,t-1}$		JAN		$R_{20,t-1}$	
0.0048		0.1896		0.1231		0.0287	
(1.705)		(4.679)		(8.163)		(0.475)	

Variance equation								
Model	δ_0	$e_{1,t-1}^2$	$h_{1,t-1}$	JAN	$e_{20,t-1}^2$	$DYLD$	$TERM$	DEF
(1)	−0.000	0.0284	0.9305	0.0005	0.0022			
	(0.998)	(2.039)	(41.915)	(0.464)	(2.741)			
(2)	−0.0001	0.0259	0.9341	0.0008	0.0021	−0.003		
	(0.470)	(1.890)	(43.648)	(0.738)	(2.629)	(1.167)		
(3)	−0.0001	0.0254	0.9316	0.0009	0.0023		−0.0001	
	(0.228)	(1.812)	(43.310)	(0.789)	(2.650)		(2.991)	
(4)	−0.0001	0.0273	0.9286	0.0008	0.0024			−0.0001
	(0.134)	(1.843)	(39.142)	(0.729)	(2.681)			(3.014)
(5)	−0.0001	0.0009	0.9694	0.0012	0.0018	−0.0005	−0.0001	−0.0001
	(0.740)	(0.092)	(82.117)	(1.193)	(3.556)	(4.160)	(0.693)	(0.751)

Note: Robust t-statistics in brackets.

Table 3.2 Large stock portfolio

Mean equation			
μ_0	$R_{20,t-1}$	JAN	$R_{1,t-1}$
0.0064	0.0497	−0.0082	0.1013
(3.867)	(1.295)	(1.413)	(6.051)

Variance equation Model	δ_0	$e^2_{20,t-1}$	$h_{20,t-1}$	JAN	$e^2_{1,t-1}$	DYLD	TERM	DEF
(1)	0.0002	0.1610	0.6511	−0.0001	0.0237			
	(2.981)	(3.347)	(10.148)	(0.194)	(2.986)			
(2)	0.0003	0.1595	0.6504	−0.0001	0.0239	−0.0001		
	(2.563)	(3.324)	(9.926)	(0.226)	(3.043)	(0.795)		
(3)	0.0001	0.1544	0.6293	−0.0001	0.0282		0.0004	
	(1.811)	(3.252)	(9.986)	(0.205)	(3.442)		(2.492)	
(4)	0.0001	0.1549	0.6460	−0.0003	0.0244			0.0003
	(1.321)	(3.214)	(9.567)	(0.089)	(4.489)			(1.989)
(5)	0.0001	0.1502	0.6322	−0.0001	0.2974	0.0002	0.0008	−0.0001
	(0.820)	(3.270)	(10.214)	(0.393)	(3.733)	(0.784)	(2.055)	(1.111)

Note: Robust t-statistics in brackets.

evident GARCH phenomenon in a bivariate system. The system of equations for the spot exchange rate, S_t, and the forward exchange rate, F_t, is specified as an extended VAR, which incorporates a forward premium into a simple VAR. In addition, the covariance of the extended VAR is time-varying which allows for and mimics volatility spillovers or transmission between the spot and forward foreign exchange markets. The model is given as follows:

$$
\begin{aligned}
\Delta s_t &= c_1 + \gamma_1(f_{t-1} - s_{t-1}) + \sum_{i=1}^{m} \alpha_{1i} \Delta s_{t-i} + \sum_{i=1}^{m} \beta_{1i} \Delta f_{t-i} + \varepsilon_{1t} \\
\Delta f_t &= c_2 + \gamma_2(f_{t-1} - s_{t-1}) + \sum_{i=1}^{m} \alpha_{2i} \Delta s_{t-i} + \sum_{i=1}^{m} \beta_{2i} \Delta f_{t-i} + \varepsilon_{2t} \\
\varepsilon_t | \Omega_{t-1} &\sim N(0, H_t)
\end{aligned}
\tag{26}
$$

where $s_t = \ln(S_t)$, $f_t = \ln(F_t)$, $\Delta s_t = s_t - s_{t-1}$, $\Delta f_t = f_t - f_{t-1}$, and H_t is the time-varying covariance matrix with the BEKK specification.

The inclusion of the forward premium is not merely to set up an ECM model – it keeps information in levels while still meeting the requirements for stationarity. Although there are arguments about the property of the forward premium, its inclusion makes the system informationally and economically complete by reserving information in levels (original variables) and reflecting expectations in the market.

The bivariate GARCH effects are, in general, strong in both the spot and forward markets, though there exists a clear asymmetry in the volatility spillover patterns.

That is, there are, to a lesser extent, volatility spillovers from the spot market to the forward market, compared with the other way round. Table 3.3 presents the results based mainly on the second moment.

In addition, the parameter for the forward premium is also reported, as it would validate the cointegration between the spot and forward exchange rates and the need to incorporate the forward premium. Consider the British pound first. a_{12} and a_{21} are both significant at the 1 per cent level, but the magnitude of the former is about half the size of the latter, implying that the effect of the shock in the forward market on the spot market volatility is bigger than that on the forward market induced by the shock in the spot market. Turning to the effects of the previous uncertainty, while b_{21} is significant, b_{12} is not significant at all, so the volatility spillovers are one-directional from the forward to the spot. Notice, b_{22} is also insignificant, which means there is only ARCH in the forward exchange rate. Further scrutiny on the signs of a_{12} and a_{22} suggests that the future volatility in the forward market would be higher if the two shocks have different signs. In the case of the German mark, the asymmetry is more apparent, where a_{12} is not significant at all but a_{21} is significant at the 1 per cent level. As such, the shock in the forward market would affect the future volatility in the spot market, but the shock in the spot market has no influence on the future volatility in the forward market. In addition, a_{11} and a_{21} have different signs, so the shock with opposite signs in these two markets would be inclined to increase the future volatility in the spot market. As far as the previous variance is concerned, b_{12} and a_{21} are both significant, but the size of the former is much smaller than that of the latter, so the asymmetry exists in this respect too. Again, b_{22} is not significant; the forward rate would only have the ARCH effect if it were not considered in a bivariate system. The strongest asymmetry occurs in the exchange rates of the Canadian dollar. The volatility spillovers are absolutely one-directional from the forward rate to the spot rate. That is, a_{12} and b_{12} are not significant at any conventional levels, whereas a_{21} and b_{21} are both significant at the 1 per cent level. Similar to the British pound, in the case of French franc, the influence of the previous variance is clearly one directional from the forward to the spot rate measured by b_{12} and b_{21}. Although the GARCH effect is strong in the forward rate as well as in the spot rate, b_{22} is close to being twice as big as b_{11}. Regarding the previous shocks, the influence is also more from forward to spot; both a_{12} and a_{21} are significant but a_{21} is much bigger than a_{12}. Therefore, the four currencies have similar asymmetric volatility spillover patterns. Another interesting point in the example of French franc is that the premium is not significant in either the spot or forward equations when the covariance matrix is assumed constant. The premium is significant in the forward equation when estimated in a multivariate GARCH framework. This suggests that the rejection/acceptance of a cointegration relationship is, to certain extent, subject to the assumption on the properties of the covariance.

In Table 3.4, all four eigenvalues for each currency are reported. Their positioning on the complex plane is displayed in Figure 3.1. It can been seen that the biggest of the eigenvalues for each currency is around 0.96 in modules, so the time-varying volatility is highly persistent. In the French franc case, the biggest module

Table 3.3 Volatility spillovers between spot and forward FX rates

$$\Delta s_t = c_1 + \gamma_1(f_{t-1} - s_{t-1}) + \sum_{i=1}^{m} \alpha_{1i}\,\Delta s_{t-i} + \sum_{i=1}^{m} \beta_{1i}\,\Delta f_{t-i} + \varepsilon_{1t}$$

$$\Delta f_t = c_2 + \gamma_2(f_{t-1} - s_{t-1}) + \sum_{i=1}^{m} \alpha_{2i}\,\Delta s_{t-i} + \sum_{i=1}^{m} \beta_{2i}\,\Delta f_{t-i} + \varepsilon_{2t}$$

$$\varepsilon_t|\Omega_{t-1} \sim N(0, H_t)$$

$$
\begin{bmatrix} h_{11,t} & h_{12,t} \\ h_{21,t} & h_{22,t} \end{bmatrix}
=
\begin{bmatrix} c_{11} & c_{12} \\ c_{21} & c_{22} \end{bmatrix}
+
\begin{bmatrix} a_{11} & a_{12} \\ a_{21} & a_{22} \end{bmatrix}'
\begin{bmatrix} \varepsilon_{1,t-1}^2 & \varepsilon_{1,t-1}\varepsilon_{2,t-1} \\ \varepsilon_{1,t-1}\varepsilon_{2,t-1} & \varepsilon_{2,t-1}^2 \end{bmatrix}
\begin{bmatrix} a_{11} & a_{12} \\ a_{21} & a_{22} \end{bmatrix}
$$

$$
+
\begin{bmatrix} b_{11} & b_{12} \\ b_{21} & b_{22} \end{bmatrix}'
\begin{bmatrix} h_{11,t-1} & h_{12,t-1} \\ h_{21,t-1} & h_{22,t-1} \end{bmatrix}
\begin{bmatrix} b_{11} & b_{12} \\ b_{21} & b_{22} \end{bmatrix}
$$

	BP	DM	FF	CD
c_1	0.00025**	−0.00058***	0.00012	0.00013**
	(2.3740)	(4.3591)	(1.2106)	(2.2491)
γ_1	−0.12034***	−0.23731***	−0.03214	−0.05255
	(3.9301)	(5.5473)	(1.3884)	(1.8081)*
c_2	0.00027**	−0.00057***	0.00014	0.00015**
	(2.5077)	(4.0781)	(1.4735)	(2.5582)
γ_2	−0.12536***	−0.23203***	−0.05197**	−0.05436*
	(4.0293)	(5.1272)	(2.2460)	(1.8156)
a_{11}	0.51775***	−0.20555***	1.00020***	0.53282***
	(13.3029)	(3.8590)	(148.5928)	(8.4157)
a_{12}	−0.24576***	0.00539	0.03776***	−0.05055
	(6.8053)	(0.1062)	(5.4583)	(0.8144)
a_{21}	0.45452***	1.17328***	−0.06149***	0.40725***
	(11.5872)	(22.2677)	(8.7868)	(6.5068)
a_{22}	1.21688***	0.96138***	0.89990***	0.98706***
	(33.3811)	(19.1147)	(124.5143)	(16.0892)
b_{11}	0.43475***	1.00966***	0.24888***	0.52226***
	(4.8987)	(16.8606)	(8.0209)	(8.0757)
b_{12}	−0.10742	−0.18033***	−0.04565	0.01389
	(1.2389)	(3.5195)	(1.4180)	(0.2278)
b_{21}	−0.66683***	−1.16582***	0.10881***	−0.22376***
	(7.5985)	(19.1740)	(3.5734)	(3.5935)
b_{22}	−0.13151	−0.05456	0.40644***	0.28611***
	(1.5358)	(1.0563)	(12.7895)	(4.7730)

Notes
  * Significant at the 10% level.
 * * Significant at the 5% level.
* * * Significant at the 1% level.
   t-statistics in brackets.
   Constant terms in the second moment are not reported.

Table 3.4 Verifying covariance stationarity: the eigenvalues. Unconditional covariance:
$$E(\sigma_t^2) = [I - (A^* \otimes A^*)' - (B^* \otimes B^*)']^{-1} \text{vec}(C_0^{*'} C_0^*)$$

$(A^* \otimes A^*)'$ $+(B^* \otimes B^*)'$	BP	DM	FF	CD
λ_1 (real, imaginary)	0.963, 0.000	0.969, 0.000	1.003, 0.000	0.969, 0.000
λ_1 (mod)	0.963	0.969	1.003	0.969
λ_2 (real, imaginary)	0.852, 0.000	0.570, 0.000	0.995, −0.022	0.699, 0.000
λ_2 (mod)	0.852	0.570	0.996	0.699
λ_3 (real, imaginary)	0.628, 0.000	0.022, 0.000	0.995, 0.022	0.698, 0.000
λ_3 (mod)	0.628	0.022	0.996	0.698
λ_4 (real, imaginary)	0.608, 0.000	0.017, 0.000	0.988, 0.000	0.600, 0.000
λ_4 (mod)	0.608	0.017	0.988	0.600

Note: In a situation where all eigenvalues are smaller than one in modules, the covariance is confirmed as being stationary.

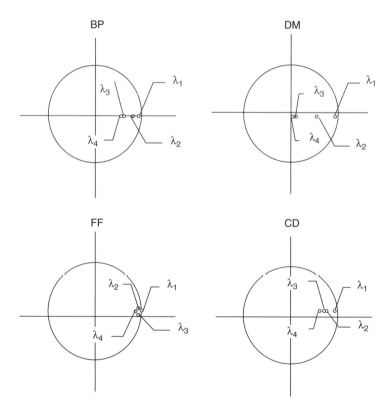

Figure 3.1 Eigenvalues on the complex plane. The horizontal axis is for the real part, and the vertical axis is for the imaginary part of the eigenvalue. The reference circle is the unit circle.

of eigenvalue is just above unity, suggesting that the unconditional covariance does not exist. There are two explanations to provide for this. First, according to Nelson (1990), Bougerol and Picard (1992) and Lumsdaine (1991), even if a GARCH (IGARCH) model is not covariance stationary, it is strictly stationary or ergodic, and the standard asymptotically-based inference procedures are generally valid. Second, the derivation of eigenvalues is based on the assumption that the spot variance and forward variance are equal in size. Nevertheless, the forward variance is smaller than the spot variance in the French franc case. Taking this into account, all of the modules of eigenvalue for the French franc become less than one and covariance stationarity exists. The analysis of the eigenvalues of the Kroneker product of the covariance matrices reveals that time-varying volatility is also highly persistent in a bivariate setting for foreign exchange rate data. In addition, though the BEKK specification has proved to be a helpful analytical technique for investigating volatility transmissions, especially the impact of the signs of the shocks in different markets, in empirical research, covariance stationarity is not so easy to satisfy and is not always guaranteed.

3.5   Empirical literature

While time-varying volatility has found applications in almost all time series modelling in economics and finance, it attracts most attention in the areas of financial markets and investment where a vast empirical literature has been generated, which has in turn brought about new forms and variations of this family of models. Time-varying volatility has become the norm in financial time series modelling, popularly accepted and applied by academics and professionals alike since the 1990s. Moreover, analysis of interactions between two or more variables in the first moment, such as in VAR and ECM, is extended through the use of time-varying volatility models to the second moment, to examine such important issues as volatility spillovers or transmissions between different markets.

One of the most extensively researched topics is time-varying volatility universally found in stock market indices. Although findings vary from one market to another, a pattern of time-varying volatility, which is also highly persistent, is common to most of them. Nevertheless, many of studies attempt to exploit new features and add variations in model specifications to meet the specific need of empirical investigations. To examine the characteristics of market opening news, Gallo and Pacini (1998) apply the GARCH model to evaluate the impact of news on the estimated coefficients of the model. They find that the differences between the opening price of one day and the closing price of the day before have different characteristics and have the effect of modifying the direct impact of daily innovations on volatility which reduces the estimated overall persistence of innovations. It is also claimed that the inclusion of this news variable significantly improves out-of-sample forecasting, compared with the simple GARCH model's performance. Brooks *et al.* (2000) adopt the power ARCH (PARCH) model proposed by Ding *et al.* (1993) to stock market returns in 10 countries and a world index. As PARCH removes the restriction implicitly imposed by ARCH/GARCH, that is, the power transformation is achieved by taking squaring operations of the residual, it can possess richer volatility patterns such as asymmetry and leverage effects. They find that the PARCH model is applicable to these return indices and that the optimal power transformation is remarkably similar across countries. Longin (1997) employs the analytical framework of Kyle (1985) where there are three types of traders: informed traders, liquidity traders and market makers. In such a setting, the paper models information as an asymmetric GARCH process so that large shocks are less persistent in volatility than small shocks. This, it is claimed, allows one to derive implications for trading volume and market liquidity. The study by Koutmos (1992) is one of the typical empirical applications of GARCH in finance in early times – risk-return trade-off in a time-varying volatility context and asymmetry of the conditional variance in response to innovations. The EGARCH in Mean (EGARCH-M) model is chosen for obvious reasons, as above, and the findings support the presence of these well-observed phenomena in 10 stock market return indices. Newly added to this literature is evidence from so-called emerging markets and the developing world. Investigating the behaviour of the Egyptian stock market in the context of pricing efficiency and the return–volatility relationship, Mecagni and Sourial (1999) employ a GARCH-M model to estimate four daily indices. Their results suggest that there is a tendency of volatility clustering in returns, and a positive but asymmetric link between risk and returns which is statistically significant during market downturns. They claim that the asymmetry in the risk–return relationship is due to the introduction of circuit breakers. Husain (1998) examines the Ramadhan effect in the Pakistani stock market using GARCH models. Ramadhan, the season of the holy month of fasting, is expected to have effects on stock market behaviour one way or another. The study finds that the market is indeed tranquil as the conditional variance declines in that month, but the season does not appear to have any impact on mean returns. Applying TGARCH models to two Eastern European markets, Shields (1997) reports findings contrary to those in the West that there is no asymmetry in the conditional variance in response to positive and negative shocks in these Eastern European markets.

International stock market linkages have attracted increasing attention in the process of so-called globalisation in a time when there are no major wars. Seeking excess returns through international diversification is one of the strategies employed by large multinational financial institutions in an ever intensifying competitive financial environment, while national markets, considered individually, appear to have been exploited to their full so that any non-trivial profitable opportunities do not remain in the context of semi-strong market efficiency. In particular, US investors have gradually given up the stand of regarding foreign markets as alien lands and changed their risk perspectives – international diversification benefits are more than off setting perceived additional risks. In the meantime, international asset pricing theory has been developed largely with a stratified approach which regards the international financial market as segmented as well as linked markets, adding additional dimensions to the original capital asset pricing model which is, ironically, universal, or in other words, global. Under such circumstances, it is not strange that applications of multivariate GARCH models have mushroomed during this period.

Investigating one of the typical features in emerging financial markets, Fong and Cheng (2000) test the information based hypothesis that the rate of information absorption in the conditional variance is faster for foreign shares (open to foreigners and locals) than for local shares (open to locals only) using a bivariate GARCH (1, 1) model for nine dual-listed stocks over the period 1991–1996. Their evidence indicates that the rate of information absorption is consistent with what was proposed by Longin (1977) that the rate of information absorption varies inversely with the number of informed traders. They claim that removing foreign ownership restrictions is likely to improve both market efficiency and liquidity. International risk transmission or volatility spillovers between two or more financial markets is by far the most intensively researched area. In this fashion, Kim and Rui (1999) examine the dynamic relationship between the US, Japan and UK daily stock market return volatility and trading volumes using bivariate GARCH models. They find extensive and reciprocal volatility spillovers in these markets. The results from return spillovers, or Granger causality in the mean equations, seem to confirm all reciprocal relationships but exclude London's influence on the New York Stock Exchange. Tay and Zhu (2000) also find such dynamic relationships in returns and volatilities in Pacific-Rim stock markets. Chou *et al.* (1999) test the hypothesis that the short-term volatility and price changes spillover from developed markets to emerging markets using the US and Taiwan data. They find substantial volatility spillover effect from the US stock market to the Taiwan stock market, especially for the model using close-to-open returns. There is also, it is claimed, evidence supporting the existence of spillovers in price changes. In contrast to the majority of the findings, Niarchos *et al.* (1999) show that there are no spillovers in means and conditional variances between the US and Greek stock markets and suggest that the US market does not have a strong influence on the Greek stock market. Many similar studies have emerged in recent years, for example, Dunne (1999) and Darbar and Deb (1997), to mention a few.

Inflation uncertainty remains one of the main application areas of GARCH modelling, following the first paper of this type on the topic by Engle (1982). In a recent study, Grier and Perry (1998), without much surprise, provide empirical evidence that inflation raises inflation uncertainty, as measured by the conditional variance of the inflation rate, for all G7 countries in the period from 1948 to 1993. Their results on the causal relationship from inflation uncertainty to inflation are mixed. In three countries, increased inflation uncertainty lowers inflation; while in two countries increased inflation uncertainty raises inflation. These findings have been extended to cover the developing world as well. Applying a similar testing procedure, Nas and Perry (2000) find evidence supporting the claim that inflation raises inflation uncertainty in Turkey over the full sample period of 1960–1998 and in the three sub-samples. They again show mixed results for the effect of inflation uncertainty on inflation, and claim that this is due to institutional and political factors in the monetary policy-making process in Turkey between 1960 and 1998. Wang *et al.* (1999) examine the causal relationships between inflation, inflation uncertainty as measured with the conditional variance of the aggregate inflation rate and relative price variability in sectoral price indices. They find that, although inflation does Granger cause inflation uncertainty, relative price variability is more a source of inflation uncertainty than the inflation level itself. In contrast, Grier and Perry (1996) present different findings in respect of these relationships and appear to contradict the results of their other studies. Various studies on the topic include Brunner and Hess (1993), and Loy and Weaver (1998).

In examining foreign exchange markets, time-varying volatility models have been widely adopted to study various issues ranging from time-varying risk premia, volatility spillovers between the spot and forward exchange market, and hedging strategies, to the effect of monetary policy. Searching for an explanation for the departure from uncovered interest parity (UIP), Tai (1999) examines the validity of the risk premium hypothesis using a GARCH-M (1, 1) model. The empirical evidence supports the notion of time-varying risk premia in explaining the deviations from UIP. It also supports the idea that foreign exchange risk is not diversifiable and hence should be priced in both the foreign exchange market and the equity market. Hu's (1997) approach is to examine the influence of macroeconomic variables on foreign exchange risk premia. The paper assumes that money and production follow a joint stochastic process with bivariate GARCH innovations based on Lucas's asset pricing model and implies that the risk premium in the foreign exchange market is due to time-varying volatilities in macroeconomic variables. Testing the model for three currencies shows that the time-varying risk premium is able to explain the deviation of the forward foreign exchange rate from the future spot rate. It is claimed that the model partially supports the efficient market hypothesis after accounting for time-varying risk premia. Investigating the effect of central bank intervention, Dominguez (1993) adopts GARCH models to test whether the conditional variance of exchange rates has been influenced by the intervention. The results indicate that intervention need not be publicly known for it to influence the conditional variance of exchange rate changes. Publicly known Fed intervention generally decreases exchange rate volatility, while secret intervention operations by both the Fed and the Bundesbank generally increase the volatility. Kim and Tsurumi (2000), Wang and Wang (1999), Hassapis (1995), Bollerslev and Melvin (1994), Copeland and Wang (1993), Mundaca (1991), Bollerslev (1990) and many other studies are also in this important area.

As mentioned earlier, time-varying volatility has become the norm in financial time series modelling, popularly accepted and applied by academics and professionals alike since the 1990s. Therefore, it does not appear to be feasible to completely list the application areas and individual cases. Among other things not covered by the brief survey in this section, there are applications in option modelling, dynamic hedging, the term structure of interest rates and interest rate-related financial instruments.

Questions and problems

1 Describe ARCH and GARCH in comparison with AR and ARMA in the mean process.
2 Discuss many variations of GARCH and their relevance to financial modelling.
3 What is the stochastic volatility model? Discuss the similarities and differences between a GARCH-type model and a stochastic volatility model.
4 Compare different specifications of multivariate GARCH models and comment on their advantages and disadvantages.
5 Collect data from Datastream to test for GARCH phenomena, using the following time series:

   a foreign exchange rates of selected industrialised nations and developing economies *vis-à-vis* the US$, taking the log or log difference transformation if necessary prior to the test;
   b CPI of the UK, US, Japan, China, Russia and Brazil, taking any necessary transformation prior to the test;
   c total return series of IBM, Microsoft, Sage, Motorola, Intel, Vodafone, and Telefonica, taking any necessary transformation prior to the test.

   What do you find of their characteristics?
6 Collect data from Datastream and apply various multivariate GARCH models to the following time series:

   a the spot and forward foreign exchange rates of selected industrialised nations and developing economies *vis-à-vis* the US$, taking the log or log difference transformation if necessary prior to the test;
   b the stock market return indices of the US (e.g. S&P 500) and the UK (e.g. FTSE 100);
   c the stock market return indices of Japan and Hong Kong.

   What do you find of their links in the second moment?
7 Discuss and comment on the new developments in modelling time-varying volatilities.

Note

1 Equation (14) becomes $h_{11,t} = \alpha_{11,0}^2 + \sum_{i=1}^{q} \alpha_{11,i}^2 \varepsilon_{t-i}^2 + \sum_{j=1}^{p} \beta_{11,j}^2$, so $\alpha_{11,0}^2$, $\alpha_{11,i}^2$ and $\beta_{11,j}^2$ are equivalent to α_0, α_i and β_j respectively, in equation (4).

References

Andersen, T. G. and Lund, J. (1997), Estimating continuous-time stochastic volatility models of the short-term interest rate, *Journal of Econometrics*, 77, 343–377.

Baba, Y., Engle, R. F., Kraft, D. F. and Kroner, K. F. (1990), Multivariate simultaneous generalised ARCH, *Mimeo*, Department of Economics, University of California, San Diego.

Bollerslev, T. (1990), Modelling the coherence in short-run nominal exchange rates: A multivariate generalized ARCH model, *Review of Economics and Statistics*, 72, 498–505.

Bollerslev, T. (1986), Generalized autoregressive conditional heteroskedasticity, *Journal of Econometrics*, 31, 307–327.

Bollerslev, T. and Melvin, M. (1994), Bid-ask spreads and volatility in the foreign exchange market: An empirical analysis, *Journal of International Economics*, 36, 355–372.

Bougerol, P. and Picard, N. (1992), Stationarity of GARCH processes and some nonnegative time series, *Journal of Econometrics*, 52, 115–127.

Brooks, R. D., Faff, R. W., McKenzie, M. D. and Mitchell, H. (2000), A multi-country study of power arch models and national stock market returns, *Journal of International Money and Finance*, 19, 377–397.

Brunner, A. D. and Hess, G. D. (1993), Are higher levels of inflation less predictable? A state-dependent conditional heteroscedasticity approach, *Journal of Business and Economic Statistics*, 11, 187–197.

Chen, N. F. (1991), Financial investment opportunities and the macroeconomy, *Journal of Finance*, 46, 529–554.

Chou, R. Y., Lin, J. L. and Wu, C. S. (1999), Modeling the Taiwan stock market and international linkages, *Pacific Economic Review*, 4, 305–320.

Copeland, L. and Wang, P. J. (1993), Estimating daily seasonals in financial time series: The use of high-pass spectral filters, *Economics Letters*, 43, 1–4.

Darbar, S. M. and Deb, P. (1997), Co-movements in international equity markets, *Journal of Financial Research*, 20, 305–322.

Ding, Z., Granger, C. W. J. and Engle, R. F. (1993), A long memory property of stock market returns and a new model, *Journal of Empirical Finance*, 1, 83–106.

Dominguez, K. M. (1993), Does central bank intervention increase the volatility of foreign exchange rates? *National Bureau of Economic Research Working Paper*. 4532.

Dunne, P. G. (1999), Size and book-to-market factors in a multivariate GARCH-in-Mean asset pricing application, *International Review of Financial Analysis*, 8, 35–52.

Engle, R. F. (1982), Autoregressive conditional heteroscedasticity with estimates of the variance of United Kingdom inflation, *Econometrica*, 50, 987–1007.

Engle, R. F. and Kroner, K. F. (1995), Multivariate simultaneous generalized ARCH, *Econometric Review*, 11, 122–150.

Engle, R. F., Lilien, D. M. and Robins, R. P. (1987), Estimating time varying risk premia in the term structure: The ARCH-M model, *Econometrica*, 55, 391–407.

Fama, E. and French, K. (1989), Business conditions and expected returns on stocks and bonds, *Journal of Financial Economics*, 25, 23–49.

Fong, W. M. and Cheng, P. L. (2000), On the rate of information absorption in the conditional variance of SES dual listed stocks, *International Journal of Theoretical and Applied Finance*, 3, 205–217.

Gallo, G. M. and Pacini, B. (1998), Early news is good news: The effects of market opening on market volatility, *Studies in Nonlinear Dynamics and Econometrics*, 2, 115–131.

Glosten, L. R., Jagannathan, R. and Runkle, D. (1993), On the relation between the expected value and the volatility of the normal excess return on stocks, *Journal of Finance*, 48, 1779–1801.

Grier, K. B. and Perry, M. J. (1996), Inflation, inflation uncertainty, and relative price dispersion: Evidence from bivariate GARCH-M models, *Journal of Monetary Economics*, 38, 391–405.

Grier, K. B. and Perry, M. J. (1998), On inflation and inflation uncertainty in the G7 countries, *Journal of International Money and Finance*, 17, 671–689.

Harvey, A., Ruiz, E. and Shephard, N. (1994), Multivariate stochastic variance models, *Review of Economic Studies*, 61, 247–264.

Hasan, I. and Francis, B. B. (1998), Macroeconomic factors and the asymmetric predictability of conditional variances, *European Financial Management*, 4, 207–230.

Hassapis, C. (1995), Exchange risk in the EMS: Some evidence based on a GARCH model, *Bulletin of Economic Research*, 47, 295–303.

Hu, X. Q. (1997), Macroeconomic uncertainty and the risk premium in the foreign exchange market, *Journal of International Money and Finance*, 16, 699–718.

Husain, F. (1998), Seasonality in the Pakistani equity market: The Ramadhan effect, *Pakistan Development Review*, 37, 77–81.

Judge, G. G., Hill, R. C., Griffiths, W. E., Lütkepohl, H. and Lee, T. C. (1988), *Introduction to the Theory and Practice of Econometrics*, John Wiley & Sons, Inc., New York.

Kim, S. and Rui, M. (1999), Price, volume and volatility spillovers among New York, Tokyo and London stock markets, *International Journal of Business*, 4, 41–61.

Kim, S. and Tsurumi, H. (2000), Korean currency crisis and regime change: A multivariate GARCH model with Bayesian approach, *Asia-Pacific Financial Markets*, 7, 31–44.

Koutmos, G. (1992), Asymmetric volatility and risk return tradeoff in foreign stock markets, *Journal of Multinational Financial Management*, 2, 27–43.

Kyle, A. S. (1985), Continuous auctions and insider trading, *Econometrica*, 53, 1315–1335.

Longin, F. M. (1997), The threshold effect in expected volatility: A model based on asymmetric information, *Review of Financial Studies*, 10, 837–869.

Loy, J. P. and Weaver, R. D. (1998), Inflation and relative price volatility in Russian food markets, *European Review of Agricultural Economics*, 25, 373–394.

Lumsdaine, R. L. (1991), Asymptotic properties of the maximum likelihood estimator in GARCH(1, 1) and IGARCH(1, 1) models, *Princeton University Department of Economics manuscript*.

Mecagni, M. and Sourial, M. S. (1999), The Egyptian stock market: Efficiency tests and volatility effects, *International Monetary Fund Working Paper*: 99-48.

Mundaca, B. G. (1991), The volatility of the Norwegian currency basket, *Scandinavian Journal of Economics*, 93, 53–73.

Nas, T. F. and Perry, M. J. (2000), Inflation, inflation uncertainty, and monetary policy in Turkey: 1960–1998, *Contemporary Economic Policy*, 18, 170–180.

Nelson, D. B. (1990), Stationarity and persistence in the GARCH (1, 1) model, *Econometric Theory*, 6, 318–334.

Nelson, D. B. (1991), Conditional heteroskedasticity in asset returns: A new approach, *Econometrica*, 59, 347–370.

Niarchos, N., Tse, Y., Wu, C. and Young, A. (1999), International transmission of information: A study of the relationship between the U.S. and Greek stock markets, *Multinational Finance Journal*, 3, 19–40.

Ruiz, E. (1994), Quasi-maximum likelihood estimation of stochastic volatility models, *Journal of Econometrics*, 63, 289–306.

Shields, K. K. (1997), Threshold modelling of stock return volatility on Eastern European markets, *Economics of Planning*, 30, 107–125.

Tai, C. S. (1999), Time-varying risk premia in foreign exchange and equity markets: Evidence from Asia-Pacific countries, *Journal of Multinational Financial Management*, 9, 291–316.

Tay, N. S. P. and Zhu, Z. (2000), Correlations in returns and volatilities in Pacific-Rim stock markets, *Open Economies Review*, 11, 27–47.

Wang, P. J. and Wang, P. (1999), Foreign exchange market volatility in Southeast Asia, *Asia Pacific Financial Markets*, 6, 235–252.

Wang, P. J. and Wang, P. (2001), Equilibrium adjustment, basis risk and risk transmission in spot and forward foreign exchange markets, *Applied Financial Economics*, 11, 127–136.

Wang, P. J., Wang, P. and Topham, N. (1999), Relative price variability and inflation uncertainty, *Applied Economics*, 31, 1531–1539.

4 Shock persistence and impulse response analysis

From the study of unit roots in Chapter 2 we have learned the distinctive characteristics of stationary and non-stationary time series. Nevertheless, although one of the main concerns in Chapter 2 was whether a time series has a unit root or not, there was no further examination regarding different properties of non-stationary time series – whether they are pure random walks or possess serial correlation. Furthermore, what is the serial correlation structure of a time series, if it is not a pure random walk? There are generally two categories of non-pure random walk time series. If the time series can be viewed as a combination of a pure random walk process and a stationary process with serial correlation, the long-run effect would be smaller than that of a pure random walk, and the time series would contain unit roots due to its non-stationary component. If there is no stationary component in the time series which is not a pure random walk either, then the first difference of the time series is a stationary process with serial correlation, and the long-run effect would be larger than that of a pure random walk. There would be, to a certain degree, a mean-reverting tendency in the former category due to its stationary component; and there would be a compounding effect in the latter. The interest in this chapter is then centred on the characteristics and behaviour of time series associated with their correlation structure, and the relative contribution and importance of the two components: the trend which is a pure random walk, and the cycle (after taking the first difference in the latter category) which is a stationary process involving serial correlation in the long run. How persistent a time series is depends on the relative contribution of these two components.

This chapter first discusses measures of persistence in time series in both univariate and multivariate cases. Then the chapter introduces impulse response analysis, which, in a similar way but from a different perspective to persistence analysis, shows graphically the path of response in a time series to a shock to itself or to another time series. Both orthogonal impulse response analysis and non-orthogonal cross-effect impulse response analysis are considered, together with their related and respective variance decomposition.

4.1 Univariate persistence measures

Economic time series are usually a combination of a non-stationary trend component and a stationary cycle component. Shocks to the two components are different in that they have remarkably different effects on future trend values. A shock to a stationary time series is transitory and the effect will disappear after a sufficiently long time. Taking a simple first-order autoregressive process for example:

$$y_{1,t} = c + \rho y_{1,t-1} + \varepsilon_{1,t} \tag{1}$$

where $\rho < 1$. Suppose there is a shock at time t with its magnitude being s, and there is no shock afterwards. Then after k periods, the time series evolves to:

$$y_{1,t+k} = \frac{1 - \rho^{k+1}}{1 - \rho} c + \rho^{k+1} y_{1,t-1} + \rho^k s = \frac{c}{1 - \rho} \quad \text{as } k \to \infty \tag{2}$$

that is, the time series reverts to its mean value and the impact of the shock disappears; the smaller the value of ρ, the quicker the impact disappears. In contrast, a shock to a trend as expressed in a pure random walk moves the time series away from its trend path permanently by an extent which is exactly the size of the shock. For example, if in the following random walk process:

$$y_{2,t} = c + y_{2,t-1} + \varepsilon_{2,t} \tag{3}$$

there is a shock at time t with a magnitude of s, and there is no further shock afterwards. Then, after k periods, the impact is to shift permanently the level of the time series by an extent of s:

$$y_{2,t+k} = (k + 1)c + y_{2,t-1} + s \tag{4}$$

The impact will not disappear even if $k \to \infty$.

If there is a third time series which is a combination of a stationary time series of the kind of equation (1) and a pure random walk such as equation (3), then the impact of a shock will not disappear, nor the impact would be exactly s. The permanent impact would usually be a figure smaller than s, depending on the relative contributions of the trend component and the cycle component. Furthermore, if $\rho > 1$ in equation (1), then the first difference of the time series is stationary and the impact of a shock will disappear after a sufficiently long time, while the impact of a shock to the time series itself would be greater than that to a pure random walk. Persistence is therefore introduced as a concept and a measure for the long run or permanent impact of shocks on time series, taking the above illustrated behaviour and patterns, which are beyond the question of testing for unit roots, into consideration. We first describe persistence with the infinite polynomial of the Wold moving average (MA) representation of time series, as adopted by Campbell and Mankiw (1987a,b); and then introduce more effective methods for its estimation and the ideas behind those methods. Persistence can be illustrated by the infinite polynomial of the Wold MA representation of a time series, $A(L)$, being evaluated at $L = 1$, that is:

$$\Delta y_t = A(L)\varepsilon_t, \quad \varepsilon_t \sim (0, \sigma_\varepsilon^2) \tag{5}$$

where

$$A(L) = 1 + A_1 L + A_2 L^2 + \cdots \tag{6}$$

is a polynomial in the lag operator L, and ε_t is zero mean and independent (not necessarily independent identical distribution (i.i.d.)) residuals. $A(1)$ ($= 1 + A_1 + A_2 + \cdots$) is $A(L)$ valued at $L = 1$. The impact of a shock in period t on the change or first difference of the time series in period $t + k$ is A_k. The impact of the shock on the level of the time series in period $t + k$ is therefore $1 + A_1 + \cdots + A_k$. The accumulated impact of the shock on the level of the time series is the infinite sum of these MA coefficients $A(1)$. The value of $A(1)$ can then be used as a measure of persistence. In a pure random walk, $A(1) = 1$; and in any stationary time series, $A(1) = 0$. For series which are neither stationary nor a pure random walk, $A(1)$ can take any value greater than zero. If $0 < A(1) < 1$, the time series would display mean-reversion tendency. If $A(1) > 1$, an unanticipated increase would be reinforced by other positive changes in the future, and the series would continue to diverge from its pre-shock expected level.

Having introduced the above straightforward representation of persistence, we discuss a second and non-parametric approach to measuring persistence proposed by Cochrane (1988), which is the ratio of the k period variance to the one period variance, being divided by $k + 1$. The method of the infinite polynomial of the Wold MA representation involves estimation of parameters $A(L)$ which are sensitive to change. The variance ratio method is non-parametric and the estimate is consequently more stable. The Cochrane (1988) persistence measure is known as V_k in the following formula:

$$V_k = \frac{1}{k+1} \frac{\text{Var}(\Delta_k y_t)}{\text{Var}(\Delta y_t)} = 1 + \frac{2}{\sigma_{\Delta y_t}^2} \sum_{\tau}^{k} \left(1 - \frac{\tau}{k+1}\right) \text{Cov}(\Delta y_t, \Delta y_{t-\tau})$$

$$= 1 + \frac{2}{\sigma_{\Delta y_t}^2} \sum_{\tau}^{k} \left(1 - \frac{\tau}{k+1}\right) R_\tau = 1 + 2 \sum_{\tau}^{k} \left(1 - \frac{\tau}{k+1}\right) \rho_\tau \tag{7}$$

where Δ_k is the k period difference operator and $\Delta_k y_t = y_t - y_{t-k}$; Δ is the usual one period difference operator and the subscript 1 is suppressed for simplicity, $R_\tau = \text{Cov}(\Delta y_t, \Delta y_{t-\tau})$ is the τth autocovariance in Δy_t and $\rho_\tau = \text{Cov}(\Delta y_t, \Delta y_{t-\tau})/\sigma_{\Delta y_t}^2$ is the τth autocorrelation in Δy_t. The right-hand side of equation (7) is in fact the spectrum of Δy_t at the zero frequency, passing through a k-size window. Interested readers can refer to Chapter 9 for detail.

In theory, the relationship between V_k and $A(1)$, ignoring any inaccuracies in estimation, is

$$V_k = A^2(1) \frac{\sigma_\varepsilon^2}{\sigma_{\Delta y_t}^2}$$

So let us define persistence consistently as follows:

$$P = V_k = A^2(1) \frac{\sigma_\varepsilon^2}{\sigma_{\Delta y_t}^2} \qquad (8)$$

But, as one cannot effectively estimate $A(1)$, one cannot effectively estimate P via $A(1)$ either. This is one of the reasons for having a V_k version of persistence. To empirically obtain the persistence measurement, approaches include ARMA, non-parametric and unobserved components methods. The ARMA approach is to estimate $A(1)$ direct, where parameters are quite sensitive to change with regard to estimation. The non-parametric approach is then widely adopted and has been written as two regressional analysis of time series (RATS) procedures by Goerlich (1992).

In the random walk circumstance, the variance of the k period difference of a time series is k times the variance of the one period difference of the time series, then the persistence measure $V_k = 1$. For any stationary series, the variance of the k period difference approaches twice the variance of the one period difference. In this case, V_k approaches zero when k becomes larger. The limit of the ratio of the two variances is, therefore, the measure of persistence. The choice of k, the number of autocorrelations to be included, is important. Too few autocorrelations may obscure the trend-reversion tendency in higher order autocorrelations; and too many autocorrelations may exaggerate the trend-reversion, since as k approaches the sample size T, the estimator approaches zero. Hence, though a larger k might be preferred, k must be small relative to the sample size.

4.2 Multivariate persistence

The persistence measures of V_k and $A(1)$ can be generalised and applied to multivariate time series. The multivariate V_k and $A(1)$ can then be jointly applied to a group of variables or sectors, for example, industrial production, construction and services, to evaluate the cross-section effects. Again, we first adopt the infinite polynomial of the Wold MA representation to demonstrate persistence measures in a way similar to equation (5):

$$\mathbf{\Delta y}_t = \mathbf{A}(\mathbf{L})\mathbf{\varepsilon}_t, \quad \mathbf{\varepsilon}_t \sim (0, \mathbf{\Sigma_\varepsilon}) \qquad (9)$$

where we use characters in bold for matrices and vectors.

$$\mathbf{A}(\mathbf{L}) = \mathbf{A}_0 + \mathbf{A}_1\mathbf{L} + \mathbf{A}_2\mathbf{L}^2 + \cdots \qquad (10)$$

is an $n \times 1$ dimension vector of infinite polynomials, $\Delta \mathbf{y}_t$ is an $n \times 1$ dimension vector of variables, $\boldsymbol{\varepsilon}_t$ is an $n \times 1$ dimension vector of residuals, and $\boldsymbol{\Sigma}_{\boldsymbol{\varepsilon}}$ is an $n \times n$ covariance matrix of residuals. Similar to the univariate case and extending equation (7), we have the multivariate persistence measure as follows:

$$P = \mathbf{A}(1)\boldsymbol{\Sigma}_{\boldsymbol{\varepsilon}}\boldsymbol{\Sigma}_{\Delta \mathbf{y}_t}^{-1}\mathbf{A}(1)' \tag{11}$$

which reduces to $A^2(1)(\sigma_\varepsilon^2/\sigma_{\Delta y_t}^2)$ in a univariate time series.

To obtain multivariate persistence measures, previous studies have attempted to scale the covariance matrix of residuals in different ways. Pesaran *et al.* (1993) use the conditional variance of $\Delta y_{j,t}$ (the jth diagonal element of $\boldsymbol{\Sigma}_{\boldsymbol{\varepsilon}}$) to normalise the jth column of the covariance matrix of residuals. Van de Gucht *et al.* (1996) use the unconditional variance of $\Delta y_{j,t}$ (the jth diagonal element of $\boldsymbol{\Sigma}_{\Delta \mathbf{y}_t}$) to scale the jth column of the covariance matrix of residuals, arguing that it is consistent with the univariate persistence measure proposed by Cochrane (1988). Both Van de Gucht *et al.* (1996) and Pesaran *et al.* (1993) regard the diagonal elements in the normalised covariance matrix as representing total persistence in individual sectors, and off-diagonal elements as the cross-effect between two sectors, for example, an element in the ith row and the jth column is the effect on the ith sector due to a shock in the jth sector. Both aim to generalise the persistence measure and have partly achieved this objective. They have extended the persistence measurement to the multivariate case. However, their normalisations use a single variance for the normalisation of a column and, whether conditional or unconditional, ignore the fact that the process is multivariate. In fact, the normalisation is as simple as in univariate cases. Instead of being scaled down by the unconditional variance, the covariance matrix of residuals should be normalised by the unconditional covariance matrix, that is, the covariance matrix for $\Delta \mathbf{y}_t$. To have an exact expression of multivariate persistence, the normalisation should be realised with matrix operations; it is not possible to achieve this with simple arithmetic division.

By considering possible effects from, and links with, other sectors, this measurement of multivariate persistence for individual sectors is more precise, compared with its univariate counterpart. With this approach, the effect on sector i due to shocks in sector j is represented by the (i, j) element in **P**, that is, **P**(i, j), while **P**(i, i) measures the sector-specific persistence.

Generalising the non-parametric persistence measure into the multivariate case, we define $\mathbf{V}_k$ as the k period covariance matrix times the inverse of the one period covariance matrix, divided by $k + 1$:

$$\mathbf{V}_k = \frac{1}{k+1}\boldsymbol{\Sigma}_{\Delta_k \mathbf{y}_t}\boldsymbol{\Sigma}_{\Delta \mathbf{y}_t}^{-1} \tag{12}$$

In a procedure equivalent to equation (7), letting $\Delta \mathbf{y}_t$ pass through a k-size window in the Fourier transform and evaluating at the zero frequency, we have:

$$
\mathbf{V}_k =
\begin{bmatrix}
1 + 2\sum_{\tau}^{k}\left(1 - \dfrac{\tau}{k+1}\right)R_{11,\tau} & \cdots & 1 + 2\sum_{\tau}^{k}\left(1 - \dfrac{\tau}{k+1}\right)R_{1n,\tau} \\
\vdots & & \\
1 + 2\sum_{\tau}^{k}\left(1 - \dfrac{\tau}{k+1}\right)R_{n1,\tau} & \cdots & 1 + 2\sum_{\tau}^{k}\left(1 - \dfrac{\tau}{k+1}\right)R_{nn,\tau}
\end{bmatrix}
$$

$$
\times
\begin{bmatrix}
R_{11,0} & \cdots & R_{1n,0} \\
\vdots & & \\
R_{n1,0} & & R_{nn,0}
\end{bmatrix}^{-1}
\tag{13}
$$

where $R_{ij,\tau} = \mathrm{Cov}(\Delta y_{i,t}, \Delta y_{j,t-\tau})$ is the covariance between $\Delta y_{i,t}$ and $\Delta y_{j,t}$ at lag τ, and $R_{ij,0} = \mathrm{Cov}(\Delta y_{i,t}, \Delta y_{j,t})$ is the contemporaneous covariance. The elements in the first matrix on the right-hand side are bivariate, but the elements in $\mathbf{V}_k$ are truly multivariate due to the second matrix on the right-hand side. So this measure of persistence takes account of the influence from all the sources in the system when considering $\mathbf{V}_k(i, j)$ in the appearance of interactions between the ith and jth time series.

Multivariate persistence analysis is more sensible in that, instead of analysing the individual variables separately as in univariate cases, it allows shocks to transmit from one variable to all the others. Therefore, multivariate persistence analysis is able to examine the sources of shocks and the effects of the shock in one sector on other sectors. Moreover, it is able to detect the effect of certain kinds of shocks, for example, a monetary shock, from that of other shocks, such as those from the real sectors. The multivariate measurement of persistence is not built on structural relations. As such, the inclusion of a specific kind of shock in persistence analysis will not lead to the violation of constraints, as it may in a system of structural equations. In addition, the effects of this specific shock can be evaluated in a VAR framework, which is relatively less complicated. A specific kind of shock can be added to the model, as in the following:

$$
\Delta \mathbf{y}_t = \mathbf{s}(\mathbf{L})\mathbf{v}_t + \mathbf{A}(\mathbf{L})\boldsymbol{\varepsilon}_t
\tag{14}
$$

where $\mathbf{v}_t$ represents specific shocks whose effects are to be analysed, which can be the demand shock, supply shock or monetary shock, depending on the way it is extracted from another fitted equation(s); and $\mathbf{s}(\mathbf{L})$ is an $n \times 1$ dimension vector of polynomials. By evaluating equation (14) with and without $\mathbf{v}_t$, one can establish whether an individual sector is subject to shock $\mathbf{v}_t$. Furthermore, in the existence of the effect of $\mathbf{v}_t$, the proportion of the persistence due to $\mathbf{v}_t$ and that due to other shocks can be identified. In theory, more than one set of specific shocks can be included; in which case, $\mathbf{v}_t$ becomes an m dimension vector with m being the number of sets of shocks, and $\mathbf{s}(\mathbf{L})$ is an $n \times m$ matrix. However, the estimation would not be feasible empirically, since greater inaccuracy would be introduced. In addition, this approach would be less appealing if it were to lose its advantages of no subjective assumptions and restrictions. Nevertheless, if there are only two types of shocks, for example, demand v. supply, or monetary v. real, then $\mathbf{v}_t$ can only be one of the two types of shocks, otherwise, equation (14) would be over-identified.

Persistence can be decomposed into separate components, that due to the specific shock and that due to other shocks:

$$\mathbf{P}_s = \mathbf{A}(1)\mathbf{s}(1)\sigma_v^2\mathbf{s}(1)'\boldsymbol{\Sigma}_{\Delta\mathbf{y}_t}^{-1}\mathbf{A}(1)' \tag{15}$$

$$\mathbf{P}_o = \mathbf{A}(1)\boldsymbol{\Sigma}_\varepsilon\boldsymbol{\Sigma}_{\Delta\mathbf{y}_t}^{-1}\mathbf{A}(1)' \tag{16}$$

and total persistence is:

$$\mathbf{P}_T = \mathbf{P}_s + \mathbf{P}_o \tag{17}$$

If the specific shock is chosen as the demand or monetary disturbance, then the underlying assumption is that the demand or monetary shock may also have a long-run effect, as the persistence measure is about the effect on the levels of variables. This assumption can be empirically ruled out or ruled in which, in effect, becomes a hypothesis. Although Blanchard and Quah (1989) arguably excluded the demand shock from having a long-run effect, their empirical work suggests that the effect of a demand shock would decline to vanish in about 25 quarters or 5–6 years. In such a long period, the probability of a structural change or break would be rather high. If a structural change does happen, it would override any supply shocks and the effects of demand and supply shocks would be mixed.

4.3   Impulse response analysis and variance decomposition

Impulse response analysis is another way of inspecting and evaluating the impact of shocks cross-section. While persistence measures focus on the long-run properties of shocks, impulse response traces the evolutionary path of the impact over time. Impulse response analysis, together with variance decomposition, forms innovation accounting for sources of information and information transmission in a multivariate dynamic system.

Considering the following vector autoregression (VAR) process:

$$\mathbf{y}_t = \mathbf{A}_0 + \mathbf{A}_1\mathbf{y}_{t-1} + \mathbf{A}_2\mathbf{y}_{t-2} + K + \mathbf{A}_k\mathbf{y}_{t-k} + \boldsymbol{\mu}_t \tag{18}$$

where $\mathbf{y}_t$ is an $n \times 1$ vector of variables, $\mathbf{A}_0$ is an $n \times 1$ vector of intercept, $\mathbf{A}_\tau$ ($\tau = 1, \ldots, k$) are $n \times n$ matrices of coefficients, $\boldsymbol{\mu}_t$ is an n dimension vector of white noise processes with $E(\boldsymbol{\mu}_t) = 0$, $\boldsymbol{\Sigma}_\mu = E(\boldsymbol{\mu}_t\boldsymbol{\mu}_t')$ being non-singular for all t, and $E(\boldsymbol{\mu}_t\boldsymbol{\mu}_s')$ for $t \neq s$. Without losing generality, exogenous variables other than lagged $\mathbf{y}_t$ are omitted for simplicity. A stationary VAR process of equation (18) can be shown to have a MA representation of the following form:

$$\mathbf{y}_t = \mathbf{C} + \boldsymbol{\mu}_t + \boldsymbol{\Phi}_1\boldsymbol{\mu}_{t-1} + \boldsymbol{\Phi}_2\boldsymbol{\mu}_{t-2} + \mathbf{K}$$

$$= \mathbf{C} + \sum_{\tau=0}^{\infty} \boldsymbol{\Phi}_\tau \boldsymbol{\mu}_{t-\tau} \tag{19}$$

where $\mathbf{C} = E(\mathbf{y}_t) = (\mathbf{I} - \mathbf{A}_1 - \cdots - \mathbf{A}_k)^{-1}\mathbf{A}_0$, and $\boldsymbol{\Phi}_\tau$ can be computed from $\mathbf{A}_\tau$ recursively $\boldsymbol{\Phi}_\tau = \mathbf{A}_1\boldsymbol{\Phi}_{\tau-1} + \mathbf{A}_2\boldsymbol{\Phi}_{\tau-2} + \mathbf{K} + \mathbf{A}_k\boldsymbol{\Phi}_{\tau-k}$, $\tau = 1, 2, \Lambda$, with $\boldsymbol{\Phi}_0 = \mathbf{I}$ and $\boldsymbol{\Phi}_\tau = 0$ for $\tau < 0$.

The MA coefficients in equation (19) can be used to examine the interaction between variables. For example, $a_{ij,k}$, the ijth element of $\boldsymbol{\Phi}_k$, is interpreted as the reaction, or impulse response, of the ith variable to a shock τ periods ago in the jth variable, provided that the effect is isolated from the influence of other shocks in the system. So a seemingly crucial problem in the study of impulse response is to isolate the effect of a shock on a variable of interest from the influence of all other shocks, which is achieved mainly through orthogonalisation.

Orthogonalisation *per se* is straightforward and simple. The covariance matrix $\boldsymbol{\Sigma}_\mu = E(\boldsymbol{\mu}_t\boldsymbol{\mu}_t')$, in general, has non-zero off-diagonal elements. Orthogonalisation is a transformation, which results in a set of new residuals or innovations $\mathbf{v}_t$ satisfying $E(\mathbf{v}_t\mathbf{v}_t') = \mathbf{I}$. The procedure is to choose any non-singular matrix $\mathbf{G}$ of transformation for $\mathbf{v}_t = \mathbf{G}^{-1}\boldsymbol{\mu}_t$ so that $\mathbf{G}^{-1}\boldsymbol{\Sigma}_\mu\mathbf{G}'^{-1} = \mathbf{I}$. In the process of transformation or orthogonalisation, $\boldsymbol{\Phi}_\tau$ is replaced by $\boldsymbol{\Phi}_\tau\mathbf{G}$ and $\boldsymbol{\mu}_t$ is replaced by $\mathbf{v}_t = \mathbf{G}^{-1}\boldsymbol{\mu}_t$, and equation (19) becomes:

$$\mathbf{y}_t = \mathbf{C} + \sum_{\tau=0}^{\infty} \boldsymbol{\Phi}_\tau \boldsymbol{\mu}_{t-\tau} = \mathbf{C} + \sum_{\tau=0}^{\infty} \boldsymbol{\Phi}_\tau \mathbf{G} \mathbf{v}_{t-\tau}, \qquad E(\mathbf{v}_t\mathbf{v}_t') = \mathbf{I} \tag{20}$$

Suppose that there is a unit shock to, for example, the jth variable at time 0 and there is no further shock afterwards, and there are no shocks to any other variables. Then after k periods, $\mathbf{y}_t$ will evolve to the level:

$$\mathbf{y}_{t+k} = \mathbf{C} + \left(\sum_{\tau=0}^{k} \boldsymbol{\Phi}_\tau \mathbf{G}\right) \mathbf{e}(\mathbf{j}) \tag{21}$$

where $\mathbf{e}(\mathbf{j})$ is a selecting vector with its jth element being one and all other elements being zero. The accumulated impact is the summation of the coefficient matrices from time 0 to k. This is made possible because the covariance matrix of the transformed residuals is a unit matrix $\mathbf{I}$ with off-diagonal elements being zero. Impulse response is usually exhibited graphically based on equation (21). A shock to each of the n variables in the system results in n impulse response functions and graphs, so there are a total of $n \times n$ graphs showing these impulse response functions.

To achieve orthogonalisation, the Choleski factorisation, which decomposes the covariance matrix of residuals Σ_μ into GG' so that G is lower triangular with positive diagonal elements, is commonly used. However, this approach is not invariant to the ordering of the variables in the system. In choosing the ordering of the variables, one may consider their statistical characteristics. By construction of G, the first variable in the ordering explains all of its one-step forecast variance, so a variable which is least influenced by other variables, such as an exogenous variable, is consigned to the first in the ordering. Then the variable with least influence on other variables is chosen as the last variable in the ordering. The other approach to orthogonalisation is based on the economic attributes of data, such as the Blanchard and Quah structural decomposition. It is assumed that there are two types of shocks, the supply shock and the demand shock. While the supply shock has permanent effect, the demand shock has only temporary or transitory effect. Restrictions are imposed accordingly to realise orthogonalisation in the residuals.

Since the residuals have been orthogonalised, variance decomposition is straightforward. The k-period ahead forecast errors in equation (19) or (20) are:

$$\sum_{\tau=0}^{k-1} \Phi_\tau G v_{t-\tau+k-1} \tag{22}$$

The covariance matrix of the k-period ahead forecast errors are:

$$\sum_{\tau=0}^{k-1} \Phi_\tau GG' \Phi_\tau' = \sum_{\tau=0}^{k-1} \Phi_\tau \Sigma_\mu \Phi_\tau' \tag{23}$$

The right-hand side of equation (23) just reminds the reader that the outcome of variance decomposition will be the same irrespective of G. The choice or derivation of matrix G only matters when the impulse response function is concerned to isolate the effect from the influence from other sources.

The variance of forecast errors attributed to a shock to the jth variable can be picked out by a selecting vector $e(j)$, with the jth element being one and all other elements being zero:

$$\text{Var}(j, k) = \left(\sum_{\tau=0}^{k-1} \Phi_\tau G e(j) \, e(j)' G' \Phi_\tau' \right) \tag{24}$$

Further, the effect on the ith variable due to a shock to the jth variable, or the contribution to the ith variable's forecast error by a shock to the jth variable, can be picked out by a second selecting vector $e(i)$ with the ith element being one and all other elements being zero.

$$\text{Var}(ij, k) = \mathbf{e}(i)' \left(\sum_{\tau=0}^{k-1} \mathbf{\Phi}_\tau \mathbf{G} \mathbf{e}(\mathbf{j}) \mathbf{e}(\mathbf{j})' \mathbf{G}' \mathbf{\Phi}_\tau' \right) \mathbf{e}(i) \tag{25}$$

In relative terms, the contribution is expressed as a percentage of the total variance:

$$\frac{\text{Var}(ij, k)}{\sum_{j=1}^{n} \text{Var}(ij, k)} \tag{26}$$

which sums up to 100 per cent.

4.4 Non-orthogonal cross-effect impulse response analysis

There are other ways to evaluate the effect of a shock. One of the main advantages of applying orthogonalised residuals is that the impact at time k due to a unit shock to the jth variable at time 0 is simply the summation of matrices $\mathbf{\Phi}_\tau \mathbf{G}$, over $0 \le \tau \le k$, being timed by the selecting vector $\mathbf{e}(\mathbf{j})$. That is, there is no need to consider the effect due to shocks to other than the jth variable because such an effect does not exist. Then it would be a reasonable idea not to perform orthogonalisation but to consider the effect arising from the non-orthogonalisation of residuals, or the cross-effect, in impulse response analysis. With non-orthogonal residuals, when there is a shock to the jth variable of the size of its standard deviation, there are shocks to other variables in the meantime through their correlations. Let δ_j stand for such shocks:

$$\delta_j = \begin{bmatrix} \rho_{1j} \\ \vdots \\ 1 \\ \rho_{nj} \end{bmatrix} \sqrt{\sigma_{jj}} = \begin{bmatrix} \sigma_{1j} \\ \vdots \\ \sigma_{jj} \\ \sigma_{nj} \end{bmatrix} \frac{1}{\sqrt{\sigma_{jj}}} = \mathbf{\Sigma}_\mu \mathbf{e}(\mathbf{j}) \frac{1}{\sqrt{\sigma_{jj}}} \tag{27}$$

With such a shock to the jth variable at time 0 and supposing there is no further shock afterwards, $\mathbf{y}_t$ will evolve to the level after k periods:

$$\mathbf{y}_{t+k} = \mathbf{C} + \left(\sum_{\tau=0}^{k} \mathbf{\Phi}_\tau \right) \mathbf{e}(\mathbf{j}) \frac{1}{\sqrt{\sigma_{jj}}} \tag{28}$$

So, it appears that orthogonalisation can be avoided. But bearing in mind that, in non-orthogonal impulse response analysis, we cannot simply give a shock of one standard deviation to the equation of interest, the jth equation, only; we should, in the meantime, give a 'shock' to each of other equations of the size of the square root of its covariance with the jth shock. It indeed means that we have to consider both the direct effect of the jth shock and the indirect effect of the jth shock through other series in the system. Moreover, the outcome would be in general different to that from orthogonal impulse response analysis.

Let us work out variance decomposition in a slightly different way. We consider single elements first. The k-period ahead forecast errors in equation (28) are:

$$\sum_{\tau=0}^{k-1} \Phi_\tau \Sigma_\mu \mathbf{e}(\mathbf{j}) \frac{1}{\sqrt{\sigma_{jj}}} \tag{29}$$

The covariance matrix of the k-period ahead forecast errors contributed to the jth shock are:

$$\text{Var}(\mathbf{j}, k) = \frac{1}{\sigma_{jj}} \sum_{\tau=0}^{k-1} \Phi_\tau \Sigma_\mu \mathbf{e}(\mathbf{j}) \mathbf{e}(\mathbf{j})' \Sigma_\mu \Phi_\tau' \tag{30}$$

The total covariance matrix is the summation of equation (30) over j:

$$\sum_{j=1}^{n} \frac{1}{\sigma_{jj}} \sum_{\tau=0}^{k-1} \Phi_\tau \Sigma_\mu \mathbf{e}(\mathbf{j}) \mathbf{e}(\mathbf{j})' \Sigma_\mu \Phi_\tau' \tag{31}$$

which is different from equation (23). The variance of the ith variable contributed to the jth shock and the total variance of the ith variable are:

$$\text{Var}(ij, k) = \frac{1}{\sigma_{jj}} \mathbf{e}(\mathbf{i})' \left(\sum_{\tau=0}^{k-1} \Phi_\tau \Sigma_\mu \mathbf{e}(\mathbf{j}) \mathbf{e}(\mathbf{j})' \Sigma_\mu \Phi_\tau' \right) \mathbf{e}(\mathbf{i}) \tag{32}$$

and

$$\text{Var}(i, k) = \sum_{j=1}^{n} \frac{1}{\sigma_{jj}} \mathbf{e}(\mathbf{i})' \left(\sum_{\tau=0}^{k-1} \Phi_\tau \Sigma_\mu \mathbf{e}(\mathbf{j}) \mathbf{e}(\mathbf{j})' \Sigma_\mu \Phi_\tau' \right) \mathbf{e}(\mathbf{i}) \tag{33}$$

respectively. The contribution by the jth shock as expressed as a percentage of the total variance is:

$$\frac{\text{Var}(ij, k)}{\text{Var}(j, k)} = \frac{\text{Var}(ij, k)}{\sum_{j=1}^{n} \text{Var}(ij, k)} \tag{34}$$

which sums up to 100 per cent.[1]

4.5   Examples and cases

Example 1

This case presents the profile of the UK property market's responses to shocks from various sources by Wang (2000). We only use and discuss the multivariate part of the study. The variables considered in the study in relation to persistence in the property market are the Jones Lang Wootten property total return index (JLW) (with necessary adjustment), the Nationwide Building Society House Price Index (NTW), the Financial Times Actuary All Share Index (FTA), Construction output on new work (CO), Total production (PDN), Services (SVC), the Unemployment rate (UER), and the Money supply (M0). All the economic data are of quarterly frequency and from the Office for National Statistics (ONS) of the UK. They are all seasonally adjusted for consistency, as not all data are available in the form of non-seasonally adjusted. Table 4.1 presents the multivariate persistence estimates with the six sectors represented by JLW, FTA, NTW, CO, PDN and SVC. The diagonal elements in the table are sector-specific persistence measures (the diagonal elements in the $\mathbf{P}$ or $\mathbf{V}_k$ matrix). FTA, the stock market index, is most close to a random walk with its $A(1)k$ being very close to unity. Total production and services do not have as large persistence measures as property, housing and construction. No direct comparison with other studies is possible, because there have been virtually no studies of persistence of shocks in the UK economy and sectors. Several US studies have reported that the services sector has a large persistence measure estimate while the production sector has a relatively low value for persistence measurement. It is also documented that utilities exhibit considerable persistence while manufacturing has a rather small value for persistence measurement. It is also documented that utilities exhibit considerable persistence while manufacturing has a rather small value for persistence measurement. In Table 4.1 the production sector's V_k of 1.3348 would be an aggregate estimate combining a higher value of persistence for utilities and lower value of persistence for manufacturing. As the intention of this multivariate persistence analysis is to investigate the cross-sectional effects between property and the broadly classified sectors, no further disaggregation is necessary and appropriate here.

The off-diagonal elements in Table 4.1 provide information that is not found in univariate persistence analysis. It has been revealed that shocks from the

Table 4.1 Multivariate persistence

Effect on	Sources of shocks					
	JLW	*FTA*	*NTW*	*CO*	*PDN*	*SVC*
JLW	2.6243	0.8744	2.7542	1.0119	1.0782	1.5273
FTA	0.7962	0.8284	1.2710	0.6919	0.1238	1.0530
NTW	3.0412	1.5032	4.4957	1.3024	1.3020	2.3466
CO	−0.3611	−0.0746	−0.9907	2.8815	0.7135	0.8976
PDN	0.4385	−0.1939	0.0468	1.5431	1.3348	0.5788
SVC	0.8457	0.6488	0.9700	1.9384	0.7768	1.5798

Note: Same as in the univariate cases, the standard error of these statistics is $(4(k+1)/3N)VC_k(i, j)$ (with the Bartlett window), where N is the number of observations. k is in fact the window size in the frequency domain. With our specification, it can be inferred the window size is about 1/4 of the total observations, so the standard error of these statistics is acceptable. See Priestley (1996). Detail from the author upon request.

housing market have the largest effect on the persistence in property, with the cross-sectional effect on JLW from NTW being 2.7542. It is followed by the services sector which is also quite substantial, the production sector and construction. Shocks in the stock market have effects on the persistence in property, but they are the smallest among all selected variables, with the cross-sectional effect on JLW being 0.8744.

Regarding the effects of the property market on other sectors, again, the largest impacts seem to be felt in the housing market, with the cross-sectional effect on NTW from JLW being 3.0412. So the commercial and non-commercial property markets have very close links in this perspective. The effects of shocks on the services sector (0.8457) are larger than those on the production sector (0.4385), as expected. A negative figure for the effects on construction suggests, in statistical terms, that the one period covariance and the n ($n \to \infty$) period covariance have different signs. This is only possible in covariance but not in variance. The empirical meaning of a negative cross-sectional persistence measure would be: a positive shock in the property market which also results in an increase in construction (i.e. a positive one period covariance is assumed) would eventually lead to a decrease in CO, or contraction in the construction industry, in the long run. This revelation of the interaction between the property market and the construction sector has profound economic implications.

The reported multivariate persistence measurement estimates are derived using an unrestricted VAR model of order 2 (the inverse of the matrix is effectively corresponding to an infinite MA process). The restricted model, which drops the regressors whose t-statistic of coefficient is less than one, is also tested. The two sets of results are similar, so the unrestricted model is adopted for reasons that it is easy to implement in the future and in slightly different situations.[2] This is consistent with Cochrane's (1988) recommendation of including all autocorrelation terms even if they are insignificant. Both models are estimated with Seemingly Unrelated Regression (SUR), though there are no efficiency gains from using an OLS procedure to applying SUR in the unrestricted model.

The paper further decomposes shocks into monetary and non-monetary components. The above tests have analysed the 'sources' of shocks, and the sources are sectors. In the following, the sources are divided into monetary and non-monetary ones. The reasons for adopting this line of research are as follows. Traditionally, the effect of a monetary shock is viewed as only being temporary or transitory, while a real shock has both permanent and transitory effects. In the long run, the effect of the monetary shock disappears and the only effect left is due to the real shock. Similarly, a demand shock is viewed as temporary and a supply shock as permanent. In separating or decomposing a monetary shock from non-monetary shocks, one is able to evaluate the long-run and short-term effects more effectively. However, the traditional view, which suggests that the monetary shock is not held responsible for any permanent or long-run effects, may be over-assertive and should be empirically tested. In this study, if the effect of the monetary shock is not long lasting, then the monetary shock would have no contribution to the persistence measure. Obviously, different test results would have different implications for policy making and practice, especially with regard to a long-run perspective.

Monetary shocks can be derived from estimating a money supply growth model and obtaining its residuals. The money supply growth model is specified as follows:

$$\Delta M_t = \alpha + \beta \Delta M_{t-1} + \gamma \Delta SVC_{t-1} + \delta UER_{t-1} + v_t \tag{35}$$

where M_t is money supply, SVC_t is services output and UER_t is the unemployment rate. M0, the narrowly defined money, is chosen as the money supply variable in this model. The reasons for using M0 instead of M4, the broad money supply, are empirical. There is a big break in the M4 series in the fourth quarter of 1981 caused by the switch between the old banking sector and the new monetary sector. In July 1989, Abbey National's conversion to a public limited company caused minor breaks to the M0 series and major breaks in the M4 series. Although the first breaks in the fourth quarter of 1981 were removed from the changes in M4, the removal of the breaks in the changes in M4 resulted in as much distortion as the retaining of the breaks in M4 levels. Besides these breaks, the M0 and M4 series had a similar pattern. Beyond the concern in breaks, M0 is more liquid and more public sensitive in representing demand factors, separated from supply factors or real factors. Table 4.2 reports the summary statistics for the money growth model.

The multivariate shock persistence model has been re-estimated with monetary shocks, the residuals from the money supply growth model, being included. All the estimates are reported in Table 4.3, and a summary with sector-specific estimates and the percentage of monetary and non-monetary effects is provided in Table 4.4. The first line for each variable in Table 4.3 is the total persistence, the second line the effects of non-monetary shocks as represented by the second term on the right-hand side of equation (17), and the third line the effects of monetary shocks represented by the first term on the right-hand side of equation (17). As above, the diagonal elements are sector-specific persistence measurement, and off-diagonal elements are cross persistence measurement. Overall, the persistence estimates are smaller than those in Table 4.1, except that for the construction sector. This

Table 4.2 Summary statistics for the money growth model

	α	β	γ	δ	Q
M0	0.0155***	0.4551***	0.3616***	−0.0011**	19.9744
	(3.2723)	(4.1013)	(2.6350)	(2.4180)	(0.2753)

Notes

Q – Ljung–Box statistic for serial correlation, the order is selected as 1/4 of the observations used. *p*-value in brackets.

  * Significant at the 10% level.
 ** Significant at the 5% level.
*** Significant at the 1% level. *t*-statistics in brackets for coefficients.

Table 4.3 Multivariate persistence: monetary shocks decomposed

Effect on	Sources of shocks					
	JLW	FTA	NTW	CO	PDN	SVC
JLW	2.2304	0.4559	2.0688	0.6253	0.6802	0.8212
	2.0389	0.3347	1.5680	0.7949	0.7011	0.7515
	0.1915	0.1212	0.5008	−0.1695	−0.0208	0.0697
FTA	0.3265	0.5301	0.5480	0.4431	−0.1140	0.6191
	0.3253	0.4216	0.3856	0.4922	−0.0267	0.5090
	0.0012	0.1084	0.1624	−0.0492	−0.0874	0.1101
NTW	2.2713	0.7616	3.3395	0.5288	0.7238	1.1391
	1.9208	0.5440	2.4043	0.8496	0.7536	1.0188
	0.3505	0.2176	0.9352	−0.3209	−0.0298	0.1204
CO	−0.4758	−0.0522	−1.2515	3.0167	0.7594	0.9497
	−0.3522	−0.0362	−1.0157	2.9111	0.7699	0.9403
	−0.1236	−0.0160	0.0849	0.1057	−0.0105	0.0094
PDN	0.1860	−0.2489	−0.2548	1.4501	1.2941	0.4737
	0.1776	−0.2774	0.3397	1.4776	1.2826	0.4481
	0.0083	0.0285	0.0849	−0.0275	0.0115	0.0256
SVC	0.1568	0.3699	−0.0256	1.6847	0.4481	1.2115
	0.2742	0.2303	−0.0559	1.7202	0.6274	1.0124
	−0.1174	0.1396	0.0303	−0.0354	−0.1794	0.1991

Table 4.4 Multivariate persistence: summary of monetary and non-monetary shocks

Effect on	Monetary shocks		Non-monetary shocks		Total
	V_K	%	V_K	%	
JLW	0.1915	8.59	2.0389	91.41	2.2304
FTA	0.1084	20.45	0.4216	79.55	0.5301
NTW	0.9352	28.00	2.4043	72.00	3.3395
CO	0.1057	3.50	2.9111	96.50	3.0167
PDN	0.0115	0.89	1.2826	99.11	1.2941
SVC	0.1991	16.43	1.0124	83.57	1.2115

is because of the inclusion of the monetary shocks, which are expected to have smaller effects in the long run, in the model. In previous estimation without an explicit monetary shock variable (or a monetary variable), the persistence effects due to monetary shocks are mixed with other shocks. Further, scrutiny has found that the decrease in the persistence measure happens in those sectors which are subject to monetary shocks to a substantial degree, for example, housing where monetary shocks account for 28 per cent in total persistence, services, 16 per cent, and the stock market, 20 per cent. Monetary shocks only account for 4 per cent of total persistence in construction, and an even smaller figure of less than 1 per cent in the production sector, so their total persistence estimates are largely unaffected. In summary, a broadly defined production sector including construction, or the real economy, or the supply side of economy, is not subject to monetary shocks in the long run; whereas the services sector, broadly defined to include housing and the stock market, or the demand side of economy, or consumption, is very much influenced by monetary shocks. Commercial property, due to its fundamental links to the real economy and financial markets, reasonably stands in between the effects of monetary shocks being responsible for 9 per cent of total persistence measurement, and a large part of persistence is from non-monetary shocks caused in the real sector of the economy.

Example 2

In a recent paper, Dekker *et al.* (2001) applied both orthogonal and non-orthogonal cross-effect, or generalised, impulse response analysis to stock market linkages in Asia-Pacific. They use daily closing data of returns for a rather short period from 1 January 1987 to 29 May 1998, on 10 market indices in the region, namely, Australia's SE All Ordinary, Hong Kong's Hang Seng, Japan's Nikkei 225 Average, Malaysia's Kuala Lumpur Composite, New Zealand's SE Capital 40, the Philippines' SE Composite, Singapore's *Straits Times* Industrial, Taiwan's SE Weighted, Thailand's Bangkok Book Club, and the US Standard & Poor 500 Composite. Their models were tested using the indices as expressed in the US dollar as well as in local currencies. It is claimed that both data sets produce consistent results so only the results from using local currencies are reported in the paper. Amongst the 10 economies, Malaysia, the Philippines, Taiwan and Thailand are classified as emerging markets and the rest as developed markets.

The models and the treatment of variables are exactly those in Pesaran and Shin (1998). Consequently, variance decomposition with the generalised impulse response procedure inevitably runs into the problem that the total variance does not sum to 100 per cent. The paper deals with the problem by standardising the total variance, or scaling the total variance to 100 per cent. Although cointegration relationships are found in the data, the authors choose to apply an unrestricted VAR in the first difference without incorporating the error correction term, having reviewed the relevant literature in which an unrestricted VAR is preferred to a vector error correction model (VECM) in short horizons. The paper performs impulse response analysis over 15 days and presents 5-, 10- and 15-day ahead forecast variance decomposition. In orthogonal response analysis, the variables are ordered according to the closing time, with the most exogenous market, which in this case is the US, being the first. Table 4.5 presents the results from orthogonal variance decomposition while Table 4.6 is for those from generalised variance decomposition. As there is no substantial variation, only the results for day 15 are provided.

The paper makes common sense comparison between the orthogonal and the generalised variance decomposition results. For example, with closing time

Table 4.5 Orthogonal decomposition of forecast error variances for daily market returns for 10 Asia-Pacific markets: 15-day horizon

Effect on	Innovations in										
	Australia	Hong Kong	Japan	Malaysia	New Zealand	Philippines	Singapore	Taiwan	Thailand	US	All foreign
Australia	61.86	1.2434	0.4190	0.7736	10.70	0.9937	0.3472	0.5010	0.1912	22.95	38.14
Hong Kong	3.7954	76.76	2.2084	0.5356	2.5652	2.4665	0.4848	0.6669	0.6602	9.8596	23.24
Japan	2.4033	0.3245	86.38	0.1338	1.9109	0.3719	0.4858	1.0619	0.2365	6.6953	13.62
Malaysia	1.4956	8.0847	1.6725	54.56	1.6234	1.8302	19.20	0.9947	0.7882	9.7527	45.44
New Zealand	2.4478	1.0501	0.5868	0.4381	77.92	0.4402	0.6593	0.3093	0.2064	15.94	22.08
Philippines	0.2580	0.7532	0.6074	1.2595	0.8184	89.93	0.4930	0.9431	0.7328	4.2023	10.07
Singapore	3.9231	9.8790	1.5353	1.0009	2.1997	3.6799	60.75	1.1406	0.6726	15.22	39.25
Taiwan	0.6490	0.3131	0.1535	0.1467	0.8570	0.2967	0.4565	94.41	0.3786	2.3381	5.59
Thailand	0.7661	2.7976	0.7318	1.6507	0.7751	2.1737	3.9772	1.1219	80.13	5.8802	19.87
US	0.8925	0.6491	0.2373	0.2788	0.3792	0.5864	0.4700	0.3024	0.6313	95.57	4.43

Table 4.6 Generalised decomposition of forecast error variances for daily market returns for 10 Asia-Pacific markets: 15-day horizon

Effect on	Innovations in										
	Australia	Hong Kong	Japan	Malaysia	New Zealand	Philippines	Singapore	Taiwan	Thailand	US	All foreign
Australia	56.45	5.6008	2.7171	2.1190	8.3087	1.1327	4.5123	0.7183	0.6586	17.78	43.55
Hong Kong	4.3553	60.87	2.7598	7.6287	1.7912	2.1004	11.01	0.6114	2.0003	6.8775	39.13
Japan	3.2464	3.5870	77.98	2.3550	1.6324	0.3189	3.3952	1.0899	0.7011	5.6973	22.03
Malaysia	1.9241	8.2482	1.8899	55.01	1.0477	1.4208	20.18	0.7355	3.2695	6.2784	44.99
New Zealand	11.43	3.5104	2.3341	1.1643	63.81	0.5837	2.6339	0.6866	0.5234	13.05	36.19
Philippines	1.1852	3.8328	0.9343	3.9294	0.7017	77.66	5.3348	0.8805	1.9679	3.5829	22.35
Singapore	3.7789	10.43	2.1103	17.71	1.3428	2.6520	49.01	0.8338	2.9020	9.2371	50.98
Taiwan	1.5537	1.3017	1.2884	1.2419	0.7931	0.5862	2.1089	87.80	1.1669	2.1549	12.20
Thailand	1.1120	4.3221	1.0063	6.1836	0.6352	2.1180	7.5476	1.0419	71.28	4.7574	28.72
US	0.8076	1.9336	1.3817	0.8446	0.3651	0.5874	1.2743	0.3742	0.9412	91.49	8.51

ordering in orthogonal variance decomposition, New Zealand is ordered before Australia. The ordering appears to have a distorting effect on the variance decomposition results: shocks in the New Zealand market explain a much larger proportion of variance of 10.70 per cent in the Australian market, compared with a rather small figure of 1.99 per cent contributed by the Australian market to the New Zealand market, on day 15. This seems to be difficult to justify, considering the relative size of the two markets. In contrast, generalised variance decomposition provides apparently reasonable results that the contribution of the New Zealand market to the Australian market is 8.31 per cent while shocks in the Australian market account for a large amount of 11.43 per cent of the total variance in the New Zealand market, on day 15. Following this common sense discussion, the paper employs Table 4.6 for further analysis. There are three main conclusions. First, the US market is the most influential in Asia-Pacific. No other market contributes more than 2 per cent of the US total forecast variance, while the contribution of the US market to other markets is significant with many of them being over 10 per cent. Second, the level of exogeneity of a market is proportional to the amount of the forecast variance explained by the market itself. The US, with over 90 per cent total forecast variance being accounted for by itself, is the most exogenous. While Singapore is the most endogenous because over 50 per cent total forecast variance is attributed to shocks in the other markets. Third, markets with strong economic ties and close geographic links, such as the pairs of Australia and New Zealand and Malaysia and Singapore, have significant interaction with each other. Impulse response graphs confirm the above results. Impulse analysis also indicates that the impact of shocks disappears quickly, usually in no more than one day.

4.6 Empirical literature

Persistence and impulse response are a mainly empirical matter. Persistence looks into the long-run behaviour of time series in response to shocks and reflects the relative contribution and importance of the trend and the cycle. Inspecting the persistence profile of a time series, the effect of shocks in the long run can be evaluated, which is of help to both macroeconomic policy formation and micro-investment decision making. The other aspects in the study of the effect of shocks are the response profile over the whole time horizon of interest, including the magnitudes of the response, termed as impulse response analysis, and the examination of the sources of the disturbance, termed as variance decomposition. Many multivariate models, such as the VAR, are complemented with impulse response analysis and variance decomposition, after the model has been set up and tested. All of these reflect the importance of this chapter in empirical studies.

Following the initiatives of Campbell and Mankiw (1987a,b) and Cochrane (1988), whose concerns are the behaviour of US aggregate GNP/GDP data, persistence in macroeconomic time series have been further investigated in the sectors, in other economies and in other economic and financial variables. Pesaran *et al.* (1993) extend measures of persistence into multivariate cases and examine the persistence profile in 10 US GNP sectors, though they do not consider the cross-effect of persistence between sectors. Most of the sectors are found to be very persistent in response to shocks with the persistence measure being greater than one, suggesting there is compounding effect. In comparison, utilities exhibit the largest compounding persistence followed by services, while persistence in manufacturing is relatively lower. Mayadunne *et al.* (1995) have carried out similar research using the Australian data and made comparison with the US results. Concerned with the random walk hypothesis in foreign exchange rates, Van de Gucht *et al.* (1996) examine persistence in seven daily foreign spot exchange rates of the Canadian dollar, the French franc, the Swiss franc, the German mark, the Italian lire, the Japanese yen and the British pound *vis-à-vis* the US dollar over the period 3 September 1974–27 May 1992. They find departure from the random walk benchmark, but the departure is not substantial when the standard errors in the persistence measure are taken into consideration. Moreover, there is an increasing mean-reverting component in more recent periods. The cross-effect of shocks is also checked and that between European currencies is found to be similar. Further, the cross-effect between European currencies is larger than that between European currencies and that of the Japanese yen and the Canadian dollar. Cashin *et al.* (2000) study the persistence of shocks to world commodity prices, using monthly IMF data on primary commodities between 1957 and 1998. They find that shocks to commodity prices typically have significantly persistent effect and the persistence profile varies, based on which the effect of national and international schemes of earnings stabilisation may be formed and evaluated. Their analysis is not in favour of a stabilisation scheme, as they argue that the cost of the stabilisation scheme will be likely to exceed any associated smoothing benefits. Other studies in the area include Greasley and Oxley (1997), Linden (1995) and Demery and Duck (1992).

Impulse response and variance decomposition have been widely employed to observe cross-effects of shocks, evaluated on the basis of a pre-specified and tested multivariate model. In the last decade, one of the extensively studied areas is capital market links and interactions, owing to an increasingly integrating global financial market offering inexhaustible opportunities that never existed before in the domestic market. Investigating capital market integration in the Pacific Basin in the context of impulse response, Phylaktis (1999) studies specifically the speed of adjustment of real interest rates to long-run equilibrium following a shock in each of these markets. It is found that countries in the region are closely linked with world financial markets. Moreover, the association of these markets with Japan is stronger than that with the US. Tse *et al.* (1996) examine information transmission in three Eurodollar futures markets of Imm, Simex and Liffe. Employing impulse response analysis and variance decomposition which explores further the common factor in the cointegration system, it is found that the common factor is driven by the last trading market in the 24-hour trading sequence. Each of the markets impounds all the information and rides on the common stochastic trend during trading hours, and the three markets can be considered as one continuously trading market. In a study of equity market linkages in ASEAN countries, Roca *et al.* (1998) use impulse response analysis and variance decomposition based on a VAR with error correction to investigate the extent and structure of price linkages among these markets. They find evidence of short-term linkages among all but the Indonesian market. But in the long run, the linkages, if any, are weak. Specifically, the Malaysian market is the most influential, that is, its shocks considerably contribute to the forecast variance in the other markets; while the Singapore and Thailand markets have the most strong interaction with other markets, that is, shocks in the Singapore and Thailand markets account for a large proportion of forecast variance in other markets and, in the meantime, shocks in other markets attribute to a large amount of forecast variance in the Singapore and Thailand markets. Finally, their results indicate that the Indonesian market is isolated and not linked with any other ASEAN market.

Impulse response has been widely applied to regional studies and real estate where the response to shocks from various sources is one of the major concerns. Baffoe-Bonnie (1998) analyses the effect of key macroeconomic variables on house prices and the stock of houses sold in the framework of VAR and impulse response analysis. The results suggest that macroeconomic variables produce cycles in housing prices and the stock of houses sold. Considerable amount of the forecast variance in the housing market can be attributed to shocks in employment growth and the mortgage rate at both national and regional levels. The study also reveals that the dynamic behaviour of housing prices and the number of houses sold vary substantially among different regions and at different time periods. Hort (2000) employs impulse response analysis based on the estimation of a VAR model of the after-tax mortgage rate, house prices and sales, to examine prices and turnover in the owner-occupied housing market. The empirical results in the paper support the view that the adjustment of house price expectations following a shock to demand is slow due to informational imperfections in the housing market. There also exist asymmetries in buyers' and sellers' responses such that sales are expected to respond prior to prices where buyers are assumed to respond prior to sellers. Tse and Webb (1999), concerned with the effectiveness of land tax and capital gain tax in curbing hoarding of land and speculation, evaluate the effects of property tax on housing in Hong Kong. Using an impulse response function, they demonstrate that the transaction tax has a dynamic negative impact on housing returns, as the imposition of capital gain tax impairs the liquidity of property transaction, lowers the rate of return on property investment, and reduces revenue from land sales. They also show that the capital gain tax is capitalised into housing prices.

Various other studies can be found in the areas of business cycles and monetary policy evaluation, real and nominal exchange rate behaviour and linkages, PPP, debt markets, employment, regions and sectors, in virtually any dynamic models involving the analysis of the effect and cross-effect of shocks.

Questions and problems

1 What is meant by persistence? How is persistence measured?
2 Compare persistence analysis and the test for unit roots.
3 Discuss the advantages of the procedure in this chapter to standardise the multivariate persistence measure and its rationale.
4 Describe impulse response analysis and its application in evaluating the impact of shocks and policy changes.
5 Why is orthogonalisation required in impulse response analysis?
6 What is meant by generalised impulse response analysis? Can generalised impulse response analysis avoid all the complication in orthogonalisation while achieving the same goal?
7 The contribution by the shock in each of the sources, as expressed as a percentage of the total variance, sums to 100 per cent in this chapter. Discuss its rationale.
8 Collect data from various sources and test for persistence in the following time series:

   a spot foreign exchange rates of selected industrialised nations and developing economies *vis-à-vis* the US$, testing one individual time series each time;
   b GDP of selected countries, testing one individual time series each time;
   c nominal interests in selected countries, testing one individual time series each time.

   What do you find of their characteristics?

9 Collect data from various sources and test for multivariate persistence in the following groups of time series:

   a spot foreign exchange rates of selected industrialised nations *vis-à-vis* the US$;
   b spot foreign exchange rates of selected developing economies *vis-à-vis* the US$;
   c GDP of selected countries;
   d nominal interests in selected countries.

   What do you find of their characteristics?

10 Collect data from various sources and carry out (orthogonal) impulse response analysis in the following groups of time series:

   a sectoral output indices in the UK;
   b GDP of the UK, the US and Japan;
   c stock market return indices of the UK, the US and Japan.

   What do you find of their characteristics?

11 Collect data from various sources and carry out generalised impulse response analysis in the following groups of time series:

   a sectoral output indices in the UK;
   b GDPs of the UK, the US and Japan;
   c stock market return indices of the UK, the US and Japan.

What do you find of their characteristics? Analyse the differences in your findings from (9) and (10).

Notes

1 Pesaran and Shin (1998) and Microfit use the total variance of the orthogonal case in the denominator, so the components do not sum up to 100%.
2 The restricted model involves deletion of the lagged variables with the t-statistic of their coefficients being less than one, and re-estimation. Therefore, the implementation of the model is complicated and the model differs in every case. Whereas the unrestricted model decides the lag length, then includes all lagged variables. So, the implementation and estimation are 'standard'.

References

Baffoe-Bonnie, J. (1998), The dynamic impact of macroeconomic aggregates on housing prices and stock of houses: A national and regional analysis, *Journal of Real Estate Finance and Economics*, 17, 179–197.

Blanchard, O. J. and Quah, D. (1989), The dynamic effects of aggregate demand and supply disturbances, *American Economic Review*, 79, 655–673.

Campbell, J. Y. and Mankiw, N. W. (1987a), Are output fluctuations transitory?, *Quarterly Journal of Economics*, 102, 857–880.

Campbell, J. Y. and Mankiw, N. W. (1987b), Permanent and transitory components in macroeconomic fluctuations, *American Economic Review*, 77 (Papers and Proceedings), 111–117.

Cashin, P., Liang, H. and McDermott, C. J. (2000), How persistent are shocks to world commodity prices? *IMF Staff Papers*, 47, 177–217.

Cochrane, J. H. (1988), How big is the random walk in GDP?, *Journal of Political Economy*, 96, 893–920.

Dekker, A., Sen, K. and Young, M. R. (2001), Equity market linkages in the Asia Pacific region: A comparison of the orthogonalised and generalised VAR approaches, *Global Finance Journal*, 12, 1–33.

Demery, D. and Duck, N. W. (1992), Are economic fluctuations really persistent? A reinterpretation of some international evidence, *Economic Journal*, 102, 1094–1101.

Goerlich, P. (1992), Cochrane.src, *RATS, Estima*.

Greasley, D. and Oxley, L. (1997), Shock persistence and structural change, *Economic Record*, 73, 348–362.

Hort, K. (2000), Prices and turnover in the market for owner-occupied homes, *Regional Science and Urban Economics*, 30, 99–119.

Linden, M. (1995), Finnish GNP series 1954/I–1990/IV: Small shock persistence or trend stationarity? Some evidence with variance ratio estimates, *Empirical Economics*, 20, 333–349.

Mayadunne, G., Evans, M. and Inder, B. (1995), An empirical investigation of shock persistence in economic time series, *Economic Record*, 71, 145–156.

Pesaran, M. H., Pierse, R. G. and Lee, K. C. (1993), Persistence, cointegration and aggregation: A disaggregated analysis of output fluctuations in the US economy, *Journal of Econometrics*, 56, 67–88.

Pesaran, M. H. and Shin, Y. (1998), Generalized impulse response analysis in linear multivariate models, *Economics Letters*, 58, 17–29.

Priestley, M. B. (1996), *Sprectral Analysis and Time Series*, 9th printing (1st printing 1981), Academic Press, London.

Phylaktis, K. (1999), Capital market integration in the Pacific Basin region: An impulse response analysis, *Journal of International Money and Finance*, 18, 267–287.

Roca, E. D., Selvanathan, E. A. and Shepherd, W. F. (1998), Are the ASEAN equity markets interdependent?, *Asean Economic Bulletin*, 15, 109–120.

Tse, R. Y. C. and Webb, J. R. (1999), Property tax and housing returns, *Review of Urban and Regional Development Studies*, 11, 114–126.

Tse, Y., Lee, T. H. and Booth, G. G. (1996), The international transmission of information in eurodollar futures markets: A continuously trading market hypothesis, *Journal of International Money and Finance*, 15, 447–465.

Van de Gucht, L. M., Dekimpe, M. G. and Kwok, C. C. Y. (1996), Persistence in foreign exchange rates, *Journal of International Money and Finance*, 15, 191–220.

Wang, P. J. (2000), Shock persistence in property and related markets, *Journal of Property Research*, 17, 1–21.

5 Modelling regime shifts

Markov switching models

Recent renewed interest in Markov chain processes and Markov switching models was largely stimulated by Hamilton (1989, 1994). While the major contributors with economic significance to the popularity of this family of models are the intensified studies in business cycles in the last two decades on the frontiers of macro and monetary economics, and the proliferating use of mathematical tools in the exploitation of excess returns in a seemingly efficient while volatile financial market. The regime shift or state transition features of Markov switching, when applied properly, are able to illustrate and explain economic fluctuations around boom–recession or more complicated multiphase cycles. In financial studies, the state transition process can be coupled with bull–bear market alternations, where regimes are less clearly defined but appear to have more practical relevance. However, estimation of Markov switching models may be technically difficult and the results achieved may be sensitive to the settings of the procedure. Probably, rather than producing a set of figures of immediate use, the approach helps improve our understanding about an economic process and its evolving mechanism constructively, as with many other economic and financial models.

5.1 Markov chains

A Markov chain is defined as a stochastic process $\{S_t, t = 0, 1, \ldots\}$ that takes a finite or countable number of integer values denoted by i, j, and that the probability of any future value of S_{t+1} equals j, that is, the conditional distribution of any future state S_{t+1}, given the past state $S_0, S_1, \ldots, S_{t-1}$ and the present state S_t, is only dependent on the present state and independent of the past states. That is:

$$P\{S_{t+1} = j \mid S_t = i_t, S_{t-1} = i_{t-1}, S_1 = i_1, S_0 = i_0\}$$
$$= P\{S_{t+1} = j \mid S_t = i_t\} = p_{ij} \tag{1}$$

where p_{ij} is the probability that the state will next be j when the immediate preceding state is i, and can be called the transition probability from i into j. Suppose there are N states, then all the transitions can be expressed in a transition matrix:

$$
\mathbf{P} = \begin{bmatrix} p_{11} & p_{12} & \cdots & p_{1N} \\ p_{21} & p_{22} & \cdots & p_{2N} \\ \vdots & & & \\ p_{N1} & p_{N2} & \cdots & p_{NN} \end{bmatrix} \tag{2}
$$

The probability is non-negative and the process must transit into some state, including the current state itself, so that:

$$
\sum_{j=1}^{N} p_{ij} = 1, \quad i = 1, 2, \ldots, N \tag{3}
$$

These are one-step transition probabilities. It is natural for us to extend the one-step case and consider n-step transitions that are clearly functions and results of several one-step transitions. For example, a two-step transition $P\{S_{t+2} = j \mid S_t = i\}$ probability is the summation of the probabilities of transitions from state i into all the states, then from all the states into state j:

$$
\sum_{k=1}^{N} P\{S_{t+2} = j \mid S_{t+1} = k\} P\{S_{t+1} = k \mid S_t = i\}
$$

More generally, define the n-step transition probability as:

$$
P\{S_{t+n} = j \mid S_t = i\} = p_{ij}^n \tag{4}
$$

A formula called the Chapman–Kolmogorov equation holds for calculating multi-step transition probabilities:

$$
p_{ij}^{m+n} = \sum_{k=1}^{N} p_{ik}^n p_{kj}^m, \quad i, j = 1, 2, \ldots, N \tag{5}
$$

5.2 Estimation

The estimation of a Markov chain process or Markov switching model is achieved, naturally, by considering the joint conditional probability of each of future states, as a function of the joint conditional probabilities of current states and the transition probabilities. This procedure is called filtering: the conditional probabilities of current states are input, passing through or being filtered by the system of dynamic transformation that is the transition probability matrix, to produce the conditional probabilities of future states as output. The conditional likelihood function can be obtained in the meantime, and the parameter can be estimated accordingly.

Suppose there is a simply two-state Markov chain process:

$$
y_t = \mu_1 S_1 + \mu_2 S_2 + \varepsilon_t \tag{6}
$$

where $S_1 = 1$ when in state 1 and 0 otherwise, $S_2 = 1$ when in state 2 and 0 otherwise, and ε_t is a white noise residual. We are interested to know how the joint probability of y_t and S_t transits over time. This can be achieved in two major steps. The first step is to have an estimate of the conditional probability $P(S_t = s_t \mid y_{t-1})$, that is, the probability of being in state s_t, based on information available at time $t - 1$. According to the transition probability and property, that is straightforward. The second step is to consider the joint probability density distribution of y_t and S_t, so the probability of being in state s_t is updated to $P(S_t = s_t \mid y_t)$, using information available at time t. The procedure is as follows:

1   Estimating the probability of being in state s_t, conditional on information at $t - 1$:

$$P(S_t = s_t \mid y_{t-1}) = P(S_t = s_t \mid S_{t-1} = s_{t-1}) \times P(S_{t-1} = s_{t-1} \mid y_{t-1})$$

2   a   Calculating the joint density distribution of y_t and S_t:

$$
\begin{aligned}
f(y_t, S_t = s_t \mid y_{t-1}) \\
= f(y_t \mid S_t = s_t, y_{t-1}) \times P(S_t = s_t \mid y_{t-1}) \\
= f(y_t \mid S_t = s_t, y_{t-1}) \times P(S_t = s_t \mid S_{t-1} = s_{t-1}) \\
\times P(S_{t-1} = s_{t-1} \mid y_{t-1})
\end{aligned}
\tag{7}
$$

b   Calculating the density distribution of y_t:

$$f(y_t \mid y_{t-1}) = \sum_{s_t=1}^{2} f(y_t, S_t = s_t \mid y_{t-1}) \tag{8}$$

c   Calculating the following:

$$P(S_t = s_t \mid y_t) = \frac{f(y_t, S_t = s_t \mid y_{t-1})}{f(y_t \mid y_{t-1})} \tag{9}$$

that is, the updated joint probability of y_t and S_t.

Consider now a general N-state Markov chain process y_t that has autoregression of order r in its residual ε_t and is also the function of the exogenous variable x_t and its lags. This is the typical dynamic process of autoregression, frequently encountered in contemporary empirical economics and finance, if there is only one state. When variable y_t in a Markov chain process has autoregression of order r, the joint conditional probability of the current state and r previous states, based on the information set including all its lags up to r periods before period 0, that is:

$$P(S_t = s_t, S_{t-1} = s_{t-1}, \ldots, S_{t-1} = s_{t-r} \mid \Omega_{t-1}) \tag{10}$$

should be considered, where $\Omega_{t-1} = (y_{t-1}, y_{t-2}, \ldots, y_{-r}, x_{t-1}, x_{t-2}, \ldots, x_{-r})$ is the information set available at time $t - 1$. The filtering procedure, which is to update the joint conditional probability of equation (7) from the previous joint conditional probability, is as follows:

1   Calculating the joint density distribution of y_t and S_t:

$$
\begin{aligned}
f(y_t, S_t &= s_t, S_{t-1} = s_{t-1}, \ldots, S_{t-r-1} = s_{t-r-1} \mid \Omega_{t-1}) \\
&= f(y_t \mid S_t = s_t, S_{t-1} = s_{t-1}, \ldots, S_{t-r-1} = s_{t-r-1}, \Omega_{t-1}) \\
&\quad \times P(S_t = s_t, S_{t-1} = s_{t-1}, \ldots, S_{t-r-1} = s_{t-r-1} \mid \Omega_{t-1}) \\
&= f(y_t \mid S_t = s_t, S_{t-1} = s_{t-1}, \ldots, S_{t-r-1} = s_{t-r-1}, \Omega_{t-1}) \\
&\quad \times P(S_t = s_t \mid S_{t-1} = s_{t-1}) \\
&\quad \times P(S_{t-1} = s_{t-1}, \ldots, S_{t-r-1} = s_{t-r-1} \mid \Omega_{t-1})
\end{aligned}
\tag{11}
$$

2   Calculating the density distribution of y_t:

$$
\begin{aligned}
&f(y_t \mid \Omega_{t-1}) \\
&= \sum_{s_t=1}^{N} \sum_{s_{t-1}=1}^{N} \cdots \sum_{s_{t-r}=1}^{N} f(y_t, S_t = s_t, S_{t-1} = s_{t-1}, \ldots, S_{t-r-1} = s_{t-r-1} \mid \Omega_{t-1})
\end{aligned}
\tag{12}
$$

3   Calculating the following that, unlike the non-serial correlation residual case, is not yet the output of the filter:

$$
\begin{aligned}
&P(S_t = s_t, S_{t-1} = s_{t-1}, \ldots, S_{t-r-1} = s_{t-r-1} \mid \Omega_t) \\
&= \frac{f(y_t, S_t = s_t, S_{t-1} = s_{t-1}, \ldots, S_{t-r-1} = s_{t-r-1} \mid \Omega_{t-1})}{f(y_t \mid \Omega_{t-1})}
\end{aligned}
\tag{13}
$$

4   The output of the filter is then the summation over the states at lag r:

$$
\begin{aligned}
&P(S_t = s_t, S_{t-1} = s_{t-1}, \ldots, S_{t-r} = s_{t-r} \mid \Omega_t) \\
&= \sum_{s_{t-r-1}=1}^{N} P(S_t = s_t, S_{t-1} = s_{t-1}, \ldots, S_{t-r-1} = s_{t-r-1} \mid \Omega_t)
\end{aligned}
\tag{14}
$$

During the above course, the probability of the states at time t, based on currently available information, is obtained:

$$
\begin{aligned}
&P(S_t = s_t \mid \Omega_t) \\
&= \sum_{s_t=1}^{N} \sum_{s_{t-1}=1}^{N} \cdots \sum_{s_{t-r}=1}^{N} P(S_t = s_t, S_{t-1} = s_{t-1}, \ldots, S_{t-r} = s_{t-r} \mid \Omega_t)
\end{aligned}
\tag{15}
$$

The log likelihood function is also derived:

$$
L(\theta) = \sum_{t=1}^{T} f(y_t \mid \Omega_{t-1}; \theta)
\tag{16}
$$

where θ represents the vector of parameters. There are few techniques that are singled out for estimating the log likelihood function, such as the Gibbs sampling and the EM algorithm, but maximum likelihood remains a useful, convenient and largely appropriate method in practice. Maximising equation (16) leads to the derivation of the estimates with regard to the parameters and states.

Using the simple instance of the two-state Markov chain process of equation (6) and assuming a normally distributed residual, we write down its maximum likelihood function explicitly, that can be routinely extended to more complicated cases, as follows:

$$
\begin{aligned}
L(\theta) &= \sum_{t=1}^{T} f(y_t \mid y_{t-1}; \theta) \\
&= \sum_{t=1}^{T} \sum_{s_t=1}^{2} f(y_t \mid S_t = s_t, y_{t-1}; \theta) \times P(S_t = s_t \mid y_{t-1}) \\
&= \sum_{t=1}^{T} \sum_{s_t=1}^{2} \sum_{s_{t-1}=1}^{2} \{ f(y_t \mid S_t = s_t, y_{t-1}; \theta) \times P(S_t = s_t \mid S_{t-1} = s_{t-1}) \\
&\quad \times P(S_{t-1} = s_{t-1} \mid y_{t-1}) \} \\
&= \sum_{t=1}^{T} \left\{ \frac{1}{\sqrt{2\pi}\sigma_\varepsilon} \exp\left(\frac{-(y_t - \mu_1)^2}{2\sigma_\varepsilon^2} \right) \times [p_{11} \times P_{tL}(1) + p_{21} \times P_{tL}(2)] \right. \\
&\quad \left. + \frac{1}{\sqrt{2\pi}\sigma_\varepsilon} \exp\left(\frac{-(y_t - \mu_2)^2}{2\sigma_\varepsilon^2} \right) \times [p_{21} \times P_{tL}(1) + p_{22} \times P_{tL}(2)] \right\}
\end{aligned}
$$

$$(17)$$

where $P_{tL}(1) = P(S_{t-1} = 1 \mid y_{t-1})$ and $P_{tL}(2) = P(S_{t-1} = 2 \mid y_{t-1})$ for simplicity.

5.3   Smoothing

Similar to the case of the Kalman filter to be introduced in Chapter 7, the states at time t have been estimated based on the information set at t in the above procedure. It may be of interest to review the states at a later time when more information is available, or infer the states using the whole information set up to the last observation at time T. An inference made about the present states using future information is called smoothing, with the inference made with the whole information set being full smoothing, or simply smoothing. Smoothing may be of no use to problems such as real time control in cybernetics, but it provides more desirable results when an insightful understanding of the process is the major concern; for example, in the economic science for revealing the working mechanism of dynamic economic systems and shaping future policies.

Smoothing is to revise $P(S_t = s_t \mid \Omega_t)$, the probability of the states at time t based on currently available information, to $P(S_t = s_t \mid \Omega_T)$, the probability of the states at time t based on the whole information set. Put it simply, it replaces Ω_t by Ω_T. Smoothing involves two steps when there is no lag in y_t, and three steps and one approximation when there are lags in y_t. We again show the procedure for the simple case of equation (6) first:

1   Calculating (to save space, $S_t = s_t$ has been simplified as S_t):

$$
\begin{aligned}
& P(S_{t-r}, \dots, S_t, S_{t+1} \mid \Omega_T) \\
&= P(S_{t-r+1}, \dots, S_t, S_{t+1} \mid \Omega_T) \times P(S_{t-r} \mid S_{t-r+1}, \dots, S_t, S_{t+1}, \Omega_T) \\
&= P(S_{t-r+1}, \dots, S_t, S_{t+1} \mid \Omega_T) \times P(S_{t-r} \mid S_{t-r+1}, \dots, S_t, S_{t+1}, \Omega_t) \\
&= \frac{P(S_{t-r+1}, \dots, S_{t+1} \mid \Omega_T) \times P(S_{t-r}, \dots, S_{t+1}, \Omega_t)}{P(S_{t-r+1}, \dots, S_t, S_{t+1} \mid \Omega_t)} \\
&= \frac{P(S_{t-r+1}, \dots, S_{t+1} \mid \Omega_T) \times P(S_{t-r}, \dots, S_t, \Omega_t) \times P(S_{t+1} \mid S_t)}{P(S_{t-r+1}, \dots, S_t, S_{t+1} \mid \Omega_t)} \quad (18)
\end{aligned}
$$

The second equality involving $P(S_{t-r} \mid S_{t-r+1}, \dots, S_t, S_{t+1}, \Omega_T) = P(S_{t-r} \mid S_{t-r+1}, \dots, S_t, S_{t+1}, \Omega_t)$ is exact only if:

$$
\begin{aligned}
& f(y_{t+1}, \Omega_{Tt} \mid S_{t-r}, S_{t-r+1}, \dots, S_t, S_{t+1}, \Omega_t) \\
&= f(y_{t+1}, \Omega_{Tt} \mid S_{t-r+1}, \dots, S_t, S_{t+1}, \Omega_t) \quad (19)
\end{aligned}
$$

holds. It is because, define $\Omega_{Tt} = \Omega_T - \Omega_t$, it follows:

$$
\begin{aligned}
& P(S_{t-r} \mid S_{t-r+1}, \dots, S_t, S_{t+1}, \Omega_T) = P(S_{t-r} \mid S_{t-r+1}, \dots, S_t, S_{t+1}, \Omega_t, \Omega_{Tt}) \\
&= \frac{f(y_{t+1}, S_{t-r}, \Omega_{Tt} \mid S_{t-r+1}, \dots, S_t, S_{t+1}, \Omega_t)}{f(Y_{t+1}, \Omega_{Tt} \mid S_{t-r+1}, \dots, S_t, S_{t+1}, \Omega_t)} \\
&= \frac{f(y_{t+1}, \Omega_{Tt} \mid S_{t-r}, \dots, S_t, S_{t+1}, \Omega_t) \times P(S_{t-r} \mid S_{t-r+1}, \dots, S_t, S_{t+1}, \Omega_t)}{f(y_{t+1}, \Omega_{Tt} \mid S_{t-r+1}, \dots, S_t, S_{t+1}, \Omega_t)}
\end{aligned}
$$

$$
(20)
$$

2   Summing up over $S_{t+1} = 1, 2, \dots, N$:

$$
P(S_{t-r}, \dots, S_t \mid \Omega_T) = \sum_{s_{t+1}=1}^{N} P(S_{t-r}, \dots, S_t, S_{t+1} \mid \Omega_T) \quad (21)
$$

Equation (21) is already the smoothed states when there is no serial correlation in the residual or there is no lagged y_t involved. When there are lags, smoothing is, similar to equation (15), finally achieved through the following summation:

$$P(S_t \mid \Omega_T) = \sum_{s_t=1}^{N} \sum_{s_{t-1}=1}^{N} \cdots \sum_{s_{t-r}=1}^{N} P(S_t, S_{t-1}, \ldots, S_{t-r} \mid \Omega_T) \tag{22}$$

5.4   Time-varying transition probabilities

It is natural to extend the above analysis to allow the Markov chain model additional flexibility, by introducing time-varying transition probabilities. Let us define the time-varying transition probability as follows:

$$P\{S_{t+1} = j \mid S_t = i_t, \mid \Omega_{t+1}\} = p_{ij}(t+1) \tag{1'}$$

Then the transition probability matrix is:

$$\mathbf{P(t)} = \begin{bmatrix} p_{11}(t) & p_{12}(t) & \cdots & p_{1N}(t) \\ p_{21}(t) & p_{22}(t) & \cdots & p_{2N}(t) \\ \vdots & & & \\ p_{N1}(t) & p_{N2}(t) & \cdots & p_{NN}(t) \end{bmatrix} \tag{2'}$$

The choice of types of time-varying transition probabilities is an empirical issue, though those used in binary choice models in the form of probit and logit are logically adopted, with the similar rationale argued for the probit and logit model. In addition, there is the exponential function and the cumulative normal distribution function. The exponential function and the cumulative normal distribution function are symmetric, with the mirror image on the vertical axis, so any departure from the mean value will increase the probability. While a logic function is asymmetric with a positive departure, a negative departure from the mean value has opposite effects. These time-varying functions are also similar to what are widely used in smoothing transition models. The use of time-varying transition probabilities has an additional advantage, that is, such specifications limit the value of the probability in the range of [0, 1] at the same time, or indeed, in any desirable ranges. This prevents unreasonable outcome from occurring in the execution of a programme. Even if the transition probability is not time varying, using some functional forms to set the range of the probability is always helpful.

The logit function of transition probabilities is:

$$p_{ij}(t) = \frac{1}{1 + \exp\{-\Omega_t \boldsymbol{\beta}'_{ij}\}} \tag{23}$$

where $\boldsymbol{\beta}'_{ij}$ is a vector of coefficients on the set of dependent and exogenous variables. $\exp\{-\Omega_t \boldsymbol{\beta}'_{ij}\}$ can change from 0 to ∞, containing the probability in the range of [0, 1]. In a simple example, when $-\Omega_t \boldsymbol{\beta}'_{ij} = \omega_{ij0} - \gamma_{ij} y_{t-1}$, equation (23) becomes:

$$p_{ij}(t) = \frac{1}{1 + \exp\{\omega_{ij0} - \gamma_{ij}y_{t-1}\}}$$

It has a mean value of 0.5 when $y_t = \omega_{ij}/\gamma_{ij}$ and will increase when $y_t > \omega_{ij}/\gamma_{ij}$ with $p_{ij}{}_{y_{t-1}\to\infty}(t) \to 0$, and decrease when $y_t < \omega_{ij}/\gamma_{ij}$ with $p_{ij}{}_{y_{t-1}\to\infty}(t) \to 1$, provided γ_{ij} is positive. A cumulative normal distribution has the similar pattern.

An exponential type transition probability is specified as follows:

$$p_{ij}(t) = 1 - \exp\{-(\Omega_t \boldsymbol{\beta}'_{ij})^2\} \tag{24}$$

$\exp\{-(\Omega_t \boldsymbol{\beta}'_{ij})^2\}$ can change from 1 to 0, limiting the probability in the range of [0, 1]. Using the same example of $-\Omega_t \boldsymbol{\beta}'_{ij} = \omega_{ij0} - \gamma_{ij}y_{t-1}$, equation (24) becomes:

$$p_{ij}(t) = 1 - \exp\{-(\omega_{ij0} - \gamma_{ij}y_{t-1})^2\}$$

It has the maximum value of unity when $y_t = \omega_{ij}/\gamma_{ij}$, and will decrease when γ_t departs from ω_{ij}/γ_{ij}, no matter whether $y_t - \omega_{ij}/\gamma_{ij}$ is positive or negative.

The above two specifications have direct economic meanings and implications, for example, symmetric responses related only to the distance of departure from a central point or the equilibrium, no matter what the direction or the sign of departure is, and asymmetric effects where both the distance and the sign are relevant. If the purpose is to restrict the value of the probability only, then many simpler and more straightforward specifications, such as the one used in Example 1 in Section 5.5, can perform satisfactorily.

5.5 Examples and cases

Example 1

We use the Markov chain model to illustrate regime shifts in business cycle conditions in UK GDP data at the factor price running from the first quarter of 1964 to the fourth quarter of 1999. The model has two means for recessions and normal times, respectively. The residual follows an autoregressive process of order 1 and has different volatility or variance in the two regimes. Let y_t be the logarithm of GDP, S_1 be the state for normal times, and S_2 be the state for recessions:

$$\Delta y_t = \mu + \mu_2 S_2 + \rho \Delta y_{t-1} + \omega_t$$
$$\omega_t \sim (0, S_1\sigma_1^2 + S_2\sigma_2^2) \tag{25}$$

With this specification, the growth rate is μ in normal times, and $\mu + \mu_2$ in recessions, while the variance is σ_1^2 in normal periods and σ_2^2 in recessions. We adopt equation (23) to restrict the transition probability to the range of [0, 1], though the transition probability is not time varying. The results from estimating the model are reported in Table 5.1.

Table 5.1 Estimation of UK GDP with a two-regime Markov
switching model: 64Q1–99Q4

μ_1	$0.7491e^{-2***}$	$(0.1281e^{-2})$
μ_2	$-0.1517e^{-1***}$	$(0.5446e^{-2})$
σ_1	$0.8591e^{-4***}$	$(0.7592e^{-5})$
σ_2	$0.6626e^{-4}$	$(0.4354e^{-4})$
$\omega_{11}{}^a$	$3.2153***$	(1.1569)
$\omega_{22}{}^b$	0.7245	(1.0248)

Notes
    * Significant at the 10% level.
   ** Significant at the 5% level.
 *** Significant at the 1% level. Standard errors in brackets.
    a The parameter from using a simple function, $p = e^{\omega}/(1+e^{\omega})$,
      to impose restrictions on the range of the probability. p_{11}, the
      transition probability of staying in normal periods, is 0.9613,
      according to the function.
    b Equivalent to a p_{22}, the transition probability of remaining in
      a recession, of 0.6736.

It has been found that UK GDP growth is about 0.7 per cent per quarter (μ_1),
translating into an annual growth rate of 3 per cent, during normal times in the estimation period. In recessions, the growth rate is a negative 0.7 per cent ($\mu_1 + \mu_2$),
or a negative 3 per cent per annum. The transition probability of staying in normal periods, or from normal to normal is 0.9613, being calculated from $\omega_{11,0}$ and
using a simple function, $p = e^{\omega}/(1 + e^{\omega})$, to impose restrictions on the range of
the probability. With similar transformation, the transition probability of remaining in a recession is 0.6736. This transition probability is, however, statistically
insignificant and therefore unreliable. One of the reasons is that the duration of
recessions is relatively short, so the probability of staying in the recession varies,
especially when the economy is nearing the end of a recession. The duration of
being in normal times is

$$\frac{1}{1 - p_{11}} = \frac{1}{1 - 0.9613} \approx 26$$

quarters or 6.5 years.

The duration of an average recession is

$$\frac{1}{1 - p_{22}} = \frac{1}{1 - 0.6736} \approx 3$$

quarters.

As observed before, the errors associated with p_{22} are large so the duration
of recessions could well deviate from three-quarters by a large margin. The two
regimes also have different volatility. In normal times, the standard deviation of the
residual is $0.8591e^{-4}$ (σ_1), or about 0.009 per cent per quarter, being statistically
significant at the 1 per cent level. While the standard deviation seems smaller in
recessions with σ_2 being $0.6626e^{-4}$, it does not suggest lower volatility as the

statistic is statistically insignificant. Since recession periods are relatively short with much fewer observations being available, this statistic is unreliable. We can see from Table 5.1 that the standard error of it is $0.4354e^{-4}$. So the standard deviation of the residual can be very large as well as very small. This does cast more uncertainty in recessions.

The business cycle regime characteristics of UK GDP are exhibited in Figure 5.1. Notice the probability of being in one of the states is time varying, regardless whether the transition probabilities are constant or not. Panel (a) in the figure is the growth rate of UK GDP between the first quarter in 1964 and the fourth quarter in 1999. Panel (b) shows the probability of being in the state of recession without smoothing, and panel (c) is the full sample smoothed probability for the same state. As in most empirical studies, there is only a very small difference between the two representations of probability.

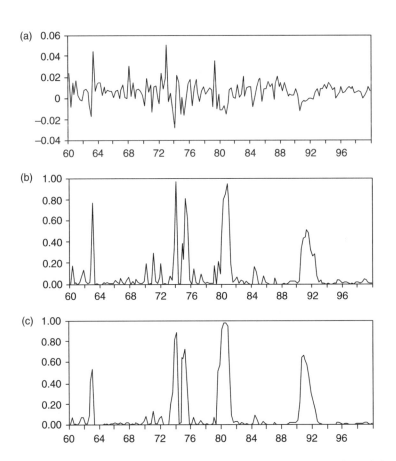

Figure 5.1 Business cycle regime characteristics of UK GDP. (a) Growth in GDP, (b) Probability and (c) Probability, full sample smoothed.

Example 2

Oil price volatility has long been considered a factor influencing the state of business cycles and, in particular, plunging the economy into recessions when there is a sharp increase in the oil price, or an oil price crisis. Therefore, the oil price is frequently used as a variable of impact in time-varying transition probabilities. One of the examples is a study by Raymond and Rich (1997) entitled 'Oil and the macroeconomy: a Markov state-switching approach'. Their modelling of time-varying transition probabilities follows Filardo (1994); and the treatment of the oil price series follows Hamilton (1996), having considered the asymmetric effects of oil price changes on business cycles. The net oil price increase variable proposed by Hamilton (1996) is equal to the percentage change in the current real oil price above the maximum of the previous four quarters if positive and zero otherwise. Bearing this characteristic in mind, their mean equation is:

$$\Delta y_t = \alpha_0 + \alpha_1 S_t + \sum_{i=1}^{n} \beta_i o_{t-i}^{+} + \varepsilon_t, \qquad \alpha_1 < 0, \quad \varepsilon_t \sim (0, \sigma_\varepsilon^2) \qquad (26)$$

where $S_t = 0$ is the state for the normal period or with the higher growth rate, $S_t = 1$ is the state for recessions, and o_t^{+} is the net oil price increase variable explained above. There is no lagged real GDP growth entering the mean equation. The specification does not distinguish the volatility or variance of the residual between the higher growth period and recession. The time-varying transition probabilities are designed as follows:

$$P\{S_t = 0 \mid S_{t-1} = 0, o_{t-1}^{+}, o_{t-2}^{+}, \ldots\} = q_t = \Phi\left(\delta_0 + \sum_{i=1}^{d} \delta_i o_{t-i}^{+}\right)$$

$$P\{S_t = 1 \mid S_{t-1} = 1, o_{t-1}^{+}, o_{t-2}^{+}, \ldots\} = p_t = \Phi\left(\gamma_0 + \sum_{i=1}^{d} \gamma_i o_{t-i}^{+}\right) \qquad (27)$$

where $\Phi(\cdot)$ is the cumulative normal distribution function with the same purpose as in Example 1 to limit the range of the transition probability between 0 and 1.

The data sample period in the study is from the first quarter of 1951 to the third quarter in 1995 for both US real GDP and the real price of oil. The empirical results are summarised in Table 5.2, where the quarterly growth rate has been multiplied by 100.

The unrestricted model, where the net oil price increase variable enters both the mean equation for real GDP growth and the transition probability, has achieved the highest log likelihood function value. Comparing the two restricted versions with the general model of no restriction by the statistic of the likelihood ratio test however, it is found that the time-varying transition probability model is of no difference from a constant transition probability model. That is, the validity of the restriction cannot be rejected at any conventional statistical significance level, with the log likelihood ratio being $LR = 0.894$. Nevertheless, the oil variable

Table 5.2 Estimation of US real GDP with a time-varying transition probability Markov switching model: 51Q1–95Q3

	Restricted: oil has no effect on transition probabilities	Restricted: oil has no effect in the mean equation	No restrictions: the general model
α_0	1.066***	0.929***	1.018***
	(0.097)	(0.076)	(0.081)
$\alpha_0 + \alpha_1$	−0.068	−0.593**	−0.081
	(0.310)	(0.294)	(0.341)
β_1	−0.031***	—	−0.026**
	(0.012)		(0.012)
β_2	−0.013	—	−0.008
	(0.012)		(0.013)
β_3	−0.027**	—	−0.032***
	(0.012)		(0.013)
β_4	−0.046***	—	−0.021
	(0.011)		(0.014)
δ_0	1.484***	1.866***	1.750***
	(0.375)	(0.322)	(0.361)
δ_3	—	−0.053	−0.044
		(0.069)	(0.051)
δ_4	—	−0.154**	−0.139
		(0.073)	(0.090)
γ_0	0.334	1.012	0.779
	(0.387)	(1.008)	(0.704)
γ_3	—	0.918	0.948
		(0.846)	(1.043)
γ_4	—	−0.485	−0.502
		(0.344)	(0.410)
σ_ε	0.714***	0.753***	0.732***
	(0.050)	(0.047)	(0.048)
Log likelihood	−209.320	−214.944	−208.873

Notes
* Significant at the 10% level.
** Significant at the 5% level.
*** Significant at the 1% level. Standard errors in brackets.

plays a role in the mean equation and the restriction is rejected by a log likelihood ratio test statistic of 12.142. The above analysis suggests that the net oil price increase variable has a negative impact on the growth of real GDP but provides little valid information about future switches between the two regimes and their timing. Indeed, none of the coefficients for lagged net oil price increases are statistically significant in the transition probabilities with the general model; and only the coefficient for the net oil price increase variable at lag 4 in the transition probability of remaining in the normal time (δ_4) is significant at the 5 per cent level with the model where restrictions are imposed on the mean equation. But, as indicated earlier, restrictions on the coefficients in the mean equation are rejected, so estimates obtained with that model are questionable. Besides, none of the parameters in the transition probability of remaining in recession, either the constant or the coefficients for lagged oil price increases, are statistically significant. This is consistent with the findings in Example 1.

From applying equation (27) and the estimates in Table 5.2, q, the average transition probability of remaining in the normal period, is 0.931; and p, the average transition probability of remaining in recession, is 0.631. The average duration of being in normal times is

$$\frac{1}{1-q} = \frac{1}{1-0.931} \approx 14.5$$

quarters or slightly more than 3.5 years.

The duration of an average recession is

$$\frac{1}{1-p} = \frac{1}{1-0.631} \approx 2.7$$

quarters.

These durations, especially the duration of normal periods, are relatively shorter than those in Example 1 with the UK case. The difference may suggest that the UK economy has a longer duration of normal periods but suffers more severely in recessions, or may arise from the sensitivity of the parameters to estimation procedures and data sets.

5.6 Empirical literature

Markov switching approaches have attracted much attention in financial and economic modelling in recent years, due to business cycle characteristics highlighted in macroeconomics and monetary economics, and a changing business and investment environment featured by bull–bear market alternations in financial studies. Collectively, these cyclical movements can be termed as regime shifts, common to most modern market economies. As the Markov switching model clearly defines two or more states or regimes, it can vividly reveal the dynamic process of the variables in concern and provide the researcher and policy maker with a clue of how these variables have evolved in the past and how they may change in the future. Nevertheless, the implementation and execution of a Markov switching model, though not complicated, may be technically difficult as it is rather sensitive to the choice of initial values, other settings such as the lag length, and even the data sample.

Stock market behaviour is one of the areas to which Markov switching has been widely applied. In a paper entitled 'Identifying bull and bear markets in stock returns', Maheu and McCurdy (2000) use a Markov switching model to classify returns into a high-return stable state and a low-return volatile state. They call the two states bull and bear markets, respectively. Using the US monthly data of 160 years, they find that bull markets have a declining hazard function although the best market gains come at the start of a bull market. Volatility increases with duration in bear markets. Driffill and Sola (1998) investigate whether there is an intrinsic bubble in stock prices so that stock prices deviate from the values predicted by the present value model or deviate from the fundamental relationship between income and value. They claim that a Markov switching model is a more appropriate representation of dividends. Allowing for dividends to switch between regimes, they show that stock prices can be better explained than by the bubble hypothesis. When both the bubble and the regime switching in the dividend process are considered, the incremental explanatory contribution of the bubble is low. Assoe (1998) examines regime switching in nine emerging stock market returns. The author claims that changes in government policies and capital market reforms may lead to changes in return generating processes of capital markets. The results show strong evidence of regime switching behaviour in emerging stock market returns with regard to volatility which concerns foreign investors most. Other research includes Dewachter and Veestraeten (1998) on jumps in asset prices which are modelled as a Markov switching process in the tradition of event studies; Scheicher's (1999) investigation into the stock index of the Vienna Stock Exchange with daily data from 1986 to 1992, adopting Markov switching and GARCH alternatives; and So *et al.* (1998) who examine the S&P 500 weekly return data with the Markov switching approach to modelling stochastic volatility, and have identified high, medium and low volatility states associated with the return data.

The business and investment environment can be reasonably characterised by switching between different regimes as well. In this regard, Asea and Blomberg (1998) investigate the lending behaviour of banks over lending cycles, using the Markov switching model with a panel data set consisting of approximately two million commercial and industrial loans granted by 580 banks between 1977 and 1993. They demonstrate that banks change their lending standards from tightness to laxity systematically over the cycle. Town (1992), based on the well-observed phenomenon that mergers take place in waves, fits the merger data into a Markov switching model with shifts between two states of high and low levels of activity and claims improvements over ARIMA models.

The changing pattern of interest rates is indicative to business cycle conditions and could be subject to regime shifts itself. To investigate how real interest rates shift, Bekdache (1999) adopts a time-varying parameter model with Markov switching conditional heteroscedasticity to capture two sources of shifts in real interest rates: shifts in the coefficients and shifts in the variance. The former relates the *ex ante* real rate to the nominal rate, the inflation rate and a supply shock variable, and the latter is unconditional shifts in the variance of the stochastic process. The results prefer a time-varying parameter model to Markov switching with limited states. Dewachter (1996) studies interest rate volatility by examining both regime shifts in the variance and links between volatility and levels of the interest rate. While regime shifts are found in the variance, the contribution of volatility-level links cannot be ignored. The above findings suggest that univariate or single element regime shifts in interest rate modelling fail to fully characterise interest rate dynamics.

Probably the majority of this sort of applied research is in the area of business cycles where recent studies are still burgeoning. In addition to classifying the economy into two states of booms and recessions, Kim and Nelson (1999) further investigate whether there has been a structural break in postwar US real GDP growth towards stabilisation. They employ a Bayesian approach to identifying a structural break at an unknown change-point in a Markov switching model. Their empirical results suggest a break in GDP growth towards stabilisation at the first quarter of 1984, and a narrowing gap between growth rates during recessions and booms. Filardo and Gordon (1998) specify a time-varying transition probability model where the information contained in the leading indicator is used to forecast transition probabilities and, in turn, to calculate expected business cycle durations. Both studies employ Gibbs sampling techniques. Other research in the category covers Diebold *et al.* (1993), Filardo (1994), Ghysels (1994), Luginbuhl and de Vos (1999), Kim and Yoo (1996), and Raymond and Rich (1997) as illustrated in Example 2.

It should be noted that the empirical application of Markov switching models is not always superior to an alternative simple model, and is not without deficiencies. Aware of these problems, Boldin (1996) explores the robustness of Hamilton's (1989) two-regime Markov switching model framework. Applying Hamilton's exact specification to a revised version of real GNP, the author finds that parameter estimates are similar to those reported by Hamilton only when the author uses the same sample period (1952–1984) and a particular set of initial values for the maximum likelihood procedure. Two other local maximums exist that have higher likelihood values, and neither corresponds to the conventional recession–expansion dichotomy. When the sample period is extended, there is no longer a local maximum near the parameter set reported by Hamilton. Exploring the model and data further, the author rejects the cross-regime restrictions of the Hamilton specification, but also finds that relaxing these restrictions increases the number of local maximums. In a study on the prediction of US business cycle regimes, Birchenhall *et al.* (1999) compare the use of logistic classification methods and Markov switching specifications for the identification and prediction of postwar US business cycle regimes as defined by the NBER reference turning point dates. They examine the performance of logistic procedures in reproducing the NBER regime classifications and in predicting one and three months ahead growth rates using leading indicator variables. They show that the logistic classification model provides substantially more accurate business cycle regime predictions than the Markov switching model. Nevertheless, as said at the beginning of this chapter, one of the major contributions the Markov switching approach has made is probably to help improve our understanding about an economic process. This may partly explain its contemporary popularity. In addition to the empirical literature discussed above, a variety of applications can be further found in foreign exchange rates, bond yields, inflation and so on.

Questions and problems

1 Describe the state and the state transition probability in a Markov chain.
2 What is the Chapman–Kolmogorov equation for calculating multi-step transition probabilities?

3 Cite examples of economic and financial variables which can be shown as a Markov process.

4 What is smoothing in the estimation of a Markov process? Why is smoothing required?

5 Discuss the advantages of adopting time-varying transition probabilities in the Markov process?

6 Collect data from various sources, and estimate a two-state constant transition probability model in the following time series (using RATS, GAUSS or other packages):

    a Industrial production of selected countries;

    b CPI of the G7;

    c GDP of the US, Argentina, France, Algeria and India.

7 Estimate a two-state time-varying transition probability model in the above time series.

References

Asea, P. K. and Blomberg, B. (1998), Lending cycles, *Journal of Econometrics*, 83(1–2), 89–128.

Assoe, K. G. (1998), Regime-switching in emerging stock market returns, *Multinational Finance Journal*, 2(2), 101–132.

Bekdache, B. (1999), The time-varying behaviour of real interest rates: A re-evaluation of the recent evidence, *Journal of Applied Econometrics*, 14(2), 171–190.

Birchenhall, C. R., Jessen, H., Osborn, D. R. and Simpson, P. (1999), Predicting U.S. business-cycle regimes, *Journal of Business and Economic Statistics*, 17(3), 313–323.

Boldin, M. D. (1996), A check on the robustness of Hamilton's Markov switching model approach to the economic analysis of the business cycle, *Studies in Nonlinear Dynamics and Econometrics*, 1(1), 35–46.

Dewachter, H. (1996), Modelling interest rate volatility: Regime shifts and level links, *Weltwirtschaftliches Archiv*, 132(2), 236–258.

Dewachter, H. and Veestraeten, D. (1998), Expectation revisions and jumps in asset prices, *Economics Letters*, 59(3), 367–372.

Diebold, F. X., Lee, J. H. and Weinbach, G. C. (1993), Regime switching with time varying transition probabilities, *Federal Reserve Bank of Philadelphia Research Working Paper* 93-12.

Driffill, J. and Sola, M. (1998), Intrinsic bubbles and regime-switching, *Journal of Monetary Economics*, 42(2), 357–373.

Filardo, A. J. (1994), Business cycle phases and their transitional dynamics, *Journal of Business and Economic Statistics*, 12(3), 299–308.

Filardo, A. J. and Gordon, S. F. (1998), Business cycle durations, *Journal of Econometrics*, 85(1), 99–123.

Ghysels, E. (1994), On the periodic structure of the business cycle, *Journal of Business and Economic Statistics*, 12(3), 289–298.

Hamilton, J. D. (1989), A new approach to the economic analysis of nonstationary time series and the business cycle, *Econometrica*, 57(2), 357–384.

Hamilton, J. D. (1994), *Time Series Analysis*, Princeton University Press, Princeton, New Jersey.

Hamilton, J. D. (1996), This is what happened to the oil price–macroeconomy relationship, *Journal of Monetary Economics*, 38, 215–220.

Kim, C. J. and Nelson, C. R. (1999), Has the U.S. economy become more stable? A bayesian approach based on a Markov-switching model of the business cycle, *Review of Economics and Statistics*, 81(4), 608–616.

Kim, M. J. and Yoo, J. S. (1996), A Markov switching factor model of coincident and leading indicators, *Journal of Economic Research*, 1(2), 253–272.

Luginbuhl, R. and de Vos, A. (1999), Bayesian analysis of an unobserved-component time series model of GDP with Markov-switching and time-varying growths, *Journal of Business and Economic Statistics*, 17(4), 456–465.

Maheu, J. M. and McCurdy, T. H. (2000), Identifying bull and bear markets in stock returns, *Journal of Business and Economic Statistics*, 18(1), 100–112.

Raymond, J. E. and Rich, R. W. (1997), Oil and the macroeconomy: A Markov state-switching approach, *Journal of Money, Credit, and Banking*, 29(2), 193–213.

Scheicher, M., (1999), Nonlinear dynamics: evidence for a small stock exchange, *Empirical Economics*, 24, 45–59.

So, M. K. P., Lam, K. and Li, W. K. (1998), A stochastic volatility model with Markov switching, *Journal of Business and Economic Statistics*, 16(2), 244–253.

Town, R. J. (1992), Merger waves and the structure of merger and acquisition time series, *Journal of Applied Econometrics*, 7(suppl.), S83–S100.

6 Present value models and tests for rationality and market efficiency

The present value model states that the present value of an asset is derived from its earning power, or the ability to generate future income. This crucially depends on the expectations about future income and the discount rate at which people or investors would sacrifice a portion of their current income for future consumption, after adjusting for uncertainty or risk involved in the process. Although the present value of an asset, or economic value as against accounting value, is the best to reflect its true value, it involves expectations on future income, the discount rate and rationality of people. Therefore, the present value model is difficult to apply properly in practice. Linking the present value of an asset to its future income in the framework of cointegration analysis, as proposed by Campbell and Shiller (1987), has provided a useful tool for testing expectations and rationality in financial markets.

6.1 The basic present value model and its time series characteristics

The present value of an asset is its all future income discounted:

$$V_t = \sum_{\tau=1}^{\infty} \frac{1}{(1+r_t)\cdots(1+r_{t+\tau})} E_t I_{t+\tau} \tag{1}$$

where V_t is the present value of the asset, I_{t+1} is income derived from possessing this asset in period $(t, t+1]$, E_t is expectations operator, and r_t is the discount rate in period $(t, t+1]$.

When the discount rate is constant, that is, $r_t = r$, equation (1) becomes:

$$V_t = \sum_{\tau=1}^{\infty} \frac{1}{(1+r)^\tau} E_t I_{t+\tau} \tag{1'}$$

Subtracting $V_t/(1+r)$ from both sides leads to:

$$V_t - \frac{V_t}{1+r} = \sum_{\tau=1}^{\infty} \frac{1}{(1+r)^\tau} E_t I_{t+\tau} - \sum_{\tau=1}^{\infty} \frac{1}{(1+r)^\tau} E_t I_{t+\tau-1} + \frac{I_t}{1+r}$$

Rearrangement of the above yields:

$$V_t - \frac{I_t}{r} = \frac{1+r}{r} \sum_{\tau=1}^{\infty} \frac{1}{(1+r)^\tau} E_t \Delta I_{t+\tau} \tag{2}$$

Equation (2) states that if V_t and I_{t+1} are $I(1)$ series, then a linear combination of them is stationary too and the two series are cointegrated. Campbell and Shiller (1987) define $V_t - I_t/r$ as spread, S_t. Obviously, the spread links a stock variable, V_t, to a flow variable, I_t. It is not strange that a flow variable divided by the rate of flow (in this case r) is a stock variable; or a stock variable times the rate of flow is a flow variable. If income is constant over time, then total wealth or value of an asset is simply the current income flow divided by the rate at which income is generated, that is, the spread is equal to zero. Otherwise, the spread is a function of the expected changes in future income discounted. A positive spread reflects an overall growth in future incomes, and a negative spread is associated with income declines.

Nevertheless, the seeming stationarity of the right-hand side in equation (2) is problematic, or at least unrealistic. The growth or change in income as expressed in equation (2) is in an absolute term, $I_t - I_{t-1}$, instead of a relative term, $(I_t - I_{t-1})/I_{t-1}$. Let us adopt a version of the Gordon dividend growth model:

$$V_t = \sum_{\tau=1}^{\infty} \frac{E_t I_{t+\tau}}{(1+r)^\tau} = \sum_{\tau=1}^{\infty} \frac{(1+g)^\tau I_t (1 + E_t u_{t+\tau})}{(1+r)^\tau} \tag{3}$$

subtracting $(1+g)V_t/(1+r)$ from both sides, we have:

$$V_t - \frac{(1+g)V_t}{1+r} = \sum_{\tau=1}^{\infty} \frac{(1+g)^\tau I_t (1 + E_t u_{t+\tau})}{(1+r)^\tau}$$

$$- \sum_{\tau=1}^{\infty} \frac{(1+g)^\tau I_t (1 + E_t u_{t+\tau-1})}{(1+r)^\tau} + \frac{(1+g)I_t}{1+r}$$

and rearrangement yields:

$$V_t - \frac{(1+g)I_t}{r-g} = \frac{1+r}{r-g} \sum_{\tau=1}^{\infty} \frac{(1+g)^\tau E_t \Delta u_{t+\tau}}{(1+r)^\tau} \tag{4}$$

where $\Delta u_{t+\tau} = \Delta \ln I_{t+\tau} - g$. Equation (4) reduces to the Campbell and Shiller (1987) formulation when $g = 0$. ΔI_t is in general non-stationary.

Define $V_t - ((1+g)I_t)/(r-g)$ as the full spread, Sf_t. Equation (4) says total wealth or value of an asset is simply the current income flow (notice $I_{t+1} = (1+g)I_t$ is the income in the current period) divided by, instead of the discount rate, the difference between the discount rate and the growth rate. Equation (4) is, in fact, the Gordon valuation model for constantly growing perpetuities. The important message here is that there exists a cointegration or long-run relationship between the value and the income, as revealed by equations (2) and (4). Moreover, if income obeys a constant growth process, the spread in the sense of Campbell and Shiller (1987) is not stationary, but the full spread as defined above is stationary. Therefore, caution has to be taken in explaining and interpreting the cointegration vector. If $(1+g)/(r-g)$ is mistaken as $1/r$, then $(r-g)/(1+g)$ might be mistaken as the discount rate r and the practice would *under*estimate the true discount rate if there is growth in income.[1] Later in this chapter, we will see how to impose restrictions and carry out empirical tests.

Equation (2) can also be written as:

$$S_t = V_t - \frac{1}{r}I_t = \frac{1+r}{r}E_t\Delta V_{t+1} \tag{5}$$

If there is a rational bubble b_t, satisfying $b_t = (1/(1+r))E_t b_{t+1}$, that is:

$$b_{t+1} = (1+r)b_t + \zeta_{t+1}, \quad \zeta_t \sim \text{i.i.d.}(0, \sigma_\zeta^2) \tag{6}$$

in equation (1'), it will appear on the right-hand side of equation (2), but will not appear on the right-hand side of equation (5). b_t has a root outside the unit circle and is explosive or non-stationary. Consequently, even if ΔI_t is stationary, the spread is non-stationary if there is a rational bubble in equation (1'), inducing non-stationarity in ΔV_t through equation (5). Therefore, testing for rationality is equivalent to testing for cointegration between the present value variable, V_t, and the income variable, I_t.

6.2 The VAR representation

Equations (2) and (5) also suggest a way to compute the variables in a vector auto-regression (VAR). Let $z_t = [S_t \cdots S_{t \ p|1} \ \Delta I_t \cdots \Delta I_{t \ p|1}]'$, the VAR can be written in the companion form:

$$\begin{bmatrix} \mathbf{S}_t \\ \Delta\mathbf{I}_t \end{bmatrix} = \begin{bmatrix} \mathbf{a}_{11}(L) & \mathbf{a}_{12}(L) \\ \mathbf{a}_{21}(L) & \mathbf{a}_{22}(L) \end{bmatrix} \begin{bmatrix} \mathbf{S}_{t-1} \\ \Delta\mathbf{I}_{t-1} \end{bmatrix} + \begin{bmatrix} \mu_{1t} \\ \mu_{2t} \end{bmatrix} \tag{7}$$

where

$$\mathbf{S}_t = [S_t \cdots S_{t-p+1}]', \qquad \Delta\mathbf{I}_t = [\Delta I_t \cdots \Delta I_{t-p+1}]'$$
$$\mu_{1t} = [v_{1t} \ 0 \ \cdots]', \qquad \mu_{2t} = [v_{2t} \ 0 \ \cdots]'$$

$$\mathbf{a}_{11}(L) = \begin{bmatrix} a_{11,1} & \cdots & & a_{11,p} \\ 1 & \ddots & & \\ & & \ddots & \\ & & & 1 \end{bmatrix}, \quad \mathbf{a}_{12}(L) = \begin{bmatrix} a_{12,1} & \cdots & & a_{12,p} \\ 0 & \ddots & & \\ & & \ddots & \\ & & & 0 \end{bmatrix}$$

$$\mathbf{a}_{21}(L) = \begin{bmatrix} a_{21,1} & \cdots & & a_{21,p} \\ 0 & \ddots & & \\ & & \ddots & \\ & & & 0 \end{bmatrix}, \quad \mathbf{a}_{22}(L) = \begin{bmatrix} a_{22,1} & \cdots & & a_{22,p} \\ 1 & \ddots & & \\ & & \ddots & \\ & & & 1 \end{bmatrix}$$

Or, in a compact form:

$$\mathbf{z}_t = \mathbf{A}\mathbf{z}_{t-1} + \mu_t \tag{8}$$

The implication of this representation is that the spread, S_t, must linearly Granger cause ΔI_t, unless S_t is itself an *exact* linear combination of current and lagged ΔI_t. Therefore, S_t would have incremental predicting power for ΔI_t. Further, let $e1'$ and $e2'$ be $(1 \times 2p)$ row vectors with zero in all cells except unity in the first element for the former and in the $(p + 1)$ element for the latter, respectively, that is:

$$S_t = e1'\mathbf{z}_t \tag{9}$$

$$\Delta I_t = e2'\mathbf{z}_t \tag{10}$$

Notice:

$$E\{\mathbf{z}_{t+k}|H_t\} = \mathbf{A}^k \mathbf{z}_t \tag{11}$$

where H_t is the information set with all available information about S_t and ΔI_t at time t. Applying equations (9)–(11) to (2) yields:

$$e1'\mathbf{z}_t = \frac{1}{r}\sum_{i=1}^{\infty}\frac{1}{(1+r)^i}e2'\mathbf{A}^i\mathbf{z}_t = e2'\frac{1}{r(1+r)}\mathbf{A}\left[\mathbf{I} - \frac{1}{1+r}\mathbf{A}\right]^{-1}\mathbf{z}_t \tag{12}$$

Equation (12) imposes restrictions on the VAR parameters if rationality is to hold, that is:

$$e1'\left[\mathbf{I} - \frac{1}{1+r}\mathbf{A}\right] = e2'\frac{1}{r(1+r)}\mathbf{A} \tag{13}$$

Accordingly, the 'theoretical' spread can be introduced as:

$$S_t^* = e2'\frac{1}{r(1+r)}\mathbf{A}\left[\mathbf{I} - \frac{1}{1+r}\mathbf{A}\right]^{-1}\mathbf{z}_t \tag{14}$$

It can be seen that the difference between the actual and 'theoretical' spreads is:

$$S_t - S_t^* = \sum_{i=1}^{\infty} \frac{1}{(1+r)^i} E(\xi_{t+i}|H_t) \tag{15}$$

where $\xi_t = V_t - [(1+r)V_{t-1} - I_t] = V_t - E_{t-1}V_t$ is the innovation in forecasting V_t. Testing the restrictions in equation (13) is equivalent to testing that the right-hand side of equation (15) is just white noise with a mean of zero. Also, using the volatility test, the variance ratio $\text{var}(S_t)/\text{var}(S_t^*)$ should not be significantly larger than unity if the present value model is to hold. In addition, the volatility test can be carried out with the innovation ξ_t and the innovation in the expected present value:

$$\xi_t^* \equiv \frac{1}{r} \sum_{i=0}^{\infty} \frac{1}{(1+r)^i} [E(\Delta I_{t+i}|H_t) - E(\Delta I_{t+i}|H_{t-1})]$$

$$= S_t^* - (1+r)S_{t-1}^* + \frac{1}{r} \Delta I_t \tag{16}$$

The variance ratio $\text{var}(\xi_t)/\text{var}(\xi_t^*)$ can be viewed as the 'innovation variance ratio', and $\text{var}(S_t)/\text{var}(S_t^*)$ as the 'level variance ratio'. Notice ξ_t can also be written in the similar expression of (16):

$$\xi_t \equiv V_t - [(1+r)V_{t-1} - I_t]$$

$$= V_t - \frac{1}{r} I_{t+1} + \frac{1}{r} I_{t+1} - (1+r)V_{t-1} + (1+r)I_t - \frac{1}{r} I_t$$

$$= S_t - (1+r)S_{t-1} + \frac{1}{r} \Delta I_{t+1} \tag{17}$$

The implications of the above equations can be summarised in the following. If the market is rational for an asset, then its value/price and income variables should be cointegrated and its spread should be stationary. Without a cointegration relation between the price and income, the spread is non-stationary and a 'rational bubble', which by definition is explosive, would exist in the market. If the market is efficient and the present value model holds, then the 'theoretical' spread should not systematically differ from the actual spread, and neither variance ratio should be significantly larger than unity. The prediction power of the spread for ΔI_t is conditional on agents' information set. If agents do not have information useful for predicting ΔI_t beyond the history of ΔI_t, then S_t is a linear combination of current and lagged ΔI_t without prediction ability. Prediction may or may not be improved simply because the price and income variables are cointegrated. Therefore, in this chapter, we use cointegration between the price and income as a criterion for rationality against the existence of bubbles in the market. In addition, we use the VAR representation and the variance ratios derived from the VAR system to examine whether the present value model holds and how far the market is from being efficient.

6.3   The present value model in logarithms with time-varying discount rates

The previous section has shown that a ratio relationship between the value and income variables is more appropriate than a 'spread' relationship between the two variables, in the context of a constant discount rate and growth in income. As most economic and financial variables grow exponentially, linear relationships are only appropriate for variables in their logarithm, not for variables in their original form. This is equivalent to saying that variables in their original form have ratio relationships, instead of linear relationships. In a sense, a right modelling strategy reflects impeccably both the economic and financial characteristics and the data generating process and makes these two considerations fit into each other. In this section, we further generalise the present value model along this line and allow for a time-varying rate of return or discount rate in the model.

In this section, we deliberate value, income and their relationship explicitly in a context of stock market investment, that is, value and income variables are characterised by observable share prices and dividends. Let us express the rate of total return in the logarithmic form:

$$r_t = \ln\left(\frac{P_{t+1} + D_{t+1}}{P_t}\right) \tag{18}$$

Notice r_t is an approximation of the exact rate of total return. However, this expression is in common with general practice and leads, conventionally, to the linear relationship among all variables involved.

As already known, total return can be split into price appreciation and dividend yield. The idea is also valid in the log-linear form. To see this, expanding equation (18) as:

$$r_t = \ln\left(\frac{P_{t+1} + D_{t+1}}{P_t}\right) = \ln\left[\frac{P_{t+1}}{P_t}\left(1 + \frac{D_{t+1}}{P_{t+1}}\right)\right]$$

$$= \ln\left(\frac{P_{t+1}}{P_t}\right) + \ln\left(1 + \frac{D_{t+1}}{P_{t+1}}\right)$$

$$\approx (\ln P_{t+1} - \ln P_t) + \frac{D_{t+1}}{P_{t+1}}$$

$$= (p_{t+1} - p_t) + e^{(d_{t+1} - p_{t+1})} \tag{19}$$

where $p_t = \ln P_t$ and $d_t = \ln D_t$. The first term on the right-hand side is price appreciation, and the last term on the right-hand side reflects the dividend yield (notice the exact dividend yield is D_{t+1}/P_t). As the last term on the right-hand side is not linear, further transformation and approximation are required. Finally, after a series of development, the rate of total return can be expressed as:

$$r_t \approx \kappa + (1 - \lambda)p_{t+1} - p_t + \lambda d_{t+1} \tag{20}$$

where $\lambda = e^{(d-p)'} = D/P$ is a constant between the minimum and maximum dividend yields, and

$$\kappa = (d - p)'e^{(d-p)'} = \ln\left(\frac{D}{P}\right) \times \left(\frac{D}{P}\right)$$

is also a constant.

With the rate of total return, price and dividend being linked in a log-linear relationship as in equation (20), it is now possible to express the present value model in a log-linear form too. Furthermore, no restriction on the rate of return r_t to be constant is required to derive the log-linear form present value model. Thus, the model could accommodate the time-varying rate of return or discount rate and is more general and closer to reality.

Solving equation (20) forward, we obtain:

$$p_t = \frac{\kappa}{\lambda} + \sum_{\tau=0}^{T}\{(1 - \lambda)^{\tau}(\lambda d_{t+1+\tau} - r_{t+\tau})\} + (1 - \lambda)^{T} p_{T+1} \tag{21}$$

when $T \rightarrow \infty$, the last term on the right-hand side $\rightarrow 0$: and equation (21)

$$p_t = \frac{\kappa}{\lambda} + \sum_{\tau=0}^{\infty}(1 - \lambda)^{\tau}(\lambda d_{t+1+\tau} - r_{t+\tau}) \tag{22}$$

Equation (22) is the log-linear counterpart of equation (1), and is not advantageous compared with the latter. Both are able to deal with the time-varying discount rate, but equation (1) is exact whereas equation (22) is an approximation. However, the benefit would be seen when the value–income or price–dividend relationship is examined. Extracting d_t from both sides of equation (22) and rearrangement yield:

$$p_t - d_t = -(d_t - p_t) = \frac{\kappa}{\lambda} + \sum_{\tau=0}^{\infty}(1 - \lambda)^{\tau}(\Delta d_{t+1+\tau} - r_{t+\tau}) \tag{23}$$

It can be observed that if d_t is $I(1)$ and r_t is $I(0)$, the left-hand side of equation (23) is also $I(0)$, or stationary. That is, the price and dividend in their logarithm are cointegrated. Notice that no conditions are placed on r_t to derive the cointegration relationship, in contrast with equation (2). This is obviously advantageous, compared with the 'spread' form specification.

Equations (22) and (23) are derived as *ex post*, but they also hold *ex ante*. Taking expectations operations on both sides of equations (22) and (23), we have:

$$p_t = \frac{\kappa}{\lambda} + E_t\left\{\sum_{\tau=0}^{\infty}(1 - \lambda)^{\tau}(\lambda d_{t+1+\tau} - r_{t+\tau})\right\} \tag{22'}$$

and

$$p_t - d_t = -(d_t - p_t) = \frac{\kappa}{\lambda} + E_t\left\{\sum_{\tau=0}^{\infty}(1 - \lambda)^{\tau}(\Delta d_{t+1+\tau} - r_{t+\tau})\right\} \tag{23'}$$

Previously in Section 6.1, we have shown that value (price) and income (dividend) would be cointegrated with a cointegration vector $[1, -1/r]$, if the *absolute* changes in income are stationary or constant. If the income stream has a constant growth rate, instead of constant absolute increase, then they would be cointegrated with a cointegration vector $[1, -1/(r - g)]$. Recall that the derivation of a cointegration relationship is dependent on $r_t \equiv r$, so the cointegration relationship is rather restrictive. With the log-linear form present value model, the cointegration vector is always $[1, -1]$. The proportional relation for the price and dividend is reflected by the constant and variables on the right-hand side of equation (23) or (23′), which are time varying in general. The cointegration between price and dividend is not affected by whether the discount rate is assumed to be constant or not as in Section 6.1. As we know prices, dividends and most other financial variables grow exponentially, there should be a log-linear relationship among them. Consequently, models in the log-linear form are generally sound, financially and statistically.

6.4 The VAR representation for the present value model in the log-linear form

The VAR representation of the log-linear form is similar to that of the original form. Let $\mathbf{z}_t = [\, s_t \cdots s_{t-p+1} \; r_t - \Delta d_{t+1} \cdots r_{t-p} - \Delta d_{t-p+1}]'$, where $s_t = d_t - p_t \cdot s_t$ is, roughly, the log-dividend yield (the exact log-dividend yield is $d_{t+1} - p_t$). Compared with Section 6.2, the spread S_t is replaced by the log-dividend yield, and the absolute changes in dividends are replaced by the difference between the percentage changes in dividends and the discount rate (recall, in Sections 6.1 and 6.2, r_t is restricted to a constant and did not appear in the $\mathbf{z}_t$ vector). With the same $\mathbf{A}$ matrix as in Section 6.2, the compact form is:

$$\mathbf{z}_t = \mathbf{A}\mathbf{z}_{t-1} + \mu_t \tag{8′}$$

The selecting vector $\mathbf{e}1$ picks up s_t from $\mathbf{z}_t$ and the following holds, conditional on H_t, the information in the VAR:

$$s_t = \mathbf{e}1'\mathbf{z}_t = \sum_{\tau=0}^{\infty}(1 - \lambda)^{\tau}\mathbf{e}2'\mathbf{A}^{\tau+1}\mathbf{z}_t = \mathbf{e}2'\mathbf{A}[\mathbf{I} - (1 - \lambda)\mathbf{A}]^{-1}\mathbf{z}_t \tag{24}$$

Therefore:

$$\mathbf{e}1' = \mathbf{e}2'\mathbf{A}[\mathbf{I} - (1 - \lambda)\mathbf{A}]^{-1} \tag{25}$$

or:

$$\mathbf{e}1'[\mathbf{I} - (1 - \lambda)\mathbf{A}] - \mathbf{e}2'\mathbf{A} = 0 \tag{26}$$

The log-dividend yield satisfying the conditions in equation (25) or (26) is the theoretical log-dividend yield, written as s_t^*. Notice again there are no restrictions imposed on r_t, so tests on the validity of the present value model in the log-linear form are not subject to the assumption about the discount rate. That is, the present value model can be accepted or rejected no matter whether the discount rate is treated as time varying or not. The variance ratio test on s_t^* and s_t can be carried out to examine whether the present value model holds.

Furthermore, dividend volatility and return volatility can also be tested, respectively. If the discount rate is constant over time, it could be excluded from the $\mathbf{z}_t$ vector, and the theoretical log-dividend yield with a constant discount rate, $s_{d,t}^*$, is obtained. The hypothesis for a constant discount rate is $H_{r0} : s_{d,t}^* = s_t^*$. In a separate study, Campbell and Shiller (1989) reject a constant discount rate in the US stock market, employing the Cowles/S&P data set (1871–1986) and the NYSE data set (1926–1986). In a similar way, if $\Delta d_t = g$, that is, the dividend growth is constant, then Δd_t can be excluded from the $\mathbf{z}_t$ vector too, and the theoretical log-dividend yield with the constant dividend growth, $s_{r,t}^*$, emerges. The hypothesis for dividend growth to be constant is $H_{d0} : s_{r,t}^* = s_t^*$, though it has little financial meaning. The variance ratio test can also be employed to test these two hypotheses.

6.5   Variance decomposition

As returns may be volatile, we are interested in the sources of volatility. Substituting equation (22′) into (20) yields an expression for innovation in the total rate of return:

$$
r_t - E_t\{r_t\} = E_{t+1}\left\{\sum_{\tau=0}^{\infty}(1-\lambda)^{\tau}\Delta d_{t+1+\tau}\right\} - E_t\left\{\sum_{\tau=0}^{\infty}(1-\lambda)^{\tau}\Delta d_{t+1+\tau}\right\}
$$
$$
- \left[E_{t+1}\left\{\sum_{\tau=1}^{\infty}(1-\lambda)^{\tau}r_{t+\tau}\right\} - E_t\left\{\sum_{\tau=1}^{\infty}(1-\lambda)^{\tau}r_{t+\tau}\right\}\right]
$$

(27)

Equation (27) can be written in compact notations, with the left-hand side term being v_t, the first term on the right-hand side $\eta_{d,t}$, and the second term on the right-hand side $\eta_{r,t}$:

$$
v_t = \eta_{d,t} - \eta_{r,t}
$$

(28)

where v_t is the innovation or shock in total returns, $\eta_{d,t}$ represents the innovation due to changes in expectations about future income or dividends, and $\eta_{r,t}$ represents the innovation due to changes in expectations about future discount rates or returns.

Again, we use VAR to express the above innovations. Vector $\mathbf{z}_t$ contains, first of all, the rate of total return or discount rate. Other variables included are relevant to forecast the rate of total return:

$$
\mathbf{z}_t = \mathbf{A}\mathbf{z}_{t-1} + \varepsilon_t
$$

(29)

with the selecting vector $\mathbf{e}1$ which picks out r_t from $\mathbf{z}_t$, we obtain:

$$
v_t = r_t - E_t\{r_t\} = \mathbf{e}1'\varepsilon_t
$$

(30)

Bringing equations (29) and (30) into the second term on the right-hand side of equation (27) yields:

$$\eta_{r,t} = E_{t+1} \left\{ \sum_{\tau=1}^{\infty} (1-\lambda)^{\tau} r_{t+\tau} \right\} - E_t \left\{ \sum_{\tau=1}^{\infty} (1-\lambda)^{\tau} r_{t+\tau} \right\}$$

$$= \mathbf{e}\mathbf{1}' \sum_{\tau=1}^{\infty} (1-\lambda)^{\tau} \mathbf{A}^{\tau} \varepsilon_t = \mathbf{e}\mathbf{1}'(1-\lambda)\mathbf{A}[\mathbf{I} - (1-\lambda)\mathbf{A}]^{-1}\varepsilon_t \qquad (31)$$

$\eta_{d,t}$ can be easily derived according to the relationship in equation (28) as follows:

$$\eta_{d,t} = \nu_t + \eta_{r,t} = \mathbf{e}\mathbf{1}'\{\mathbf{I} + (1-\lambda)\mathbf{A}[\mathbf{I} - (1-\lambda)\mathbf{A}]^{-1}\}\varepsilon_t \qquad (32)$$

The variance of innovation in the rate of total return is the sum of the variance of $\eta_{r,t}$, innovation due to changes in expectations about future discount rates or returns, $\eta_{d,t}$, innovation due to changes in expectations about future income or dividends, and their covariance, that is:

$$\sigma_{\nu}^2 = \sigma_{\eta,d}^2 + \sigma_{\eta,r}^2 - 2\operatorname{Cov}(\eta_{d,t}, \eta_{r,t}) \qquad (33)$$

6.6   Examples and cases

The present value model discussed in this chapter has provided a powerful approach to modelling value–income or price–dividend relationships via exploiting their time series characteristics, namely, cointegration and restrictions on the VAR. In this section, several examples in financial markets and international economics and finance are presented to illustrate how the research is empirically carried out.

Example 1

This is a case in US stock market behaviour in Campbell and Shiller (1987). The price and dividend data were of annual frequency from 1971 to 1986 in a broad stock index mainly represented by Standard and Poor's with adjustments. The model used was in the original form, that is, without logarithmic operations. The main results are summarised in Tables 6.1 and 6.2.

The unit root test, which uses one of the Perron–Phillips test statistics, confirms that the stock price and dividend are $I(1)$ variables. The spread is stationary, when it is calculated with a discount rate of 3.2 per cent estimated with cointegration, but the spread is non-stationary when a discount rate of 8.2 per cent from the sample mean is applied. Based on these results, Campbell and Shiller suggest that a 'rational bubble' is not present but the evidence for cointegration between the stock price and dividend is weak as the stationarity of the spread is rejected if a 'more reasonable' discount rate is used. However, as has been pointed out in Section 6.1, the stock price and dividend, if cointegrated, will not always be cointegrated at $[1, -1/r]$. With growth in dividends, they are more likely to be

Table 6.1 Tests of stationarity, cointegration and rationality

	With trends	*Without trends*
I_t	−2.88	−1.28
V_t	−2.19	−1.53
ΔI_t	−8.40***	−8.44***
ΔV_t	−9.91***	−9.96***
$S_t = (V_t - 1/0.032I_t)$	−4.35***	−4.31***
$r = 3.2\%$		
$S_t\ (=V_t - 1/0.082I_t)$	−2.68	−2.15
$r = 8.2\%$		

Notes
  * Significant at the 10% level.
 ** Significant at the 5% level.
*** Significant at the 1% level.
    V_t represents the stock price variable and I_t represents the
    dividend variable.

Table 6.2 Tests of the present value model

$r\ (\%)$	*VAR restrictions*	$\mathrm{Var}(S_t)/\mathrm{Var}(S_t^*)$	$\mathrm{Var}(\xi_t)/\mathrm{Var}(\xi_t^*)$
3.2	5.75	4.786	1.414
	(0.218)	(5.380)	(0.441)
8.2	15.72	67.22	11.27
	(0.0047)	(86.04)	(4.49)

Note: p-value in brackets for testing VAR restrictions which obeys the χ^2
distribution. Standard errors in brackets for variance ratio tests.

cointegrated at $[1, -1/(r - g)]$, and an estimate of 3.2 per cent for $(r - g)$ may not
be too low. Therefore, the estimate should be interpreted as $(r - g)$ instead of r.

Although the US stock market is not subject to a 'rational bubble' and the stock
market behaviour is rational, the present value model may not hold. This is examined by testing variance ratios of the unrestricted and theoretical specifications,
and imposing restrictions on the VAR and testing for their validity. Selected testing
statistics in Table 6.2 suggest the present value model is rejected for the US stock
market. The variance ratio test statistics are greater than unity, though only the
innovation variance ratio is statistically significant. Tests for VAR restrictions in
equation (13) accept the model with the 3.2 per cent discount rate and reject it with
the 8.2 per cent discount rate. As mentioned above, the US stock price and dividend
during this period are more likely to be cointegrated at $[1, -1/(r-g)]$, so when the
discount rate from the sample mean is applied, the right-hand side of equation (2)
may not be stationary, or in fact, it is the right-hand side of equation (3). So, the
mixed results tilt to imply the validity of the VAR model. As expected, with the
8.2 per cent discount rate, the variance ratios are much greater than unity, but with
very large standard errors.

Example 2

This is an example of the applications of the present value model in the real estate market. The data used are capital value and rental indices from Jones Lang Wootten (JLW). The JLW index is one of the major UK real estate indices. The data sets are of quarterly frequency from the second quarter in 1977 to the first quarter in 1997, at the aggregate level as well as the disaggregate level for office, industrial and retail sectors. After confirming both capital value and rent variables are $I(1)$ series, cointegration between the capital value and the rent, or stationarity of the spread, is examined. The study uses the Johansen procedure for testing the cointegration relationship. Although there are only two variables, it is beneficial to use the Johansen procedure in a dynamic setting. The cointegration test is carried out with the variables in their original form and in logarithms, the latter being able to deal with a time-varying rate of return or discount rate. However, the two sets of results in Tables 6.3 and 6.4 are virtually the same, implying that the model in the original form is acceptable in this case. The results suggest that there are no bubbles in

Table 6.3 Check for stationarity of S_t – cointegration of V_t and I_t

	λ_{max}	λ_{trace}
Office	25.66***	28.63***
Industrial	12.29	18.54
Retail	16.83	25.20*
All	34.15***	38.23***

Source: Model with unrestricted constant and restricted trend. Lag lengths are selected with a compromise of the Akaike, Schwarz and Hannan-Quinn criteria. Critical values from Osterwald-Lenum (1992). Critical values for one cointegration vector are: for λ_{max}: 16.85 (90%), 28.96 (95%) and 23.65 (99%), for λ_{trace}: 22.76 (90%), 25.32 (95%) and 30.45 (99%).

Notes:
   * Significant at the 10% level.
*** Significant at the 1% level.
   V_t represents capital value and I_t represents rent.

Table 6.4 Check for stationarity of S_t – cointegration between the logarithm of $V_t(v_t)$ and the logarithm of $I_t(i_t)$

	λ_{max}	λ_{trace}
Office	24.16***	26.98**
Industrial	14.67	17.66
Retail	14.81	23.88*
All	28.67***	33.11***

See notes in Table 6.3.

the office, retail and aggregate property markets; but the existence of bubbles in the industrial property market cannot be ruled out. Industrial property is probably the most illiquid and indivisible among all types of property, and as a consequence, its price/capital value fails to reflect its future income in transactions. Though this phenomenon is generally ruled as the existence of bubbles, it should not simply be made equal to speculation. A 'thin' market for industrial property transactions may reasonably explain a large part of this particular statistical result for industrial property.

The validity of the present value model is examined and the testing statistics are reported in Tables 6.5 and 6.6. The validity of the VAR model is rejected in all types of properties except office property. In general, the spread causes the change in the rent, implying that the spread can help predict future rents; but changes in rents do not cause the spread in the aggregate and industrial properties, and they cause the spread in office and retail properties at a lower significance level. The rejection of the VAR model is also reflected in Table 6.6 for variance ratio tests. The ratio of the variance of the spread to that of the 'theoretical' spread, that is, the 'levels variance ratio', is statistically significant in all types of properties. The 'innovation variance ratio' is also significant in all the cases, but the value is usually smaller. Observing these statistical numbers in detail, it is found that the market

Table 6.5 Tests with the VAR model

	S_t causes ΔI_t	ΔI_t causes S_t	Restrictions on VAR	$Q(18)$	
				ΔI_t	S_t
Office	17.6613***	3.3616**	1.1121	15.2080	14.2482
Industrial	9.4856***	1.5721	2.5610***	17.9259	17.7638
Retail	11.3278***	3.2626**	3.5616***	13.8085	10.6911
All	23.3608***	2.0033	1.9635**	16.3478	11.8133

Notes
** Significant at the 5% level.
*** Significant at the 1% level.

Test statistics are F-test for causality test and restrictions on the VAR model, with respective degrees of freedom. $Q(18)$ is the Ljung–Box statistic for serial correlation up to 18 lags, in the rent equation (ΔI_t) and the spread equation (S_t) respectively.

Table 6.6 Variance ratios

	$\mathrm{Var}(S_t)/\mathrm{Var}(S_t^*)$	$\mathrm{Var}(\xi_t)/\mathrm{Var}(\xi_t^*)$
Office	$144.82/66.29 = 2.1846$***	$73.96/39.95 = 1.8513$***
Industrial	$273.90/24.64 = 11.1161$***	$59.36/27.74 = 2.1399$***
Retail	$512.83/113.00 = 4.538$***	$207.76/53.07 = 3.9148$***
All	$184.15/85.19 = 2.1616$***	$67.34/33.23 = 2.0265$***

Notes
*** Significantly different at the 1% level.

for office property is the least inefficient with the smallest 'innovation variance ratio'; and the markets for industrial and retail property are the most inefficient. This phenomenon is also reflected in the cointegration test, where capital value and rent are not cointegrated for the industrial property, and capital value and rent are cointegrated at a less significant level of 10 per cent for the retail property judged by the value of λ_{trace}.

Example 3

The present value model with cointegration can also be applied to international economics and finance. An example is in MacDonald and Taylor (1993) on the monetary model for exchange rate determination. We need some transformation before getting the present value representation for the monetary model. The flexible price monetary model is based on the following three equations:

$$m_t' - p_t' = \gamma y_t' - \lambda i_t' \tag{34}$$

$$s_t = p_t' \tag{35}$$

$$i_t' = E_t(\Delta s_{t+1}) = E_t(s_{t+1}) - s_t \tag{36}$$

where m_t' is money supply, p_t' is the price level, y_t' is income, i_t' is the interest rate, s_t is the exchange rate, γ is the income elasticity, and λ is the interest rate (semi) elasticity. All variables are in the logarithm; and except for the exchange rate, all variables are the difference between the domestic variable and the foreign variable, for example, $p_t' = p_t - p_t^*$. Equation (34) states a relative money market equilibrium requirement, equation (35) is the purchasing power parity (PPP) condition, and equation (36) is the uncovered interest rate parity (UIP) condition. Let $x_t = m_t' - \gamma y_t'$, then the exchange rate can be expressed as:

$$s_t = p_t' = x_t + \lambda i_t' = x_t + \lambda(E_t(s_{t+1}) - s_t) \tag{37}$$

or:

$$s_t = \frac{x_t}{1+\lambda} + \frac{\lambda}{1+\lambda} E_t(s_{t+1}) \tag{38}$$

Equation (38) can be solved forward and lead to:

$$s_t = \sum_{\tau=0}^{\infty} \frac{\lambda^\tau}{(1+\lambda)^{\tau+1}} E_t(x_{t+\tau+1}) \tag{39}$$

as $(\lambda/1+\lambda)^T E_t(s_{t+1}) \to 0$ when $T \to \infty$. Equation (39) has the same structure as the present value model, and it is easy to work out the following 'spread':

$$s_t - x_t = \sum_{\tau=0}^{\infty} \frac{\lambda^\tau}{(1+\lambda)^\tau} E_t(\Delta x_{t+\tau+1}) \tag{38'}$$

Applying the same logic as in Section 6.1, the implication of equation (38') is that the exchange rate and x_t should be cointegrated and the 'spread' should be

Table 6.7 Tests of the VAR restrictions in the monetary model

λ	VAR restrictions	$\mathrm{Var}(S_t)/\mathrm{Var}(S_t^*)$
0.050	0.29e + 07 (0.000)	0.11e + 03 (0.000)
0.030	0.81e + 07 (0.000)	0.30e + 03 (0.000)
0.015	0.33e + 08 (0.000)	0.12e + 04 (0.000)
0.001	0.73e + 10 (0.000)	0.29e + 06 (0.000)

Note: *p*-value in brackets. The test statistic for the VAR restrictions obeys the χ^2 distribution. The variance ratio test employs the *F*-statistic.

Table 6.8 Variance decomposition for returns in REITs

	σ_ε^2	Proportion of			
		$\sigma_{\eta,d}^2$	$\sigma_{\eta,r}^2$	$-2\,\mathrm{Cov}(\eta_{d,t}, \eta_{r,t})$	$\mathrm{corr}(\eta_{d,t}, \eta_{r,t})$
REITs	22.66	0.798	0.467	−0.265	0.217
		(0.40)	(0.40)	(0.66)	(0.41)
VWStk	21.97	0.381	0.333	0.386	−0.401
		(0.21)	(0.20)	(0.19)	(0.38)
SmStk	41.41	0.297	0.947	−0.244	0.230
		(0.13)	(0.52)	(0.61)	(0.47)

Note: VWStk stands for return on value-weighted stock portfolio; SmStk stands for return on small stock portfolio. Standard errors are in brackets. The VAR models were estimated with two lags and three lags, respectively; only the former is reported here.

stationary, if the monetary model is to hold and a rational bubble does not exist in the foreign exchange market.

MacDonald and Taylor use the Johansen procedure for the cointegration test, as $s_t - x_t$ involves five variables. Using the exchange rate data for the Deutsche mark *vis-à-vis* the US dollar, they rule out rational bubbles in the mark–dollar exchange market. However, with four estimates of λ, they firmly reject the VAR model with the imposed restrictions. These are summarised in Table 6.7.

Example 4

Previous cases have paid attention to rationality in the market and the validity of the VAR representation of the present value model. The following example uses the present value model in the logarithmic form to decompose variance or risk in returns. Liu and Mei (1994) apply the approach to the US equity Real Estate Investment Trusts (REITs) data. The data set is monthly and runs from January 1971 to December 1989. In addition to REITs, they included returns on a value-weighted stock portfolio and on a small stock portfolio in the VAR as other forecasting variables. The main results are summarised in Table 6.8.

The general message is that the variance of shocks in returns can be decomposed via the present value model in logarithms and the relative impacts of shocks or news in income (cash-flow risk as they are called) and shocks or news in discount rates (discount-rate risk) can be assessed. Specifically, this study suggests that cash-flow risk accounts for a much larger proportion (79.8 per cent) in the total risk, compared with value-weighted stocks (38.1 per cent) and small stocks (29.7 per cent). As the correlation of the cash-flow shock and the discount-rate shock is positive, the total variance tends to decline when the two shocks are of opposite signs (since the contribution of the covariance is $-2\,\mathrm{cov}(\eta_{d,t}, \eta_{r,t})$). This is again different from the value-weighted stock portfolio which has a negative correlation between the two shocks, but is similar to small stocks. This study follows the paper 'A variance decomposition for stock returns' by Campbell (1991) which proposes and applies the approach to the US stock market.

6.7   Empirical literature

The present value model links the (present) value of an asset to the future income or cash flows generated from possessing that asset in a fundamental way. Study of the validity of the present value model with cointegration analysis is a powerful method in empirical finance research. The analysis can be extended to investigate issues in bond markets, foreign exchange markets and other securities markets as well, where the relationships between the variables do not appear to be straightforward.

One of the important financial variables is the interest rate, which is central to the valuation of many other financial securities. As such, the term structure of interest rates, that is, the relationships between long-term and short-term interest rates, or generally speaking, between interest rates of various maturities, has been a focus of study in a volatile financial investment environment. Applying the present value model, Veenstra (1999) investigates the relationship between spot and period freight rates for the ocean dry bulk shipping market, where the period rate is formulated as expectations of future spot rates. Formal tests on the VAR model reject the restriction imposed by the present value model. But the author argues that there is considerable evidence that the present value model is valid in ocean dry bulk shipping market after having considered alternative and informal test results. Nautz and Wolters (1999) test the expectations theory of the term structure focusing on the question of how monetary policy actions, indicated by changes in the very short rate, affect long-term interest rates. They claim that the expectations hypothesis implies that very long rates should only react to unanticipated changes of the very short rate, which only requires rational expectations but not stationary risk premia. That is, they challenge the view that there should be a cointegration relationship between very short rates and very long rates, and provide their explanation for the determinants of the term structure of interest rates.

There are a number of studies on foreign exchange rate determination similar to Example 3 in Section 6.6. Smith (1995) applies the present value model to formulate nominal exchange rates as discounted expected future fundamentals. The author rejects the validity of the present value relationship based on the findings that the discount rate obtained is statistically significantly negative. Nagayasu (1998) analyses Japanese long-run exchange rates using several exchange rate models, including the present value model. The author finds that the long-run specification is sensitive to the specification of the model. A relevant area of study is how the current account is determined and influenced by the forcing variables. In this regard, Otto (1992) examines the postwar data for the US and Canada, applying the present value relationship based upon the permanent income hypothesis of private consumption behaviour under rational expectations. The study strongly rejects the stringent restrictions imposed on the present value model with the US and Canadian data.

Research on the stock market remains one of the most active areas in which the present value model is empirically investigated, as the relationships between the price and dividends are explicitly defined and stock market investment accounts for the largest amount of all types of investment in the world. Investigating stock prices on the Shanghai Stock Exchange, Chow *et al.* (1999) adopt the log-linear version of the present value model. Surprisingly they find that the model explains well the prices of 47 traded stocks as observed at the beginning of 1996, 1997 and 1998. However, there is some doubt cast on the use of such a data sample. Chow and Liu (1999) claim that stock prices can move in a more volatile fashion than could be warranted by future dividend movements, when there is memory in the duration of dividend swings, if a constant discount rate is used in the present value model. The memory in the duration of a dividend swing will generate a spurious bias in the stock price and induce excess volatility in the stock price as if rational bubbles exist. More studies can be found in the papers by, for example, Crowder and Wohar (1998) and Lee (1995).

Due to the unique characteristics of low liquidity and high transaction costs, the behaviour of farmland and housing prices has been subject to extensive studies with regard to rationality and the existence of bubbles in the market. Bearing this in mind, Lence and Miller (1999) investigate whether the farmland 'constant-discount-rate present-value-model (CDR-PVM) puzzle' is due to transaction costs. They first discuss the theoretical implications of transaction costs for the CDR-PVM of farmland, then test the model with Iowa farmland prices and rents. Their empirical results regarding the validity of the CDR-PVM in the presence of typical transaction costs are not conclusive. Meese and Wallace (1994) examine the efficiency of residential housing markets by inspecting price, rent and cost of capital indices generated from a transactions level database for Alameda and San Francisco Counties in Northern California. They reject both constant and non-constant discount rate versions of the price present value model in the short term. Nevertheless, long-run results are consistent with the present value relation when they adjust the discount factor for changes in both tax rates and borrowing costs. Their explanation for the short-term rejection and the long-run consistency is the high transaction costs in the housing market. Clayton (1996), Lloyd (1994) and Pindyck (1993) are also in this category of empirical research.

Questions and problems

1 Why and how could the underlying economic processes and characteristics be better represented and reflected in an appropriate modelling strategy and framework? How could the consideration on statistics and the consideration on economics and finance be fitted into each other?

2 What are the advantages of linking value and income in the original form present value model? What are the shortcomings associated with this kind of modelling?

3 What are the advantages of linking value and income with the present value model in the logarithm form? Is modelling with the logarithm form an overall improvement over that of the original form, and why? Is it perfect?

4 It is often claimed that cointegration of two or more financial time series means market inefficiency. But in this chapter, cointegration between the price and dividend is a prerequisite for market efficiency, though it does not guarantee market efficiency. Explain.

5 Collect data from Datastream to test for cointegration between the price and dividend, using UK market indices

   a with the original data;
   b data in logarithm.

6 Collect data from two companies from Datastream to test for cointegration between the price and dividend. One of the companies is a fast growing firm, and the other is rather stable. Again data are in the following forms:

   a the original data;
   b data in logarithm.

   Discuss the two sets of results you have obtained. Do they differ? Explain.

Note

1 Estimated with the cointegration regression, Campbell and Shiller (1987) reported a 3.2% discount rate for the US broad stock market index from 1871 to 1986, which was substantially lower than the estimated mean rate of return of 8.2% during this period. The difference in the two estimates, in fact, implies a 4.8% growth in dividends.

References

Campbell, J. Y. (1991), A variance decomposition for stock returns, *The Economic Journal*, 101, 157–179.

Campbell, J. Y. and Shiller, R. J. (1987), Cointegration and tests of present value models, *Journal of Political Economy*, 95, 1062–1088.

Campbell, J. Y. and Shiller, R. J. (1989), The dividend–price ratio and expectations of future dividends and discount factors, *Review of Financial Studies*, 1, 195–228.

Chow, G. C., Fan, Z. Z. and Hu, J. Y. (1999), Shanghai stock prices as determined by the present-value model, *Journal of Comparative Economics*, 27(3), 553–561.

Chow, Y. F. and Liu, M. (1999), Long swings with memory and stock market fluctuations, *Journal of Financial and Quantitative Analysis*, 34(3), 341–367.

Clayton, J. (1996), Rational expectations, market fundamentals and housing price volatility, *Real Estate Economics*, 24(4), 441–470.

Crowder, W. J. and Wohar, M. E. (1998), Stock price effects of permanent and transitory shocks, *Economic Inquiry*, 36(4), 540–552.

Johansen, S. (1988), Statistical analysis of cointegration vectors, *Journal of Economic Dynamics and Control*, 12(2/3), 231–254.

Johansen, S. and Juselius, K. (1990), Maximum likelihood estimation and inference on cointegration – with applications to the demand for money, *Oxford Bulletin of Economics and Statistics*, 52(2), 169–210.

Lee, B. S. (1995), Fundamentals and bubbles in asset prices: Evidence from U.S. and Japanese asset prices, *Financial Engineering and the Japanese Markets*, 2(2), 89–122.

Lence, S. H. and Miller, D. J. (1999), Transaction costs and the present value model of farmland: Iowa, 1900–1994, *American Journal of Agricultural Economics*, 81(2), 257–272.

Liu, C. H. and Mei, J. (1994), An analysis of real-estate risk using the present value model, *Journal of Real Estate Finance and Economics*, 8, 5–20.

Lloyd, T. (1994), Testing a present value model of agricultural land values, *Oxford Bulletin of Economics and Statistics*, 56(2), 209–223.

MacDonald, R. and Taylor, M. (1993), The monetary approach to the exchange rate – rational expectations, long-run equilibrium, and forecasting, *IMF Staff Papers*, 40, 89–107.

Meese, R. and Wallace, N. E. (1994), Testing the present value relation for housing prices: Should I leave my house in San Francisco?, *Journal of Urban Economics*, 35(3), 245–266.

Nagayasu, J. (1998), Japanese effective exchange rates and determinants: prices, real interest rates, and actual and optimal current accounts, *International Monetary Fund Working Paper*: WP/98/86.

Nautz, D. and Wolters, J. (1999), The response of long-term interest rates to news about monetary policy actions: Empirical evidence for the U.S. and Germany, *Weltwirtschaftliches Archiv*, 135(3), 397–412.

Osterwald-Lenum, M. (1992), A note with quantiles of the asymptotic distribution of the maximum likelihood cointegration rank test statistics, *Oxford Bulletin of Economics and Statistics*, 54, 461–472.

Otto, G. (1992), Testing a present-value model of the current account: Evidence from the U.S. and Canadian time series, *Journal of International Money and Finance*, 11(5), 414–430.

Pindyck, R. (1993), The present value model of rational commodity pricing, *Economic Journal*, 103, 511–530.

Smith, G. W. (1995), Exchange rate discounting, *Journal of International Money and Finance*, 14, 659–666.

Timmermann, A. (1995), Cointegration tests of present value models with a time-varying discount factor, *Journal of Applied Econometrics*, 10, 17–31.

Veenstra, A. W. (1999), The term structure of ocean freight rates, *Maritime Policy and Management*, 26(3), 279–293.

7 State space models and the Kalman filter

A dynamic system can be described by changes in the state of its components. The variables concerned, which are observable, are represented as dynamic functions of these components, which are unobservable. The unobserved components, also called state variables, transit from one state to another or evolve according to certain rules which are not easily or straightforwardly applied to the observed variables themselves. This kind of dynamic modelling of systems is called the state space method. It explains the behaviour of externally observed variables by examining the internal, dynamic and systematic properties of the unobserved components. Therefore, this modelling strategy, if applied properly, may reveal the nature and cause of dynamic movement of variables in an effective and fundamental way.

State space models can be estimated using the Kalman filter, named after Kalman (1960, 1963), which was originally for and is still widely used in automatic control and communications. Initial application results are in Kalman and Bucy (1961) and subsequent developments are summarised by Kalman (1978). Clark (1987) was among the first to apply the state space model, using the Kalman filter, to economic analysis. Harvey (1989) and Hamilton (1994) contain a substantial element of this modelling method.

7.1 State space expression

The state space representation of a dynamic system can be formulated as:

$$\mathbf{y}_t = \mathbf{H}\boldsymbol{\xi}_t + \mathbf{A}\mathbf{x}_t + \boldsymbol{\mu}_t \tag{1}$$

$$\boldsymbol{\xi}_{t+1} = \mathbf{F}\boldsymbol{\xi}_t + \mathbf{B}\mathbf{x}_{t+1} + \mathbf{v}_{t+1} \tag{2}$$

where $\mathbf{y}_t$ is an $n \times 1$ vector of observed variables, $\boldsymbol{\xi}_t$ is a $r \times 1$ vector of state variables, $\mathbf{x}_t$ is a $k \times 1$ vector of exogenous variables, and $\mathbf{H}$, $\mathbf{A}$ and $\mathbf{F}$ are coefficient matrices of dimension $n \times r$, $n \times k$ and $r \times r$, respectively. $\boldsymbol{\mu}_t$ and $\mathbf{v}_t$ are vectors of residuals of dimension $n \times 1$ and $r \times 1$, with the following covariance matrices:

$$\text{Cov}(\boldsymbol{\mu}_t \boldsymbol{\mu}_t) = \mathbf{R}, \qquad \text{Cov}(\mathbf{v}_t \mathbf{v}_t) = \mathbf{Q}, \qquad \text{Cov}(\boldsymbol{\mu}_t \mathbf{v}_t) = 0 \tag{3}$$

Equation (1) is the observation equation or measurement equation; and equation (2) is the state equation or transition equation. They can be estimated by the Kalman filter algorithm to be illustrated in the next section.

7.2   Kalman filter algorithm

The Kalman filter can be better demonstrated in three steps, though at least the first two steps can be easily combined. The three steps are prediction, updating and smoothing.

Predicting

This step is to predict, based on information available at $t - 1$, the state vector $\boldsymbol{\xi}_{t\,|\,t-1}$, its covariance matrix $\mathbf{P}_{t\,|\,t-1}$ and derive an estimate of $\mathbf{y}_t$ accordingly:

$$\boldsymbol{\xi}_{t,t-1} = \mathbf{F}\boldsymbol{\xi}_{t-1\,|\,t-1} \tag{4}$$

$$\mathbf{P}_{t,t-1} = \mathbf{F}\mathbf{P}_{t-1\,|\,t-1}\mathbf{F}' + \mathbf{Q} \tag{5}$$

$$\mathbf{y}_{t\,|\,t-1} = \mathbf{H}\boldsymbol{\xi}_{t\,|\,t-1} + \mathbf{A}\mathbf{x}_{t\,|\,t-1} \tag{6}$$

Updating

At this stage, the inference about $\boldsymbol{\xi}_t$ is updated using the observed value of $\mathbf{y}_t$:

$$\boldsymbol{\psi}_t = \mathbf{H}\mathbf{P}_{t\,|\,t-1}\mathbf{H}' + \mathbf{R} \tag{7}$$

$$\mathbf{K}_t = \mathbf{P}_{t\,|\,t-1}\mathbf{H}'(\boldsymbol{\psi}_t)^{-1} \tag{8}$$

$$\boldsymbol{\varepsilon}_t = \mathbf{y}_t - \mathbf{y}_{t\,|\,t-1} \tag{9}$$

$$\boldsymbol{\xi}_{t,t} = \boldsymbol{\xi}_{t\,|\,t-1} + \mathbf{K}_t\boldsymbol{\varepsilon}_t \tag{10}$$

$$\mathbf{P}_{t,t} = (I - \mathbf{K}_t\mathbf{H})\mathbf{P}_{t\,|\,t-1} \tag{11}$$

where $\mathbf{K}_t$ is the Kalman filter gain, $\boldsymbol{\psi}_t$ can be regarded as the system wide variance/covariance matrix, and $\boldsymbol{\varepsilon}_t$ is the system wide vector of residuals. Then, estimation of the Kalman filter is straightforward. The conditional density function is:

$$f(\mathbf{y}_t \mid I_{t-1}) = (2\pi)^{-n/2} |\boldsymbol{\psi}_t|^{-1/2} \exp\left(-\frac{\boldsymbol{\varepsilon}_t'\boldsymbol{\psi}_t\boldsymbol{\varepsilon}_t}{2}\right) \tag{12}$$

where I_{t-1} is the information set at time $t - 1$. The Kalman filter can be estimated by maximising the log likelihood of the density function (ignoring the constant part):

$$\text{Max:} \sum_{t=1}^{T} \log f(\mathbf{y}_t \mid I_{t-1}) = -\frac{nT}{2} \log(2\pi)$$

$$+ \text{Max:} \quad -\frac{1}{2} \sum_{t=1}^{T} \{\log(\boldsymbol{\psi}_t) + (\boldsymbol{\varepsilon}_t' \boldsymbol{\psi}_t \boldsymbol{\varepsilon}_t)\} \tag{13}$$

Estimated parameters and state variables can be obtained accordingly.

At the prediction stage, inference is made based on the information contained in state variables only. This inference, however, has to be revised, based on the realisation of, and interaction with, observable variables. This is done at the updating stage. State variables evolve in their own way and the filter is like a black box at the prediction stage. But the purposes of introducing state variables are estimation, presentation and revelation of the governing stochastic process of $\mathbf{y}_t$ in an alternative, if not a better way. These can only be achieved by comparing the actual value of $\mathbf{y}_t$ and that predicted by state variables. Corresponding error correction is made to update the state variables so that they closely track the dynamic system. The linkage between state variables and observed variables is maintained this way.

Smoothing

The state variables estimated during the above two stages use all past information and the current realisation of $\mathbf{y}_t$, not the whole sample information which includes future information which has not arrived at the time. For real time control and similar applications, these are all required and can be expected. For some other applications, however, it may be of interest to know the estimate of a state variable at any given time t, based on the whole information set up to the last observation at time T. This procedure is smoothing which updates state variables backwards instead of forwards from $T - 1$:

$$\boldsymbol{\xi}_{t,T} = \boldsymbol{\xi}_{t|t} + \mathbf{V}_t(\boldsymbol{\xi}_{t+1|T} - \boldsymbol{\xi}_{t+1|t}) \tag{14}$$

$$\mathbf{P}_{t,T} = \mathbf{P}_{t|t} + \mathbf{V}_t(\mathbf{P}_{t+1|T} - \mathbf{P}_{t+1|t})\mathbf{V}_t' \tag{15}$$

where

$$\mathbf{V}_t = \mathbf{P}_{t|t}\mathbf{F}'\mathbf{P}_{t+1|t}^{-1} \tag{16}$$

$\boldsymbol{\xi}_{t|T}$ is an inference of $\boldsymbol{\xi}_t$ based on the whole sample and $\mathbf{P}_{t|T}$ is its covariance matrix. As the inference of the state variable vector and its covariance matrix at T, $\boldsymbol{\xi}_{T|T}$ and $\mathbf{P}_{T|T}$, is known from equations (10) and (11), all of $\boldsymbol{\xi}_{t|T}$ and $\mathbf{P}_{t|T}$ can be recursively obtained through equations (14)–(16).

7.3   Time-varying coefficient models

Previously, we have used state variables as unobserved components of $\mathbf{y}_t$ – the observable economic or financial variables – in the analysis of dynamic systems.

We can also use state variables for other purposes to better describe a system or relax some untested restrictions in the formulation of the system. One of the most common restrictions is that coefficients of a model are constant. State space models can easily set up a dynamic model that lets the coefficients time-vary. If we modify equations (1) and (2) as follows:

$$\mathbf{y}_t = \mathbf{H}(\mathbf{z}_t)\boldsymbol{\xi}_t + \mathbf{A}\mathbf{z}_t + \boldsymbol{\mu}_t \tag{17}$$

$$\boldsymbol{\xi}_{t+1} = \mathbf{F}(\mathbf{z}_t)\boldsymbol{\xi}_t + \mathbf{v}_{t+1} \tag{18}$$

that is, the matrices $\mathbf{H}$ and $\mathbf{F}$, which are constants in equations (1) and (2), become functions of $\mathbf{z}_t$, which includes lagged $\mathbf{y}_t$ and exogenous variables $\mathbf{x}_t$. This treatment allows state variables $\boldsymbol{\xi}_t$ to be time-varying coefficients. Equation (17) is a usual regressional model except that its coefficients are time varying. Equation (18) is the unobserved process governing the evolution of the coefficients.

A simplest time-varying coefficient model is to let $\boldsymbol{\xi}_t$ follow a random walk:

$$\boldsymbol{\xi}_{t+1} = \boldsymbol{\xi}_t + \mathbf{v}_{t+1} \tag{19}$$

Other specifications include autoregressive processes so that the coefficients are mean-reverting. In all these case, $\mathbf{F}(\mathbf{z}_t)$ is just a constant.

7.4   State space models of commonly used time series processes

7.4.1   AR(p) process

$$
\begin{aligned}
\mathbf{y}_t &= c + \mathbf{v}_t \\
\mathbf{v}_t &= \rho_1 \mathbf{v}_{t-1} + \cdots + \rho_p \mathbf{v}_{t-p} + \boldsymbol{\varepsilon}_t, \quad \boldsymbol{\varepsilon}_t \sim N(0, \sigma_\varepsilon^2)
\end{aligned}
\tag{20}
$$

There are a few expressions, one of them is as follows.

The observation equation is:

$$\mathbf{y}_t = c + [1 \quad 0 \quad \cdots \quad 0]
\begin{bmatrix}
\mathbf{v}_t \\
\mathbf{v}_{t-1} \\
\vdots \\
\mathbf{v}_{t-p}
\end{bmatrix}
\tag{21}$$

The state equation is:

$$
\begin{bmatrix}
\mathbf{v}_{t+1} \\
\mathbf{v}_t \\
\vdots \\
\mathbf{v}_{t-p+1}
\end{bmatrix}
=
\begin{bmatrix}
\rho_1 & \rho_2 & \cdots & & \rho_p \\
1 & 0 & \cdots & & 0 \\
0 & 1 & 0 & \cdots & 0 \\
\vdots & & & & \\
0 & \cdots & & 1 & 0
\end{bmatrix}
\begin{bmatrix}
\mathbf{v}_t \\
\mathbf{v}_{t-1} \\
\vdots \\
\mathbf{v}_{t-p}
\end{bmatrix}
\tag{22}
$$

Therefore, the construction elements of the model are:

$$\mathbf{y}_t = y_t, \qquad \boldsymbol{\xi}_t' = [v_t \quad v_{t-1} \quad \cdots \quad v_{t-p}], \qquad \mathbf{x}_t = c$$

$$\mathbf{H} = [1 \quad 0 \quad \cdots \quad 0], \qquad \mathbf{F} = \begin{bmatrix} \rho_1 & \rho_2 & \cdots & & \rho_p \\ 1 & 0 & \cdots & & 0 \\ 0 & 1 & 0 & \cdots & 0 \\ \vdots & & & & \\ 0 & \cdots & & 1 & 0 \end{bmatrix},$$

$$\mathbf{A} = 1, \qquad \mathbf{B} = 0,$$

$$\boldsymbol{\mu}_t = 0, \qquad \mathbf{v}_t' = [\varepsilon_t \quad 0 \quad \cdots \quad 0]$$

$$\mathbf{Q} = \begin{bmatrix} \sigma_\varepsilon^2 & 0 & \cdots & 0 \\ 0 & 0 & \cdots & 0 \\ \vdots & & & \\ 0 & \cdots & & 0 \end{bmatrix}, \qquad \mathbf{R} = 0$$

7.4.2   ARMA(p, q) process

$$y_t = c + \rho_1 y_{t-1} + \cdots + \rho_p y_{t-p} + \varepsilon_t + \theta_1 \varepsilon_{t-1} + \cdots + \theta_{t-q} \varepsilon_{t-q}, \quad \varepsilon_t \sim N(0, \sigma_\varepsilon^2)$$

$$(23)$$

The observation equation is:

$$y_t = [1 \quad \theta_1 \quad \cdots \quad \theta_q] \begin{bmatrix} \varepsilon_t \\ \varepsilon_{t-1} \\ \vdots \\ \varepsilon_{t-q} \end{bmatrix} + [1 \quad \rho_1 \quad \cdots \quad \rho_p] \begin{bmatrix} c \\ y_{t-1} \\ \vdots \\ y_{t-p} \end{bmatrix} \qquad (24)$$

The state equation is:

$$\begin{bmatrix} \varepsilon_{t+1} \\ \varepsilon_t \\ \vdots \\ \varepsilon_{t-q+1} \end{bmatrix} = \begin{bmatrix} 0 & 0 & \cdots & & 0 \\ 1 & 0 & \cdots & & 0 \\ 0 & 1 & 0 & \cdots & 0 \\ \vdots & & & & \\ 0 & \cdots & & 1 & 0 \end{bmatrix} \begin{bmatrix} \varepsilon_t \\ \varepsilon_{t-1} \\ \vdots \\ \varepsilon_{t-q} \end{bmatrix} + \begin{bmatrix} \varepsilon_{t+1} \\ 0 \\ \vdots \\ 0 \end{bmatrix} \qquad (25)$$

The construction elements of the model are:

$$\mathbf{y}_t = \mathbf{y}_t, \qquad \boldsymbol{\xi}_t' = [\varepsilon_t \quad \varepsilon_{t-1} \quad \cdots \quad \varepsilon_{t-q}], \qquad \mathbf{x}_t' = [c \quad \mathbf{y}_{t-1} \quad \cdots \quad \mathbf{y}_{t-p}]$$

$$\mathbf{H} = [1 \quad \theta_1 \quad \cdots \quad \theta_q], \qquad \mathbf{F} = \begin{bmatrix} 0 & 0 & \cdots & & 0 \\ 1 & 0 & \cdots & & 0 \\ 0 & 1 & 0 & \cdots & 0 \\ \vdots & & & & \\ 0 & \cdots & & 1 & 0 \end{bmatrix}$$

$$\mathbf{A} = [1 \quad \rho_1 \quad \cdots \quad \rho_p], \qquad \mathbf{B} = 0$$

$$\boldsymbol{\mu}_t = 0, \qquad \mathbf{v}_t' = [\varepsilon_t \quad 0 \quad \cdots \quad 0]$$

$$\mathbf{Q} = \begin{bmatrix} \sigma_\varepsilon^2 & 0 & \cdots & 0 \\ 0 & 0 & \cdots & 0 \\ \vdots & & & \\ 0 & \cdots & & 0 \end{bmatrix}, \qquad \mathbf{R} = 0$$

7.4.3 Stochastic volatility

The closest equivalent to an AR or ARMA process in the second moment is probably the stochastic volatility family of models, not ARCH or GARCH. Stochastic volatility can be appropriately represented by the unobserved state variable. Unlike the previous two cases that can be and are usually estimated using traditional time series methods, such as that of the Box–Jenkins, stochastic volatility models are tested in the state space with the Kalman filter as a superior and feasible way of execution.

Define a simple time-varying variance process as:

$$\mathbf{y}_t = \omega_t$$
$$\omega_t = \sigma_t \varepsilon_t \qquad\qquad\qquad\qquad\qquad\qquad (26)$$
$$\varepsilon_t \sim N(0, \sigma_\varepsilon^2)$$

In a stochastic volatility model, $\mathbf{h}_t = \log \sigma_t^2$, the logarithm of the variance, behaves exactly as a stochastic process in the mean, such as random walks or autoregression.

$$\mathbf{h}_t = c + \lambda \mathbf{h}_{t-1} + \boldsymbol{\zeta}_t \quad \boldsymbol{\zeta}_t \sim N(0, \sigma_\zeta^2) \qquad\qquad\qquad (27)$$

Equation (26) can be expressed as:

$$\mathbf{g}_t = \mathbf{h}_t + \kappa_t \qquad\qquad\qquad\qquad\qquad\qquad (28)$$

where $\mathbf{g}_t = \ln(\mathbf{y}_t^2)$ and $\kappa_t = \ln(\varepsilon_t^2)$.

The observation equation is:

$$\mathbf{g}_t = [1 \quad 0] \begin{bmatrix} \mathbf{h}_t \\ \mathbf{h}_{t-1} \end{bmatrix} + \kappa_t \qquad\qquad\qquad\qquad (29)$$

The state equation is:

$$\begin{bmatrix} \mathbf{h}_{t+1} \\ \mathbf{h}_t \end{bmatrix} = \begin{bmatrix} \lambda & 0 \\ 1 & 0 \end{bmatrix} \begin{bmatrix} \mathbf{h}_t \\ \mathbf{h}_{t-1} \end{bmatrix} + \begin{bmatrix} 1 \\ 0 \end{bmatrix} c + \begin{bmatrix} \zeta_{t+1} \\ 0 \end{bmatrix} \tag{30}$$

The construction elements are:

$$\mathbf{y}_t = \mathbf{g}_t, \qquad \boldsymbol{\xi}_t' = [\mathbf{h}_t \quad \mathbf{h}_{t-1}], \qquad \mathbf{x}_t = c$$

$$\mathbf{H} = \begin{bmatrix} 1 & 0 \end{bmatrix}, \qquad \mathbf{F} = \begin{bmatrix} \lambda & 0 \\ 1 & 0 \end{bmatrix} \qquad \mathbf{A} = 0, \qquad \mathbf{B} = \begin{bmatrix} 1 \\ 0 \end{bmatrix}$$

$$\boldsymbol{\mu}_t = \kappa_t, \qquad \mathbf{v}_t' = [\zeta_t \quad 0]$$

$$\mathbf{Q} = \begin{bmatrix} \sigma_\zeta^2 & 0 \\ 0 & 0 \end{bmatrix}, \qquad \mathbf{R} = \sigma_\kappa^2$$

As the model is not log normal (i.e. $\mathbf{y}_t^2$ is not log normal or $\ln(\mathbf{y}_t^2)$ is not normal), it cannot be estimated by the usual maximum likelihood method. Nevertheless, when the random variables in concern are orthogonal, maximising the likelihood function will yield exactly the same estimates of the parameters, except for the standard errors of the parameters, which can be calculated by a different formula. This procedure is referred to as the quasi maximum likelihood (QML) method, suggested by White (1982). Specifically, the QML estimation of stochastic volatility models is discussed in Harvey *et al.* (1994) and Ruiz (1994). Other estimation procedures include the Monte Carlo maximum likelihood suggested by Sandmann and Koopman (1998), where the basic stochastic volatility model is expressed as a linear state space model with log χ^2 disturbances. The likelihood function is approximated by decomposing it into a Gaussian part, estimated by the Kalman filter, and the rest is evaluated by simulation.

7.4.4   Time-varying coefficients

Specify a simple market model modified by using time-varying coefficients:

$$\mathbf{R}_t = \alpha_t + \beta_t R_{mt} + \varepsilon_t$$
$$\alpha_t = \alpha_{t-1} + \mathbf{v}_{1t} \tag{31}$$
$$\beta_t = \beta_{t-1} + \mathbf{v}_{2t}$$

where $\mathbf{R}_t$ is return on an individual security, $\mathbf{R}_{mt}$ is return on the market, and the coefficients follow a random walk.

The observation equation is:

$$\mathbf{R}_t = \begin{bmatrix} 1 & R_{mt} \end{bmatrix} \begin{bmatrix} \alpha_t \\ \beta_t \end{bmatrix} + \varepsilon_t \tag{32}$$

The state equation is:

$$\begin{bmatrix} \alpha_t \\ \beta_t \end{bmatrix} = \begin{bmatrix} \alpha_{t-1} \\ \beta_{t-1} \end{bmatrix} + \begin{bmatrix} \mathbf{v}_{1t} \\ \mathbf{v}_{2t} \end{bmatrix} \tag{33}$$

Therefore, the construction elements of the model are:

$$\mathbf{y}_t = \mathbf{R}_t, \qquad \mathbf{\xi}'_t = [\alpha_t \quad \beta_t]$$

$$\mathbf{H}(\mathbf{z}_t) = [1 \quad \mathbf{R}_{mt}], \qquad \mathbf{F}(\mathbf{z}_t) = [1 \quad 1], \qquad \mathbf{A} = 0$$

$$\mathbf{\mu}_t = \mathbf{\varepsilon}_t, \qquad \mathbf{v}'_t = [\mathbf{v}_{1t} \quad \mathbf{v}_{2t}]$$

$$\mathbf{Q} = \begin{bmatrix} \sigma^2_{\mathbf{v}_{1t}} & 0 \\ 0 & \sigma^2_{\mathbf{v}_{2t}} \end{bmatrix}, \qquad \mathbf{R} = \sigma^2_{\mathbf{\varepsilon}_t}$$

7.5   Examples and cases

Example 1

This is an example of decomposing the GDP series into trend and cycle components. The data used are US GDP from the first quarter of 1950 to the fourth quarter of 1999. Unlike Clark (1987) where the growth rate is a pure random walk, the model in this example has a stochastic growth rate that can be stationary or non-stationary depending on the value of λ in equation (36). Specifically, if λ is smaller than but close to one, the growth rate is persistent in its behaviour. The model is as follows:

$$\mathbf{Y}_t = \mathbf{T}_t + \mathbf{C}_t \tag{34}$$

$$\mathbf{T}_t = \mathbf{T}_{t-1} + \mathbf{g}_{t-1} + \mathbf{u}_t \tag{35}$$

$$\mathbf{g}_t = \mathbf{g}c + \lambda \mathbf{g}_{t-1} + \mathbf{w}_t \tag{36}$$

$$\mathbf{C}_t = \varphi_1 \mathbf{C}_{t-1} + \varphi_2 \mathbf{C}_{t-2} + \mathbf{v}_t \tag{37}$$

where $\mathbf{Y}_t$ is log GDP; $\mathbf{T}_t$ is its trend component following a random walk with a stochastic drift or growth rate which is an autoregressive process; $\mathbf{C}_t$ is the cycle component. Equation (36) collapses to the Clarke growth equation when restrictions $gc = 0$ and $\lambda = 1$ are imposed. There are other reasonable assumptions. If λ is set to be zero, then the growth rate is a stationary stochastic series around a constant mean value. The growth rate is constant over time when w_t is zero as well. So, in the empirical inquiries, there are three sets of restrictions imposed against the general form of equation (36).

Writing equations (34)–(37) in the state space form, the observation equation is:

$$\mathbf{Y}_t = [1 \quad 1 \quad 0 \quad 0] \begin{bmatrix} \mathbf{T}_t \\ \mathbf{C}_t \\ \mathbf{C}_{t-1} \\ \mathbf{g}_t \end{bmatrix} \tag{38}$$

The state equation is:

$$
\begin{bmatrix} T_{t+1} \\ C_{t+1} \\ C_t \\ g_{t+1} \end{bmatrix} = \begin{bmatrix} 1 & 0 & 0 & 1 \\ 0 & \varphi_1 & \varphi_2 & 0 \\ 0 & 1 & 0 & 0 \\ 0 & 0 & 0 & \lambda \end{bmatrix} \begin{bmatrix} T_t \\ C_t \\ C_{t-1} \\ g_t \end{bmatrix} + \begin{bmatrix} 0 \\ 0 \\ 0 \\ gc \end{bmatrix} + \begin{bmatrix} v_{t+1} \\ u_{t+1} \\ 0 \\ w_{t+1} \end{bmatrix} \tag{39}
$$

The construction elements of the model are:

$$
y_t = Y_t \qquad \xi_t' = [T_t \quad C_t \quad C_{t-1} \quad g_t], \qquad x_t' = [0 \quad 0 \quad 0 \quad gc]
$$

$$
H = [1 \quad 1 \quad 0 \quad 0], \qquad F = \begin{bmatrix} 1 & 0 & 0 & 1 \\ 0 & \varphi_1 & \varphi_2 & 0 \\ 0 & 1 & 0 & 0 \\ 0 & 0 & 0 & \lambda \end{bmatrix}, \qquad A = 0, \qquad B = 1
$$

$$
\mu_t = 0, \qquad v_t' = [u_t \quad v_t \quad 0 \quad w_t]
$$

$$
Q = \begin{bmatrix} \sigma_u^2 & 0 & 0 & 0 \\ 0 & \sigma_v^2 & 0 & 0 \\ 0 & 0 & 0 & 0 \\ 0 & 0 & 0 & \sigma_w^2 \end{bmatrix}, \qquad R = 0
$$

The estimation results are reported in Table 7.1. Graphs of the trend, cycle and growth rate are plotted in Figure 7.1(a)–(c). Inspecting the three standard deviations can give us some ideas about the behaviour of the GDP series. σ_v, the standard deviation of the cycle component, measures the contribution of cycles. There are no cyclical fluctuations when σ_v is zero ($\varphi_1 + \varphi_2$ must be zero at the same time for the cycles to be stochastic). If σ_w, the standard deviation of the growth rate, and λ are zero, the time series collapses to a constant growth rate case. When $\lambda < 1$ the time series is $I(1)$ and when $\lambda = 1$, that is a random walk growth rate is assumed, the time series is $I(2)$. The time series is a pure random walk if σ_w and σ_v are both zero while σ_u, the standard deviation of the trend, is not. Therefore, the relative importance and size of σ_u, σ_v, and σ_w, together with φ_1 and φ_2, demonstrate the behaviour of the GDP series.

It can be seen in Table 7.1 that $\varphi_1 + \varphi_2 = 0.9280$, showing a stationary cycle. The average quarterly growth rate over the period is $gc/(1 - \lambda) = 0.85$ or 3.5 per cent annually. The standard deviation of the cycle, σ_v, is nearly twice of that in the trend, σ_u; nevertheless, σ_w also contributes to the total volatility of the trend. All the estimates are significant at the 1 per cent level except for σ_w, which is also much smaller than the other two standard deviations, suggesting a stable growth rate in GDP, possibly approximated by a constant. Figure 7.1(a)–(c) depicts the components of GDP. Figure 7.1(c) shows that the growth rate can swing as much as 0.2 per cent in a quarter or 0.8 per cent in one year. The growth was declining from the 1950s until the early 1980s, similar to what Clark (1987) suggested. It is most evident from the middle of the 1960s, when the US was in deep domestic

Table 7.1 Decomposition of US GDP into trend and cycle with a
stochastic growth rate using the Kalman filter

φ_1	1.4978***	$(0.3203e^{-1})$
φ_2	−0.5698***	$(0.3356e^{-1})$
gc	$0.2255e^{-2}$***	$(0.1178e^{-4})$
λ	0.7362***	$(0.1892e^{-1})$
σ_u	$0.4125e^{-2}$***	$(0.8007e^{-3})$
σ_v	$0.7789e^{-2}$***	$(0.4679e^{-3})$
σ_w	$0.1175e^{-2}$**	$(0.5716e^{-3})$
Likelihood	822.3353	
LR: $gc = 0, \lambda = 1$	4.4006	
LR: $\lambda = 0$	0.6158	
LR: $\sigma_g = 0$	4.1664	

Notes

    Standard errors are in brackets. LR is the likelihood ratio statistic, the
critical values at the 10% level are 2.7055 for df 1, 4.6052 for df 2 and
6.2514 for df 3.
  * Significant at the 10% level.
 ** Significant at the 5% level.
*** Significant at the 1% level. Standard errors in brackets.

crisis, coupled with and highlighted by the Vietnam War. Policy changes in 1981 stimulated the economy but the prosperity was proved not long lasting, due to the lack of capital investment and capital formation induced by the new policy, which contributed to the Republicans' loss in a seemingly secured presidential election in 1992. The US economy has achieved relatively good performance, setting off at lower than the trend level, in most of the 1990s with consistently increasing and stable growth in GDP, starting from the Gulf war period and the collapse of the Soviet Union.

The likelihood ratio test does not reject any restrictions, though the random walk growth hypothesis is very close to being marginally rejected. Ranking in accordance with the likelihood function value, growth is best described as a mean-reverting stochastic process, followed by a constant plus white noise growth rate, and a constant growth rate, with a random walk growth rate being the least favourable. The results show that different views on, and explanations of, some economic behaviour can be largely right at the same time.

Example 2

This is an example from Foresi *et al.* (1997) on interest rate models that are crucial to bond pricing. Only those parts relevant to the state space model are extracted here. The bond price is usually modelled as a function of the short-term interest rate in the bond pricing literature; and the short-term interest rate, usually called the short rate, follows some kind of generalised Wiener processes. The idea of the paper is simply that the nominal bond price is determined by the riskless real

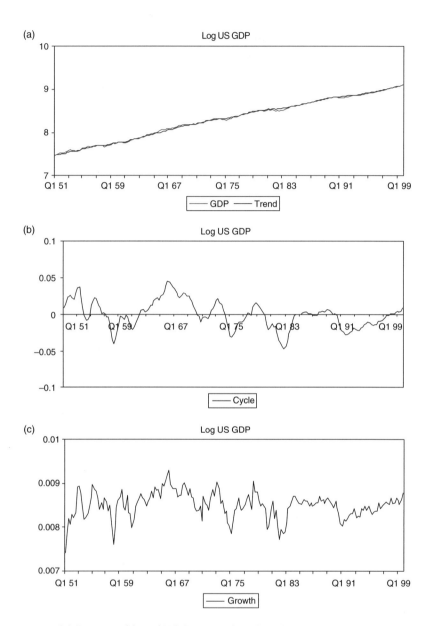

Figure 7.1 Decomposition of US GDP: trend, cycle and growth rate.

short-term interest rate and the expected instantaneous inflation rate. As the two variables are unobservable, a state space specification is proved helpful.

Basically, the paper specifies two unobserved state variables, the riskless real short-term interest rate, r_t, and the expected instantaneous inflation rate, π_t, as a vector of bivariate generalised Wiener processes (t subscript suppressed):

$$dr = (a_1 + b_{11}r + b_{12}\pi) + \sigma_r d\mathbf{z}_r$$
$$d\pi = (a_2 + b_{21}r + b_{22}\pi) + \sigma_\pi d\mathbf{z}_\pi$$

(40)

Then the continuously compounded nominal yield on zero-coupon bonds, at time t and having τ periods to maturity, $\mathbf{y}_{n,t,\tau}$, and inflation forecast at time t for $t + \tau$, $\mathbf{y}_{i,t,\tau}$, are treated as functions of above state variables (t subscript suppressed):

$$\mathbf{y}_{n,\tau} = \mathbf{j}_{n,\tau} + \alpha_{n,\tau,11}r + \alpha_{n,\tau,12}\pi + \varepsilon_n$$
$$\mathbf{y}_{i,\tau} = \mathbf{j}_{i,\tau} + \alpha_{i,\tau,21}r + \alpha_{i,\tau,22}\pi + \varepsilon_i$$

(41)

where $\mathbf{j}_{n,\tau}$ and $\mathbf{j}_{i,\tau}$ are functions of τ and independent of the state variables, which are therefore not analysed here.

The model was estimated with the steady state instantaneous real interest rate being set to 2 and 2.5 per cent, respectively. The paper only reports the estimates of the state equations' results as these estimates reveal the dynamics of the real interest rate and inflation processes. It illustrates the observation equations' results by plotting the term structure for both nominal bonds and indexed bonds. The relevant results are provided in Table 7.2.

Table 7.2 US real interest rate and expected inflation processes

	Unrestricted		Restricted $b_{11} = b_{21} = 0$	
	$r^{ss} = 2.0\%$	$r^{ss} = 2.5\%$	$r^{ss} = 2.0\%$	$r^{ss} = 2.5\%$
b_{11}	0.2938***	0.2881***	−0.0344***	−0.0344***
	(0.0820)	(0.0822)	(0.0015)	(0.0015)
b_{12}	−0.4193***	−0.4273***	0	0
	(0.0971)	(0.1000)		
b_{21}	0.8240***	0.8080***	0	0
	(0.1106)	(0.1099)		
b_{22}	−1.0930***	−1.0875***	−0.7732***	−0.7733***
	(0.0828)	(0.0831)	(0.0083)	(0.0083)
σ_r	0.0100***	0.0102***	0.0151***	0.0151***
	(0.0006)	(0.0006)	(0.0005)	(0.0005)
σ_π	0.0169***	0.0168***	0.0229***	0.0229***
	(0.0007)	(0.0007)	(0.0008)	(0.0008)
$\rho_{r\pi}$	0.8235***	0.8213***	−0.1260***	−0.1263***
	(0.2414)	(0.2439)	(0.0464)	(0.0464)
Half-life (years)				
r	6.54	6.50	20.17	20.17
π	1.07	1.06	0.90	0.90
Log likelihood	44.5038	44.4865	44.1516	44.1505

Notes
* Significant at the 10% level.
** Significant at the 5% level.
*** Significant at the 1% level. Standard errors in brackets.

With the restricted model, b_{11} is positive but b_{12} is negative and the absolute value of b_{12} is larger, so mean reversion in the interest rate appears to be caused by the effect of the expected instantaneous inflation rate. Similarly, in the inflation equation, the parameter for the interest rate b_{21} is positive, the parameter for the inflation variable b_{22} is negative, and the absolute value of b_{22} is larger. These results suggest that the riskless real short-term interest rate is likely to push itself and the expected instantaneous inflation rate away from their steady state levels, and the expected instantaneous inflation rate tends to pull both variables back to their respective steady state levels. Notice that the interest rate has a longer half-life of 6.5 years, to compare with a half-life of 1.1 years for expected inflation. This reinforces the claim that there is stronger mean-reverting tendency in expected inflation than in the interest rate. When b_{12} and b_{21} are set to zero as in the restricted model, any mean reversion in a variable must come from itself. That is, b_{11} and b_{22} must be negative. The estimates in the table are negative as expected; and the size of b_{22} is much larger, reflecting that there is far stronger mean-reverting tendency in expected inflation. Any joint movement in the two variables is now through the correlation between dz_π and dz_r, as the inter-temporal links have been cut off. In the restricted model, the instantaneous correlation between the interest rate variable and the expected inflation variable is around -0.13, a number which appears to be more reasonable that its counterpart in the unrestricted model, which is 0.82.

The authors claim that the Kalman filter method enables them to identify the separate influences of real rates of return and inflation expectations. Based on the Kalman filter parameter estimates, they could achieve improvements in constructing yield curves and calculating investors' required premia for risk from changes in real interest rates and inflation. There is one point subject to further scrutiny: the paper says that the restricted model, where b_{12} and b_{21} are set to 0, or the interest rate process and the inflation process have no inter-temporal causal relationship and any link between them is their instantaneous correlation, performs better and the yield curves constructed from the restricted model appear to be more realistic. Then the query is: can this be justified by the economics of interest rate-inflation dynamics or is this technically an estimation problem? The half-life of 20 years for the interest rate in the restricted model also seems to be rather long. The reason could be simple: changes in the real interest rate are responses to changes in the economic environment, realised, anticipated and/or unanticipated. Without other economic variables playing a role, the evolution path of the interest rate is unlikely to change or be altered, resulting in a longer half-life.

7.6   Empirical literature

There are growing applications of the Kalman filter in state space models, but the number is small relative to other popular models such as cointegration and GARCH. One of the reasons is that state space models are not easy to implement. On the one hand, most econometric software packages either do not have Kalman filter procedures or have procedures which are too basic to be of practical use. On the other hand, estimates of parameters are rather sensitive to the choice of initial values and other settings of the filter.

Recent use of the Kalman filter can be found in studies of financial markets and the economy, at micro and macro levels. In bond pricing and interest rate models, Babbs and Nowman (1998) estimate a two-factor term structure model which allows for measurement errors by using the Kalman filter. Duan and Simonato (1999) and the example above by Foresi *et al.* (1997) are similar cases. All these studies claim that the state space model provides a good fit to the yield curves concerned. Jegadeesh and Pennacchi (1996) model the target level of the interest rate, to which the short-term interest is to revert in the state space, in a two-factor equilibrium model of the term structure. They compare the term structure of spot LIBOR and Eurodollar futures volatility to that predicted by their two-factor model and find significant improvements over the one-factor model that does not include the target level of the interest rate.

On stock market behaviour, Gallagher *et al.* (1997) decompose the stock indices of 16 countries into transitory (cycles), permanent (trends) and seasonal components. They find evidence of mean-reversion in stock prices and conclude that stock prices are not pure random walks, though the transitory component is small and does not explain more than 5 per cent of stock price variations for 12 of the 16 countries. Jochum (1999) hypothesises that the risk premium on the Swiss stock market consist of two components: the amount of volatility and the unit price of risk. The unit price of risk is time varying and estimated by the Kalman filter, so investors' behaviour can be examined in different phases of market movement. McKenzie *et al.* (2000) estimate a time-varying beta model for the Australian market using the Kalman filter. The study is a typical example of the time-varying coefficient model. Using the cumulative sum of squares (CUSUMSQ) test, they find beta parameter instability for all 24 industries inspected when the world market index is the relevant benchmark of the model, as the recursively estimated residuals exceeded the 5 per cent critical boundary. They find beta instability for 20 out of the 24 industry betas when the domestic market index serves as the benchmark. They conclude that time-varying betas estimated relative to the domestic index, though not universally superior, are preferred in certain circumstances. Whether the slightly inferior performance of the world index model is caused by more instability in betas is yet to be examined, though the graphs in the paper appear to suggest so.

The dividend payment pattern is one of the areas where state space models are of empirical relevance. The information content of dividends is debatably important in practice and in research, whereas it can only be inferred. In a traditional way of interpreting dividends as a long-run performance signal arising from information asymmetry, Daniels *et al.* (1997) investigate whether and how dividends are related to earnings by decomposing earnings into permanent and transitory components using the Kalman filter. They examine the dividends and earnings of 30 firms and claim that there is a more robust relationship between dividends and permanent earnings, compared with that between dividends and current earnings. Marseguerra

(1997) models insider information regarding the firm as an unobserved state variable that can be inferred through dividends and earnings announcements, and finds that information contained in dividend announcements varies and is a supplement to the information set already available to the market.

Other various applications include Moosa (1999) who extracts the cyclical components of unemployment and output; Serletis and King (1987) on trends and convergence of EU stock markets using a time-varying parameter model; and Daniels and Tirtiroglu (1998) on decomposition of total factor productivity of US commercial banking into stochastic trend and cycle components.

Questions and problems

1 What is the state variable, unobserved component in a state space model?
2 Discuss the advantages of the state space model and the difficulties in the empirical implementation of the model.
3 Describe the three steps of the Kalman filter algorithm in estimating a state space model.
4 Collect data from various sources, and estimate the following time series using the conventional ARIMA and in the state space using the Kalman filter (using RATS, GAUSS or other packages):

   a GDP of selected countries;
   b Total return series of Tesco, Sainsbury's and ICI.

   Compare your results from the two approaches.
5 The implementation of the Kalman filter is always complicated and the results may be sensitive to even slightly different settings. To practise, collect data from various sources and repeat the same procedure of Example 1 for GDP of a few selected countries.

References

Babbs, S. H. and Nowman, K. B. (1998), Econometric analysis of a continuous time multi-factor generalized Vasicek term structure model: International evidence, *Asia-Pacific Financial Markets*, 5(2), 59–183.

Clark, P. K. (1987), The cyclical component of the U.S. economic activity, *Quarterly Journal of Economics*, 102(4), 797–814.

Daniels, K., Shin, T. S. and Lee, C. F. (1997), The information content of dividend hypothesis: A permanent income approach, *International Review of Economics & Finance*, 6(1), 77–86.

Daniels, K. N. and Tirtiroglu, D. (1998), Total factor productivity growth in U.S. commercial banking for 1935–1991: A latent variable approach using the Kalman filter, *Journal of Financial Services Research*, 13(2), 119–135.

Duan, J. C. and Simonato, J. G. (1999), Estimating and testing exponential-affine term structure models by Kalman Filter, *Review of Quantitative Finance & Accounting*, 13(2), 111–135.

Foresi, S., Penati, A. and Pennacchi, G. (1997), Estimating the cost of U.S. indexed bonds, *Federal Reserve Bank of Cleveland Working Paper* 9701.

Gallagher, L. A., Sarno, L. and Taylor, M. P. (1997), Estimating the mean-reverting component in stock prices: A cross-country comparison, *Scottish Journal of Political Economy*, 44(5), 566–582.

Hamilton, J. D. (1994), *Time Series Analysis*, Princeton University Press, Princeton, New Jersey.

Harvey, A. C. (1989), *Forecasting, Structural Time Series Models and the Kalman Filter*, Cambridge University Press, Cambridge, England.

Harvey, A. C., Ruiz, E. and Sheppard, N. (1994), Multivariate stochastic variance models, *Review of Economic Studies*, 61(2), 247–264.

Jegadeesh, N. and Pennacchi, G. G. (1996), The behavior of interest rates implied by the term structure of eurodollar futures, *Journal of Money, Credit & Banking*, 28(3), 426–446.

Jochum, C. (1999), Volatility spillovers and the price of risk: Evidence from the Swiss stock market, *Empirical Economics*, 24(2), 303–322.

Kalman, R. E. (1960), A new approach to linear filtering and prediction problems, *Transactions of ASME Series D, Journal of Basic Engineering*, 82, 35–45.

Kalman, R. E. (1963), New methods of Wiener filtering theory, in Bogdanoff, J.L. and Kozin, F. (eds) *Proceedings of the first Symposium on Engineering applications of Random Function Theory and Probability*, Wiley, New York, pp. 270–388.

Kalman, R. E. (1978), A retrospective after twenty years: From the pure to the applied, *Chapman Conference on Applications of the Kalman filter to Hydrology, Hydraulics and Water Resources*, American Geophysical Union, Pittsburgh.

Kalman, R. E. and Bucy, R. S. (1961), New results in linear filtering and prediction problems, *Transactions of ASME Series D, Journal of Basic Engineering*, 83, 95–108.

McKenzie, M. D., Brooks, R. D. and Faff, R. W. (2000), The use of domestic and world market indexes in the estimation of time-varying betas, *Journal of Multinational Financial Management*, 10(1), 91–106.

Marseguerra, G. (1997), The information content of dividends: An application of the Kalman filter, *Rivista Internazionale di Scienze Economiche e Commerciali*, 44(4), 725–751.

Moosa, I. A. (1999), Cyclical output, cyclical unemployment, and Okun's coefficient: a structural time series approach, *International Review of Economics and Finance*, 8, 293–304.

Ruiz, E. (1994), Quasi-maximum likelihood estimation of stochastic volatility models, *Journal of Econometrics*, 63(1), 289–306.

Sandmann, G. and Koopman, S. J. (1998), Estimation of stochastic volatility models via Monte Carlo maximum likelihood, *Journal of Econometrics*, 87(2), 271–301.

Serletis, A. and King, M. (1997), Common stochastic trends and convergence of European Union stock markets, *The Manchester School of Economic & Social Studies*, 65(1), 44–57.

White, H. (1982), Maximum likelihood estimation of misspecified models, *Econometrica*, 50, 1–25.

8 Frequency domain analysis of time series

Spectral analysis, or studies in the frequency domain, is one of the unconventional subjects in time series econometrics. The frequency domain method has existed for a long time and has been extensively used in electronic engineering such as signal processing, communications and automatic control. Although the application of the frequency domain method in econometrics may have as long a history as that in engineering, it has been sporadic and regarded as unorthodox and often plays a supplementary role.

Analysis in the frequency domain does not bring in new or additional information, it is simply an alternative method with which information is observed, processed and abstracted. This is sometimes helpful. Depending on the characteristics of the issues, analysis in one domain may be more powerful than in the other. For example, cycles are better and more explicitly observed and represented in the frequency domain; while correlations in the time domain and cross spectra in the frequency domain deal with the relationship between two time series from different perspectives and, in the meantime, have defined links.

This chapter first introduces the Fourier transform (FT), which is one of the most commonly used transformations of time series and the spectrum, the frequency domain expression of time series. In a similar spirit of covariance analysis, cross spectra, coherence and phases in multivariate time series are discussed next. In the last two sections of the chapter, frequency domain representations of commonly used time series processes are presented and frequency domain persistence measures are developed.

8.1 The Fourier transform and spectra

A continuous non-periodic time series has a continuous Fourier spectrum. For a periodic time series, its FT is discrete Fourier series. We only introduce the FT for non-periodic time series, as periodicity is rare in economic and financial time series. We do so to avoid confusion also. Then we quickly proceed to the discrete Fourier transform (DFT), which is most common in finance and economics. Let $f(t)$ $(-\infty < t < \infty)$ be a continuous non-periodic time series, then its FT is defined as:

$$F(\omega) = \int_{t=-\infty}^{\infty} f(t) \, e^{-j\omega t} \, dt \tag{1}$$

$F(\omega)$ is also called the spectral density function of $f(t)$. There exists an inverse Fourier transform (IFT), which is continuous, so that:

$$f(t) = \frac{1}{2\pi} \int_{-\pi}^{\pi} F(\omega) \, e^{j\omega t} \, d\omega \tag{2}$$

One of the most important and relevant properties of the FT is time delay or lags. Let $F(\omega)$ be the FT of $f(t)$, then the FT of $f(t - t_0)$ is $e^{-j\omega t_0} F(\omega)$. This can be proved briefly as follows:

$$\int_{t=-\infty}^{\infty} f(t - t_0) \, e^{-j\omega t} \, dt = \int_{t=-\infty}^{\infty} f(t) \, e^{-j\omega(t+t_0)} \, dt$$

$$= e^{-j\omega t_0} \int_{t=-\infty}^{\infty} f(t) \, e^{-j\omega t} \, dt = e^{-j\omega t_0} F(\omega)$$

In practice, for a discrete time series with N observations, such as in economics and finance, the FT would usually be the DFT. The pair of DFT and inverse discrete Fourier transform (IDFT) is:

$$F(k) = \sum_{n=-(N-1)}^{N-1} f(n) \, e^{-jn(2\pi k/N)} \tag{1'}$$

and

$$f(n) = \frac{1}{N} \sum_{k=-(N-1)}^{N-1} F(k) \, e^{jk(2\pi n/N)} \tag{2'}$$

with $\Delta\omega = 2\pi/N$, $F(k) = F(k\Delta\omega) = F(2\pi k/N)$. That is, time domain series can be expressed with different frequency components. Equation (1) or (1') is the energy spectrum. In the case of stochastic processes, the FT is concerned with the power spectrum or the power spectral density function (which can be simply called spectral density function when there is no confusion).[1] The spectral density function of a discrete random process $\Delta_1 X_t = X_t - X_{t-1}$ $(t = 1, \ldots, N)$ is:

$$h(k) = \sum_{\tau=-(N-1)}^{N-1} R(\tau) \, e^{-j\tau(2\pi k/N)} \tag{3}$$

where $R(\tau)$ is the autocovariance function of $\Delta_1 X_t$, that is, $R(\tau) = E\{(\Delta_1 X_t - \mu)(\Delta_1 X_{t-\tau} - \mu)\}$ and $\mu = E\{\Delta_1 X_t\}$. The IFT of equation (3) is:

$$R(\tau) = \frac{1}{N} \sum_{k=-(N-1)}^{N-1} h(k) \, e^{jk(2\pi \tau/N)} \tag{4}$$

Setting $\tau = 0$ in equation (4), we have:

$$R(0) = E\{(\Delta_1 X_t)^2\} = \frac{1}{N} \sum_{k=-(N-1)}^{N-1} h(k)\, e^{jk(2\pi\tau/N)} \tag{5}$$

It is the mean squared value of the process and has the meaning of power of the process, so equation (3) is called the power spectrum. Equation (1) or (1′), in contrast, is the energy spectrum as it has the features of electrical current or voltage.

$R(\tau)$ usually takes real values and is an even function, that is, $R(-\tau) = R(\tau)$. Accordingly, the spectral density function can be written as:

$$h(k) = \sigma_X^2 + 2 \sum_{\tau=1}^{N-1} R(\tau) \cos\left(\frac{2\pi\tau k}{N}\right) \tag{6}$$

Empirically, $h(k)$ has to be truncated and estimated. The simplest way of truncation is to let $R(\tau)$ pass through a rectangular window or 'truncated periodogram' window, that is:

$$\hat{h}(k) = \sum_{\tau=-M}^{M} R(\tau) \cos\left(\frac{2\pi\tau k}{N}\right) \tag{7}$$

So,

$$E\{\hat{h}(k)\} = \sum_{\tau=-M}^{M} \left(1 - \frac{|\tau|}{N}\right) R(\tau) \cos\left(\frac{2\pi\tau k}{N}\right) \rightarrow h(k), \quad \text{as } M \rightarrow \infty$$

$$\tag{8}$$

In general, the truncated spectral density function takes the form:

$$\hat{h}(k) = \sum_{\tau=-M}^{M} \lambda(\tau) R(\tau) \cos\left(\frac{2\pi\tau k}{N}\right) \tag{9}$$

where $\lambda(\tau)$ is the window function. The variance of $\hat{h}(k)$ is:

$$\text{Var}[\hat{h}(k)] \sim (1 + \delta_{k,0}) h^2(k) \frac{1}{N} \left\{ \sum_{\tau=-(N-1)}^{N-1} \lambda_N^2(\tau) \right\}$$

$$= (1 + \delta_{k,0}) h^2(k) \frac{1}{N} \sum_{\theta=(N-1)}^{N-1} W_N^2(\theta) \tag{10}$$

where

$$W_N(\theta) = \sum_{\theta=-(N-1)}^{N-1} \lambda_N^2(\tau)\, e^{-j\theta(2\pi k/N)} \tag{11}$$

is the spectral expression of the window, and $\delta_{k,0}$ is an impulse function taking the value of unity at $k = 0$.

A rectangular window, though simple, does not perform well due to its sudden change at the cut-off points which may produce some peculiar frequency components. The Bartlett window is usually used. It is defined as:

$$
\lambda(\tau) = \begin{cases} 1 - \dfrac{|\tau|}{M}, & |\tau| \le M \\ 0, & |\tau| > M \end{cases} \tag{12}
$$

With Bartlett's window, the variance of $\hat{h}(k)$ is:

$$
\mathrm{Var}[\hat{h}(k)] \sim \frac{2M}{3N} h^2(k), \quad \text{for } k \ne 0 \tag{13}
$$

and

$$
\mathrm{Var}[\hat{h}(k)] \sim \frac{4M}{3N} h^2(k), \quad \text{for } k = 0 \tag{14}
$$

If k takes the value of zero in equation (8), the truncated spectral density function becomes:

$$
E\{\hat{h}(0)\} = \sum_{\tau=-M}^{M} \left(1 - \frac{|\tau|}{N}\right) R(\tau)
$$

$$
= R(0) + 2 \sum_{\tau=1}^{M} \left(1 - \frac{|\tau|}{N}\right) R(\tau) \tag{15}
$$

Equation (15) is, in fact, the M period variance of $\Delta_M X_t = X_t - X_{t-M}$. Dividing equation (15) by the variance of $\Delta_1 X_t$, $\sigma^2_{\Delta_1 X}$, yields Cochrane's (1988) version of persistence. Therefore, the Cochrane measure is a specific case of equation (8), and assesses the long-run behaviour of time series at the zero frequency only. It appears that such measures as represented by Campbell and Mankiw (1987a,b), Cochrane (1988) and Pesaran *et al.* (1993) are the necessary condition(s) for a random walk, not sufficient conditions, as other points on the spectrum are not evaluated against the random walk hypothesis and it is possible that they deviate from unity jointly significantly. There are no significance test statistics associated with them either, though $\mathrm{Var}[\hat{h}(0)]$ is available to provide a guideline for the accuracy of the measures, which is decided by the ratio of the window size to the number of observations, M/N, only. In other words, the window size should be small relative to the number of observations to achieve reliability in the measure. To investigate persistence and associated time series properties properly, the whole spectrum of the time series should be examined, instead of just at the zero frequency point. These will be proposed and conducted in the following section.

8.2   Multivariate spectra, phases and coherence

If we replace $R(\tau)$, the autocovariance function of $\Delta_1 X_t$, by the covariance between two time series, that is, $\text{Cov}_{X,Y}(\tau) = E\{(\Delta_1 X_t - \mu_X)(\Delta_1 Y_{t-\tau} - \mu_Y)\}$, $\mu_X = E\{\Delta_1 X_t\}$ and $\mu_Y = E\{\Delta_1 Y_t\}$, then we get the cross spectrum of the two time series in the form of:

$$h_{X,Y}(k) = \sum_{\tau=-(N-1)}^{N-1} \text{Cov}_{X,Y}(\tau)\, e^{-j\tau(2\pi k/N)} \tag{16}$$

$\text{Cov}(\tau)$ is in general not an even function, so equation (16) cannot take the form of equation (6), and $h_{X,Y}(k)$ is in general a complex number:

$$h_{X,Y}(k) = c(k)\cos\left(\frac{2\pi k}{N}\tau\right) + jq(k)\sin\left(\frac{2\pi k}{N}\tau\right) \tag{17}$$

Unlike the univariate FT where the imaginary part is zero, the cross spectrum has both magnitude and phase as follows:

$$m(k) = \sqrt{c^2(k) + q^2(k)} \tag{18}$$

and

$$p(k) = \tan^{-1}\frac{q(k)}{c(k)} \tag{19}$$

Equations (18) and (19) are called the magnitude spectrum and the phase spectrum respectively. It can be seen, from the above analysis, that if $\text{Cov}_{X,Y}(\tau)$ is an even function, then the phase spectrum is zero, that is, there is no overall lead of series X_t over series Y_t, and vice versa. With equations (18) and (19), the cross spectrum can also be expressed as:

$$h_{X,Y}(k) = m(k)\, e^{jp(k)} \tag{20}$$

so that both magnitude and phase are shown explicitly.

Another measure of the closeness of two time series is coherence, defined, in a very similar way to the correlation coefficient, as:

$$\text{Co}\, h_{X,Y}(k) = \frac{h_{X,Y}(k)}{h_{X,X}^{1/2}(k) h_{Y,Y}^{1/2}(k)} \tag{21}$$

If we make comparison of the measures in the frequency domain with those in the time domain, then the cross spectrum of equation (17) is corresponding to covariance in the time domain, which is not standardised; the coherence as with equation (21) is corresponding to correlation in the time domain, which are standardised by the square roots of the two time series' spectra and the two time series' standard deviations respectively; and the phase of equation (19) addresses leads and lags. As with the non-standardised cross spectrum, the closeness of two time series is not straightforwardly observed, the measure of coherence, together with the phase measure, is widely adopted in economic and financial research.

To generalise the above bivariate analysis to the multivariate case, let:

$$\Sigma = \begin{bmatrix} \text{Cov}_{11}(\tau) & \cdots & \text{Cov}_{1m}(\tau) \\ \vdots & & \\ \text{Cov}_{m1}(\tau) & \cdots & \text{Cov}_{mm}(\tau) \end{bmatrix} \tag{22}$$

be the covariance matrix of an m-variable system of time series. Then the cross spectra of the time series can also be expressed in a matrix:

$$\mathbf{H} = \begin{bmatrix} h_{11}(k) & \cdots & h_{1m}(k) \\ \vdots & & \\ h_{m1}(k) & \cdots & h_{mm}(k) \end{bmatrix} \tag{23}$$

where $h_{il}(k)$ $(i, l = 1, \ldots, m)$ takes the form of equation (16).

8.3 Frequency domain representations of commonly used time series processes

8.3.1 AR (p) process

$$Y_t = \rho_1 Y_{t-1} + \cdots + \rho_p Y_{t-p} + \varepsilon_t, \quad \varepsilon_t \sim N(0, \sigma_\varepsilon^2) \tag{24}$$

Rearranging equation (24) as:

$$Y_t - \rho_1 Y_{t-1} - \cdots - \rho_p Y_{t-p} = \varepsilon_t \tag{24'}$$

Taking the FT and applying the property of time-delaying yield:

$$F_Y(k) \left[1 - \rho_1 e^{-j(2\pi k/N)} - \cdots - \rho_p e^{-jp(2\pi k/N)} \right] = F_\varepsilon(k) \tag{25}$$

so that the power spectrum or simply the spectrum of an AR process is:

$$\begin{aligned} h_Y(k) = \sigma_\varepsilon^2 / \Big\{ \big[1 - \rho_1 e^{-j(2\pi k/N)} - \cdots - \rho_p e^{-jp(2\pi k/N)} \big] \\ \times \big[1 - \rho_1 e^{j(2\pi k/N)} - \cdots - \rho_p e^{jp(2\pi k/N)} \big] \Big\} \end{aligned} \tag{26}$$

8.3.2 MA (q) process

$$Y_t = \varepsilon_t + \theta_1\varepsilon_{t-1} + \cdots + \theta_q\varepsilon_{t-q}, \quad \varepsilon_t \sim N(0, \sigma_\varepsilon^2) \tag{27}$$

The FT of this process is:

$$F_Y(k) = F_\varepsilon(k)\big[1 + \theta_1 e^{-j(2\pi k/N)} + \cdots + \theta_q e^{-jq(2\pi k/N)}\big] \tag{28}$$

So the spectrum is:

$$h_Y(k) = \sigma_\varepsilon^2\big[1 + \theta_1 e^{-j(2\pi k/N)} + \cdots + \theta_q e^{-jq(2\pi k/N)}\big]$$
$$\times \big[1 + \theta_1 e^{j(2\pi k/N)} + \cdots + \theta_q e^{jq(2\pi k/N)}\big] \tag{29}$$

8.3.3 VAR (p) process

$$\mathbf{Y}_t = \mathbf{A}_1\mathbf{Y}_{t-1} + \cdots + \mathbf{A}_p\mathbf{Y}_{t-p} + \boldsymbol{\varepsilon}_t, \quad \boldsymbol{\varepsilon}_t \sim N(0, \boldsymbol{\Sigma}) \tag{30}$$

where $\mathbf{Y}_t$ is an $m \times 1$ vector of variables, and $\mathbf{A}_i$, $i = 1, \ldots, p$ are $m \times m$ matrices of coefficients. Taking the FT yields:

$$\mathbf{F}_Y(\mathbf{k})\big[1 - \mathbf{A}_1 e^{-j(2\pi k/N)} - \cdots - \mathbf{A}_p e^{-jp(2\pi k/N)}\big] = \mathbf{F}_\Sigma(\mathbf{k}) \tag{31}$$

Therefore, the spectra of the VAR process is:

$$\mathbf{h}_Y(\mathbf{k}) = \big[1 - \mathbf{A}_1 e^{-j(2\pi k/N)} - \cdots - \mathbf{A}_p e^{-jp(2\pi k/N)}\big]^{-1}$$
$$\times \boldsymbol{\Sigma}\big[1 - \mathbf{A}_1 e^{j(2\pi k/N)} - \cdots - \mathbf{A}_p e^{jp(2\pi k/N)}\big]^{-1} \tag{32}$$

8.4 Test statistics for persistence and time series properties

8.4.1 Persistence spectra

Let us consider a pure random walk process in the frequency domain now. The spectral density function of a white noise process is:

$$2, \quad 0 \le \omega \le \pi \quad \text{or} \quad 0 \le k \le N \tag{33}$$

(it is 1 when in $-\pi \le \omega \le \pi$ or $-N \le k \le N$).[2] That is, a pure random walk process has equal components at every frequency point. The integrated spectrum of a pure random walk is:

$$H(\omega) = 2\omega, \quad 0 \le \omega \le \pi \tag{34}$$

or, in the DFT case:

$$H(k) = \frac{k}{N}, \quad 0 \le k \le N \tag{34'}$$

The test statistic for the white noise process, as in Priestley (1981, 1996) who follows and modifies those of Grenander and Rosenblatt (1953, 1957), is:

$$G(\omega) = \max_{0 \le \omega \le \pi} \left| \frac{\hat{H}_+(\omega)}{2\pi \sigma_X^2} - \frac{\omega}{\pi} \right| > a \sqrt{\frac{2}{N}} \tag{35}$$

and the statistic is:

$$G(k) = \max_{0 \le k \le N} \left| \frac{\hat{H}_+(k)}{\sigma_X^2} - \frac{k}{N} \right| > a \sqrt{\frac{2}{N}} \tag{35'}$$

in the DFT case. $\sqrt{N}G(\omega)$ obeys a normal distribution asymptotically. a is decided by setting $\Delta^{[1]}(a) = 1 - \alpha$, where $\Delta^{[1]}(a)$ is the value of normal distribution function and α is the significance level for the test. $G(\omega)/2\pi$ is the difference between the areas in Figures 8.1 and 8.2. In Figure 8.1, $(\hat{H}_+(\omega)/2\pi\sigma_X^2)$ is the area from 0 to ω, so $(\hat{H}_+(\pi)/2\pi\sigma_X^2) = 1$; and in Figure 8.2, the magnitude of the white noise spectrum is always unity. This implies that $G(0) \equiv 0$ and $G(\pi) \equiv 0$, and the statistic is meaningless at points 0 and π. Therefore, tests at the zero frequency only are inadequate. Replacing ω by $2k\pi/N$ in the case of DFT and the remaining analysis is similar.

In applications, the practice, which includes Durlauf (1993), is to select several points in $G(k)$ to check whether the white noise conditions are violated. The overall judgement is, therefore, rather arbitrary and may not reflect the true and whole profile. In the following, we will develop single statistics over the whole spectrum for the examination of time series properties in the context of persistence.

8.4.2   *Test statistics and associated patterns and behaviour*

In economics and finance, however, we are more interested in behaviour such as mean-reverting and the compounding effect over the whole spectrum, which cannot be reflected by statistics at the zero frequency only or at selected individual frequencies. Therefore, we propose a measure of overall persistence across the

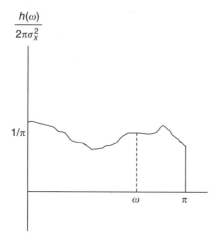

Figure 8.1 Spectrum. $\hat{H}_+(\omega)/2\pi\sigma_X^2$ is the area from origin to ω $\hat{H}_+(\pi)/2\pi\sigma_X^2 = 1$.

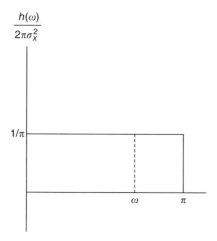

Figure 8.2 White noise spectrum. $h(\omega)/2\pi\sigma_X^2 = 1/\pi$ everywhere so $\hat{H}_+(\omega)/2\pi\sigma_X^2 = \omega/\pi$.

whole spectrum and analysis from now on is with the DFT case only. Notice that at each frequency point, $\sqrt{N}G(k)$ obeys a normal distribution $N(0, 1)$. Accordingly:

$$\Psi = \frac{1}{N}\sum_{k=1}^{N}\sqrt{N}G(k) = \overline{\sqrt{N}G(k)} \sim N\left(0, \frac{1}{N}\right) \qquad (36)$$

and the ratio:

$$\zeta = \frac{\Psi}{1/\sqrt{N}} \qquad (37)$$

has a t-distribution with $(N-1)$ degrees of freedom. With specific reference to economic and financial time series, the ζ statistic is able to reveal essential characteristics. For example, consider the following two cases in Figures 8.3 and 8.4. Figure 8.3 shows the spectrum of a time series where there are relatively more lower frequency components than higher frequency ones, whereas Figure 8.4 represents a time series whose higher frequency components dominate.

With a pure random walk $(\hat{H}_+(k)/\sigma_X^2) = k/N$ everywhere, so $G(k) = 0$ everywhere and $\zeta = 0$. If there are more lower frequency components than higher frequency components, then $G(k)$ is greater than zero; a significant and positive ζ statistic provides an overall estimate and confirms this pattern statistically. On the other hand, if there are more higher frequency components than lower frequency components, then $G(k)$ is smaller than zero; a significant and negative ζ statistic provides an overall estimate and confirms this pattern statistically.

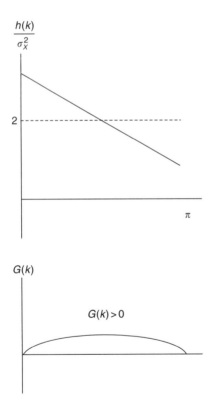

Figure 8.3 Lower frequencies dominate.

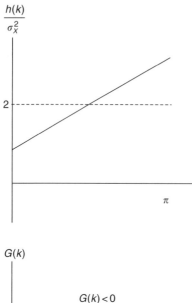

Figure 8.4 Higher frequencies dominate.

Another pattern is a non-white noise process, but unlike Figures 8.3 and 8.4, neither lower nor higher frequency components dominate overwhelmingly, as shown in Figure 8.5. In this case, $G(k)$ could be positive at some points and negative at some other points over the whole spectrum, and consequently, the ζ statistic may not be significantly different from zero. To distinguish such stochastic processes from a white noise process, we propose a second statistic, ξ. As $\sqrt{N}G(k)$ obeys a normal distribution $N(0, 1)$, then:

$$\xi = \sum_{k=1}^{N}\left[\sqrt{N}G(k)\right]^2 \sim \chi^2_{(N)} \tag{38}$$

that is, the ξ statistic has a χ^2 distribution with N degree of freedom.[3]

We end this section by summarising these typical patterns in economic and financial time series, identified by the proposed statistics, in Table 8.1.

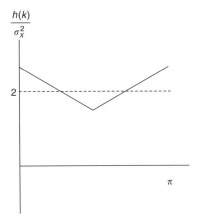

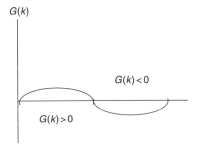

Figure 8.5 Mixed complexity.

Table 8.1 Typical patterns

Pattern	Criteria	Properties
1	$\zeta > 0$	Compounding
2	$\zeta < 0$	Mean-reverting tendency
3	$\zeta = 0$ and $\xi > 0$	Mixed complexity
4	$\zeta = 0$ and $\xi = 0$	White noise

8.5 Examples and cases

Example 1

To demonstrate the use of the frequency domain persistence statistics developed in this chapter, we scrutinise the GDP data of the two largest market economies, the US and Japan, and the exchange rate data between these two economies. The US data have been repeatedly studied and some comparison can be made. Nevertheless, we feel less comfortable if we use the US data alone to reflect the characteristics of GDP in general. Moreover, foreign exchange rate data are examined to make more general use of this approach. Both GDP data sets are quarterly series. The US data start in the first quarter of 1950 and end in the fourth quarter of 1999 and the Japanese data start in the second quarter of 1955 and end in the fourth quarter of 1999. The exchange rate series is of daily frequency running from 2 January 1976 to 31 December 1999.

The spectra of the US and Japanese GDP are exhibited in Figures 8.6(a) and 8.7(a) respectively; and the results of applying the persistence statistics are reported in Table 8.2. It is visually clear that the two GDP series do not follow random walks. The largest value of the US spectrum is 3.5516 at the zero frequency point. In general, there are more lower frequency components than the higher frequency ones, with most higher frequency points being smaller than 0.5. The Japanese spectrum at the zero frequency point is 9.7471, and it peaks with a value of 9.7969. The Japanese spectrum is largely made up of the components of very low frequencies, with little contribution being from the higher frequency end. Both US and Japanese GDP series are persistent, but the Japanese one is relatively more persistent. This intuitive analysis is confirmed by the ζ and ξ statistics in Table 8.2. Both statistics reject the null of random walks in the US and Japanese GDP decisively at the 1 per cent significance level. As the sign of ζ is positive, this statistic itself suggests that the two series are compounding, that is, they are more persistent than a pure random walk.

If we use the $G(k)$ statistic, that is, $U_T(t)$ in Durlauf (1993), to evaluate the GDP series at individual frequency points, then we are unable to get a satisfactory conclusion. It can be observed, in Figure 8.6(b), that $G(k)$ rejects the null of random walks only in a small range of $25 < k < 67$ at the 5 per cent significance level. It fails to reject the null at all other points, that is, $1 \leq k \leq 25$ or $67 \leq k \leq 129$; and it almost fails to reject the null everywhere at the 1 per cent significance level. If

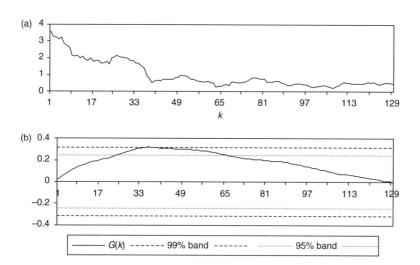

Figure 8.6 Persistence patterns: US GDP. (a) Spectrum of US GDP and (b) $G(k)$: US GDP.

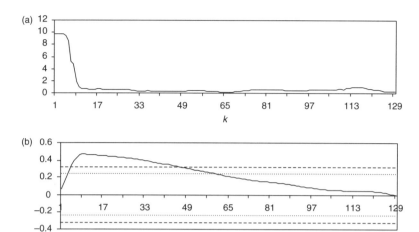

Figure 8.7 Persistence patterns: JP GDP. (a) Spectrum of JP GDP and (b) $G(k)$: JP GDP.

Table 8.2 Persistence statistics

	US GDP 50Q1–99Q4	JP GDP 55Q2–99Q4	FX rate JY v. US$
ζ	23.8786***	29.1314***	42.3804***
ξ	719.1619***	1222.2543***	2223.2376

Note
* Significant at the 10% level.
** Significant at the 5% level.
*** Significant at the 1% level.

we use the $G(k)$ statistic at seven evenly distributed points as in Durlauf (1993), then the statistic rejects the null of random walks at three points and accepts the null at the remaining points, at the 5 per cent significance level.[4] $G(k)$ or $U_T(t)$ even fails to reject the null of random walks for a time series being as far away from a random walk as Japanese GDP resolutely, though it has rejected the null at about one-thirds of all frequency points.

Finally let us examine the exchange rate series of the Japanese yen *vis-à-vis* the US dollar. It is much more like a random walk compared with the two GDP series, see Figure 8.8, where most frequency components have a value close to unity. Nevertheless, the lower frequency components make slightly more contribution than the higher frequency ones, and the value of the spectrum at the zero frequency point is 1.5732 (which is also Cochrane's (1988) V_k), greater than unity. While the ζ rejects the null of random walks, $G(k)$ or $U_T(t)$ accepts it.

Reviewing Figures 8.6–8.8 again it can be observed that, although $G(k)$ or $U_T(t)$ is not significantly different from zero according to its critical value, it is

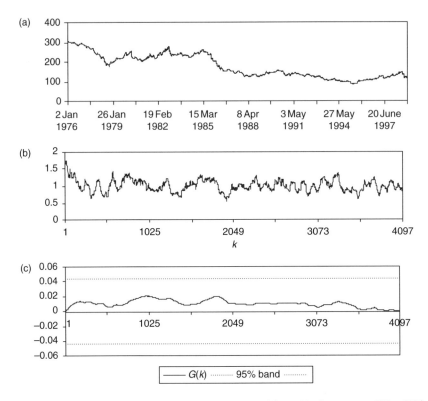

Figure 8.8 Persistence patterns: exchange rate JY v. US$. (a) Exchange rate: JY v. US$.
(b) Spectrum of Japanese yen v. US$ and (c) $G(k)$.

overwhelmingly one-sided. This fact is neglected in empirical tests – symmetrically distributed $G(k)$ or $U_T(t)$ values around the k-axis, which have an off-setting effect, are treated in the same way as one-sided $G(k)$ or $U_T(t)$ values, which either have compounding effect (when the values are positive) or mean-reverting effect (when the values are negative). The $G(k)$ or $U_T(t)$ statistic simply does not distinguish these two different cases. Moreover, as $G(k)$ or $U_T(t)$ is the integral spectrum, it does not really have a meaning at the zero frequency point, while this point is important if individual points are to be considered. The zero frequency point on the spectrum itself is also known as Cochrane's (1988) V_k, whereas the integral spectrum does not exist at the zero frequency point.[5]

Example 2

This is a case studying comovements among financial markets by means of cross spectra and phases in the frequency domain, in a paper entitled 'Pre- and post-1987 crash frequency domain analysis among Pacific Rim equity markets' by Smith (2001). The paper examines five stock markets of Australia, Hong Kong,

Japan, the US and Canada pairwise, using the individual stock market index data of Morgan Stanley International Capital Perspectives, measured in local currencies. The period surrounding the crash, that is, May 1987 through March 1988, is excluded from the sample and the author claims that this is due to the volatility during this period. Therefore, the pre-crash sample is from 18 August 1980 to 29 May 1987, and the post-crash period from 8 March 1988 to 16 December 1994.

Since the FT requires that the time series are stationary, routine unit root tests are carried out applying the KPSS procedure. The purpose is to confirm that (the logarithms of) the indices in levels are non-stationary while their first differences are stationary, which has been duly achieved.

Table 8.3 reports the frequency domain statistics of coherence for the pre- and post-crash periods and the Wilcoxon Z-statistic for testing the hypothesis that the pre- and post-crash coherences are drawn from the same population. It also provides the time domain statistics of correlation for comparison. The correlations for pairwise markets in any period are rather low, so these markets would be judged against having substantial links among them. However, the frequency domain peak coherences are much higher, ranging from 0.2415 between Japan and Hong Kong to 0.5818 between Canada and Australia in the pre-crash period. Nevertheless, the mean coherences are modest, suggesting that comovements are quite different at different frequencies – they are more coherent at some frequencies and less coherent at some other frequencies. It has been shown that coherences are low at high frequencies. In all the cases, except the pairs of US and Hong Kong, Canada and Hong Kong, and Japan and Hong Kong, the coherence falls while the frequency increases. For the pairs of US and Hong Kong, Canada and Hong Kong, and Japan and Hong Kong, the peak occurs at the frequency between 0.1 and 0.2 (5–10 days). The paper also presents phase diagrams for the pairs of the markets. Without a consistent pattern, the phase diagrams are mainly of practical interest.

The Wilcoxon Z-statistic suggests that, in every case except the pair of Australia and Hong Kong, the pre- and post-crash coherences are statistically different, or the coherences for the two periods are drawn from different populations. Moreover, both peak and mean coherences have increased in the post-crash period as against the pre-crash period in all the cases except the pair of Canada and Australia, implying increased post-crash comovements among these markets.

8.6   Empirical literature

Frequency domain analysis is most popular in business cycle research because the research object and the method match precisely. Garcia-Ferrer and Queralt's (1998) study is typical in the frequency domain – decomposing business cycles into long-, medium- and short-term cycles following Schumpeter's work. They claim that the frequency domain properties of the time series can be exploited to forecast business cycle turning points for countries exhibiting business cycle asymmetries. Cubadda (1999) examines common features in the frequency domain and

Table 8.3 Correlation and coherence

	USHK	USAU	CAJA	CAHK	CAAU	JAHK	JAAU	AUHK
Pre-correlation	0.0689	0.0661	0.0417	0.0813	0.1177	0.1394	0.1350	0.1807
Post-correlation	0.0873	0.0183	0.1715	0.1072	0.0846	0.2053	0.1676	0.1680
Pre-peak coherence	0.4010	0.5093	0.3461	0.3141	0.5818	0.2415	0.3338	0.3665
Post-peak coherence	0.4114	0.5215	0.3349	0.4313	0.4968	0.3553	0.3085	0.3511
Pre-mean coherence	0.1860	0.2482	0.1714	0.1771	0.2747	0.1502	0.1667	0.1877
Post-mean coherence	0.2250	0.2659	0.2259	0.2044	0.2371	0.2108	0.1913	0.1981
Wilcoxon Z[a]	−8.16***	−4.25***	−14.8***	−4.83***	4.40***	−17.2***	−6.94***	−1.10

Notes

*** Significant at the 1% level.

a The Wilcoxon Z-statistic tests the null that the coherences for the two periods are drawn from the same population.

the time domain. Understandably, the author has concluded that the serial correlation common feature is not informative for the degree and the lead–lag structure of their comovements at business cycle frequencies. Since the lead–lag relationship in the frequency domain is not an exact mapping of the serial correlation common feature in the time domain, the former (latter) does not contain all the information possessed by the latter (former), but does contain additional information not possessed by the latter (former). As was pointed out earlier, transformation does not generate extra new information, it simply provides another way of viewing and processing information, which may be more effective in certain aspects. Bjornland (2000) is, technically, on business cycle phases. The author finds that consumption and investment are consistently pro-cyclical with GDP in the time domain and the frequency domain. However, the business cycle properties of real wage and prices are not so clear-cut, depending on the detrending methods used. Although the number is considerably less than that in the traditional time domain, there are still a few empirical studies in the area from time to time, for example, Entorf (1993) on constructing leading indicators from non-balanced sectoral business survey data, Englund *et al.* (1992) on Swedish business cycles, Canova (1994) on business cycle turning points, and King and Rebelo (1993) on the Hodrick–Prescott filter.

As analysis in the frequency domain offers a different way of examining time series properties and patterns, it is naturally applied to issues such as unit roots, VAR and cointegrated variables. Choi and Phillips (1993) develop frequency domain tests for unit roots. Their simulation results indicate that the frequency domain tests have stable size and good power in finite samples for a variety of error-generating mechanisms. The authors conclude that the frequency domain tests have some good performance characteristics in relation to time domain procedures, although they are also susceptible to size distortion when there is negative serial correlation in the errors. Olekalns (1994) also considers frequency domain analysis as an alternative to the Dickey–Fuller test. With regard to dynamic models, error correction in continuous time is considered by Phillips (1991) in the frequency domain. Stiassny (1996) proposes a frequency domain decomposition technique for structural VAR models and argues, with an example, the benefit of adopting this technique in providing another dimension of the relationships among variables. Examining univariate impulse responses in the frequency domain, Wright (1999) estimates univariate impulse response coefficients by smoothing the periodogram and then calculating the corresponding impulse response coefficients and forms the confidence intervals of the coefficients through a frequency domain bootstrap procedure.

Other empirical studies on varied topics can be found in Cohen (1999) on analysis of government spending, Wolters (1995) on the term structure of interest rates in Germany, Koren and Stiassny (1995) on the causal relation between tax and spending in Austria, Copeland and Wang (1993) on combined use of time domain and frequency domain analyses, and Bizer and Durlauf (1990) on the positive theory of government finance, to list a few.

Questions and problems

1 What is spectral analysis of time series? Does spectral analysis render new or more information?
2 Discuss the advantages and disadvantages of the analysis in the frequency domain.
3 Describe the Fourier transform and the inverse Fourier transform.
4 What are phases and coherence in spectral analysis? Contrast them with leads/lags and correlation in the time domain.
5 Collect data from various sources and perform the Fourier transform for the following time series (using RATS, GAUSS or other packages):

   a GDP of selected countries;
   b total return series of selected companies;
   c foreign exchange rates of selected countries *vis-à-vis* the US$.

6 Collect data from Datastream and estimate phases and coherence for the following pairs of time series:

   a the spot and forward foreign exchange rates of the UK£ *vis-à-vis* the US$;
   b the spot foreign exchange rates of the UK£ and Japanese yen *vis-à-vis* the US$.

7 Collect data from various sources and estimate phases and coherence for the following pairs of time series:

   a GDP of the US and Canada;
   b GDP and retail sales of the UK.

8 Collect data from Datastream and estimate phases and coherence for the following pairs of time series:

   a total returns of Tesco and Sainsbury's;
   b total returns of Intel and Motorola.

Notes

1 This can also be the product of the FT and its conjugate.
2 We use ω because it is originally a continuous frequency matter. However, our main purpose is for the discrete frequency case.
3 Unlike the t-statistic, the χ^2 statistic increases with the degree of freedom (almost linearly when the degree of freedom becomes very large), so, most statistical tables in econometrics books only provide critical values up to a degree of freedom of 100. However, χ^2 statistics of higher degrees of freedom can be calculated with the formula when required. Critical values of higher degrees of freedom are also given in most econometric software packages, such as RATS.
4 Durlauf (1993) accepted the null of random walks at two points and rejected the null at five points for the time period of 1887–1889. He accepted the null at all points for the two sub-periods of 1887–1929 and 1947–1989, all at the 5% significance level. He used the US per capita real GNP data.
5 In our examples, V_k is 3.5516 for US GDP, 9.7471 for Japanese GDP and 1.5732 for US–Japanese exchange rates. With a flat window in FFT and the respective window

sizes, the standard error of V_k of US GDP is 0.6138, that of Japanese GDP is 1.0454, and that of US–Japanese exchange rates is 0.1745. Therefore, V_k is greater than unity at all conventional levels. Details are available upon request.

References

Bizer, D. S. and Durlauf, S. N. (1990), Testing the positive theory of government finance, *Journal of Monetary Economics*, 26, 123–141.

Bjornland, H. C. (2000), Detrending methods and stylised facts of business cycles in Norway: An international comparison, *Empirical Economics*, 25, 369–392.

Campbell, J. Y. and Mankiw, N. W. (1987a), Are output fluctuations transitory?, *Quarterly Journal of Economics*, 102, 857–880.

Campbell, J. Y. and Mankiw, N. W. (1987b), Permanent and transitory components in macroeconomic fluctuations, *American Economic Review*, 77 (Papers and Proceedings), 111–117.

Canova, F. (1994), Detrending and turning points, *European Economic Review*, 38, 614–623.

Choi, I. and Phillips, P. C. B. (1993), Testing for a unit root by frequency domain regression, *Journal of Econometrics*, 59, 263–286.

Cochrane, J. H. (1988), How big is the random walk in GDP?, *Journal of Political Economy*, 96, 893–920.

Cohen, D. (1999), An analysis of government spending in the frequency domain, *Board of Governors of the Federal Reserve System Finance and Economics Discussion Series*: 99/26.

Copeland, L. S. and Wang, P. (1993), Estimating daily seasonals in financial time series: The use of high-pass spectral filters, *Economics Letters*, 43, 1–4.

Cubadda, G. (1999), Common serial correlation and common business cycles: A cautious note, *Empirical Economics*, 24, 529–535.

Durlauf, S. (1993), Time series properties of aggregate output fluctuations, *Journal of Econometrics*, 56, 39–56.

Englund, P., Persson, T. and Svensson, L. E. O. (1992), Swedish business cycles: 1861–1988, *Journal of Monetary Economics*, 30, 343–371.

Entorf, H. (1993), Constructing leading indicators from non-balanced sectoral business survey series, *International Journal of Forecasting*, 9, 211–225.

Garcia-Ferrer, A. and Queralt, R. A. (1998), Using long-, medium-, and short-term trends to forecast turning points in the business cycle: Some international evidence, *Studies in Nonlinear Dynamics and Econometrics*, 3, 79–105.

Grenander, U. and Rosenblatt, M. (1953), Statistical spectral analysis arising from stationary stochastic processes, *Annals of Mathematical Statistics*, 24, 537–558.

Grenander, U. and Rosenblatt, M. (1957), *Statistical Analysis of Stationary Time Series*, Wiley, New York.

King, R. G. and Rebelo, S. T. (1993), Low frequency filtering and real business cycles, *Journal of Economic Dynamics and Control*, 17, 207–231.

Koren, S. and Stiassny, A. (1995), Tax and spend or spend and tax? An empirical investigation for Austria, *Empirica*, 22, 127–149.

Olekalns, N. (1994), Testing for unit roots in seasonally adjusted data, *Economics Letters*, 45, 273–279.

Pesaran, M. H., Pierse, R. G. and Lee, K. C. (1993), Persistence, cointegration and aggregation: A disaggregated analysis of output fluctuations in the US economy, *Journal of Econometrics*, 56, 67–88.

Phillips, P. C. B. (1991), Error correction and long-run equilibrium in continuous time, *Econometrica*, 59, 967–980.

Priestley, M. B. (1996), *Spectral Analysis and Time Series*, 9th printing (1st printing 1981), Academic Press, London.

Schumpeter, J. A. (1939), *Business Cycles: A Theoretical, Historical and Statistical Analysis of the Capitalist Process*, McGraw-Hill Book Co., Inc., New York and London.

Smith, K. L. (2001), Pre- and post-1987 crash frequency domain analysis among Pacific Rim equity markets, *Journal of Multinational Financial Management*, 11, 69–87.

Stiassny, A. (1996), A spectral decomposition for structural VAR models, *Empirical Economics*, 21, 535–555.

Wolters, J. (1995), On the term structure of interest rates – empirical results for Germany, *Statistical Papers*, 36, 193–214.

Wright, J. H. (1999), Frequency domain inference for univariate impulse responses, *Economics Letters*, 63, 269–277.

9 Research tools and sources of information

This chapter is intended to help the reader carry out an empirical modern financial economics or econometrics project. The chapter recommends relevant on-line information and literature on research in financial markets and financial time series. Some commonly used econometrics software packages for time series analysis are introduced. We feel that perfection of an empirical study can only be achieved against a wider background of the business environment, market operations and institutional roles, and by frequently upgrading the knowledge base. To this end, the coverage of this chapter is extended to include major monetary and financial institutions, international organisations, stock exchanges and option and futures exchanges, and professional associations and learned societies. Most materials are in the form of websites, which can be accessed almost instantly from anywhere in the world. In doing so, this chapter not only endows the reader with various tools and information for empirical research, but also prompts and/or reminds the researcher of the factors and players to be considered in the research.

9.1 Financial economics and econometrics literature on the Internet

Mostly and increasingly, finance journals are covered by lists of economics journals on the web. The following two sites are comprehensive and frequently used by academia and professionals alike: http://www.oswego.edu/~economic/journals.htm at the State University of New York (SUNY), Oswego; and http://netec.mcc.ac.uk/WebEc/journals.html at Manchester Computing, England. These sites provide editorial information, tables of contents and abstracts for most of the listed journals. To obtain access to full papers, one has to contact the publisher. More and more, there are Internet journal archive service agencies. One of the most influential is: http://www.jstor.org.

For major finance journals, it is worthwhile visiting: http://www.cob.ohio-state.edu/fin/journal/jofsites.htm#otjnl at the Ohio State University. Indeed, the Ohio State University maintains wide-ranging financial sites: http://www.cob.ohio-state.edu/fin/journal/jofsites.htm includes finance journals, institutional working paper sites, personal working paper sites, the finance profession, research centres, link collections, asset pricing and investments, derivatives, corporate finance and governance, financial institutions, research software and data, educational resources of interest to students, and miscellanies.

Not only economics journals, but also finance journals, classify paper topics by the *Journal of Economic Literature* (JEL) classification system. The JEL classification numbers are now also available on the web: http://www.aeaweb. org/journal/ elclasjn.html.

Social Science Research Network (SSRN) is very active in disseminating research output. Its website is: http://www.ssrn.com.

SSRN consists of five sub-networks: Accounting Research Network (ARN), Economics Research Network (ERN), Latin American Network (LAN), Financial Economics Network (FEN) and Legal Scholarship Network (LSN). The most relevant networks for the topics in this book are ERN and FEN. SSRN publishes working papers and abstracts of journal papers, downloadable free of charge. It encourages scholars to electronically submit their working papers and abstracts and ranks the papers by download, so it constitutes an efficient channel for gathering information on the most recent developments in the areas.

Other useful sites include:

Resources for economists on the Internet

http://www.rfe.org sponsored by the American Economic Association and maintained by the Economics Department at the SUNY, Oswego.

CRSP

http://www-gsb.uchicago.edu/research/crsp   CRSP files cover common stocks listed on the NYSE, AMEX and Nasdaq Stock Markets, US Government Treasury issues, and US Mutual Funds. The Centre has a wide variety of financial and economic indices (market, total return, cap-based and custom) and other statistics used to gauge the performance of the broader market and economy in general. CRSP also provides proxy graphs for 10K SEC filing, monthly cap-based reports and custom data sets and extractions. Data not available online but they can be purchased: datasets begin at $1,000.

Mimas

http://www.mimas.man.ac.uk   MIMAS is a JISC-supported national data centre run by Manchester Computing, at the University of Manchester, to provide the UK academic community with flexible online access to socio-economic, spatial and scientific data and to bibliographic and electronic journal data services.

Econometric Links

http://econometriclinks.com is maintained by *The Econometrics Journal*.

9.2   Econometrics packages for financial and economic time series

None of the modern financial econometrics projects can be executed without making use of an econometrics package. The following is a list of popular contemporary packages being widely, but not exclusively, used by financial economists and econometricians.

EViews

http://www.eviews.com   EViews, or Econometric Views, is a menu-driven and user-friendly package. It can easily handle most modern econometric models such as binary-dependent variable models, univariate GARCH, cross-section and panel data, and so on. Its help system in electronic form is excellent; for example, the Estimation Methods part provides detailed information on model specification and estimation, as well as the background and origin of the model. However, the menu-driven feature also means that the package is not flexible to adapt to the needs of specific requirements. Although there are many variations of GARCH available, they are all univariate. The state space model and the Kalman filter can only do basic things, which are far from enough to cope with the requirements encountered in modern empirical studies featured by sophisticated model specifications and extensions. For more detail and purchase information visit their website.

RATS

http://www.estima.com   RATS – regressional analysis of time series – is one of the most authoritative packages in the area. With RATS version 5 (WinRATS-32 5.0) there are many new features and improvements over the previous versions. Like EViews, RATS also has a User's Guide and Reference Manual in electronic form. One of the advantages of using RATS is that, while being a specialist package for time series analysis equipped with many readily executable procedures, the user can write or easily adapt a procedure for her/his own specific needs, or s/he can even write a procedure from scratch. Therefore, even if GARCH procedures were not provided, the user can write one with, for example, RATS functions and the maximum likelihood procedure. As such, virtually all kinds of contemporary time series models can be estimated with RATS, though sometimes it involves great complexity and requires much experience and skill. Mainly a time series package, one can also programme models of cross-section and panel data with RATS. In addition to conventional analysis in the time domain, RATS can estimate time series in the frequency domain, also known as spectral analysis of time series. Spectral analysis with RATS includes the Fourier transform, spectra and cross spectra and coherence and phase. All of these are at the application level capable of handling empirical issues in business cycles and other problems involving cyclical movements and phase leads. The reader is recommended to visit *Estima*'s website where informative newsletters are published and useful procedures are logged and updated with some frequency.

TSP

http://www.tspintl.com   To some extent, TSP, or time series processor, is similar to RATS. So we do not introduce it in detail and the reader can refer to the website of TSP International for information.

GAUSS

http://www.aptech.com   GAUSS is powerful in matrix operations. The GAUSS Mathematical and Statistical System is a fast matrix programming language, one of the most popular software packages for economists and econometricians as well as for scientists, engineers, statisticians, biometricians and financial analysts. Designed for computationally intensive tasks, the GAUSS system is ideally suited for the researcher who does not have the time required to develop programmes in C or FORTRAN but finds that most statistical or mathematical 'packages' are not flexible or powerful enough to perform complicated analysis or to work on large problems. Compared with RATS, GAUSS is more powerful and efficient but requires higher levels of programming knowledge and skills.

Microfit

http://www.intecc.co.uk/camfit (for sales information only)   Microfit is a menu-driven, easy to use econometric package written especially for microcomputers, and is specifically designed for the econometric modelling of time series data. The strength of the package lies in the fact that it can be used at different levels of technical sophistication. For experienced users of econometric programmes, it offers a variety of univariate and multivariate estimation methods and provides a large number of diagnostic and non-nested tests not readily available in other packages. As a result, Microfit is one of the econometric packages most frequently used by economists and applied econometricians.

SAS

http://www.sas.com   SAS is a large multi-purpose statistical package. It can process almost all model estimation problems in this book. But as it is large it is not usually available on PCs. It also requires more knowledge in software.

Matlab

http://www.mathworks.com   Matlab was initially for solving engineering problems. Now there are more and more economists and econometricians using this package.

Mathematica

http://www.wri.com   Economists and econometricians increasingly use this package as well.

9.3 Learned societies and professional associations

This section lists major learned societies and professional associations in the fields of finance, economics and econometrics, as well as real estate and accounting.

The American Finance Association (AFA)

http://www.afajof.org/   The AFA is the premier academic organisation devoted to the study and promotion of knowledge about financial economics. The AFA was planned at a meeting in December 1939 in Philadelphia. The *Journal of Finance* was first published in August 1946. Association membership has grown steadily over time and the AFA currently has over 8,000 members. The AFA sponsors an annual meeting every January, usually at the same city and during the same days as the American Economic Association (AEA).

The American Economic Association (AEA)

http://www.vanderbilt.edu/AEA/   The AEA was organised in 1885 at Saratoga, New York. Approximately 22,000 economists are members and there are some 5,500 institution subscribers. Over 50 per cent of the membership is associated with academic institutions around the world, 35 per cent with business and industry and the remainder largely with US federal, state and local government agencies. The mission statement of the AEA is: The encouragement of economic research, especially the historical and statistical study of the actual conditions of industrial life; the issue of publications on economic subjects; the encouragement of perfect freedom of economic discussion, including an Annual Meeting (in each January). The Association as such will take no partisan attitude, nor will it commit its members to any position on practical economic questions. The AEA publishes *American Economic Review*, *Journal of Economic Literature* and *Journal of Economic Perspectives*.

The American Accounting Association (AAA)

http://accounting.rutgers.edu/raw/aaa/   The AAA promotes worldwide excellence in accounting education, research and practice. Founded in 1916 as the American Association of University Instructors in Accounting, its present name was adopted in 1936. The Association is a voluntary organisation of persons interested in accounting education and research. The mission of the AAA is to foster worldwide excellence in the creation, dissemination and application of accounting knowledge and skills. The AAA publishes *The Accounting Review*, *Accounting Horizons* and *Issues in Accounting Education*.

The Econometric Society

http://www.econometricsociety.org/es/   The Econometric Society is an international society for the advancement of economic theory in its relation to statistics and mathematics. The Econometric Society was founded in 1930, at the initiative of the Yale economist Irving Fisher (the Society's first president) and the Norwegian economist Ragnar Frisch, who some forty years later was the first economist (together with Jan Tinbergen) to be awarded the Nobel Prize. The first organisational meeting of the Society was held in Cleveland, Ohio, on 29 December 1930. The first scientific meetings of the Society were held in September 1931, at the University of Lausanne, Switzerland, and in December 1931, in Washington DC.

The journal *Econometrica* published its first issue in 1933, with Frisch as editor-in-chief, and with a budget that was initially subsidised by the financier Alfred Cowles. Frisch had coined the word 'econometrics' only a few years earlier in 1926. The journal started out publishing four issues of 112 pages per year and did not grow beyond 500 pages per year until the 1950s. Since the 1970s, *Econometrica* has published six issues per year containing roughly 1,600 annual pages.

Financial Management Association International (FMA)

http://www.fma.org/   Established in 1970, the FMA is a global leader in developing and disseminating knowledge about financial decision making. The mission of the FMA is to broaden the common interests between academicians and practitioners, provide opportunities for professional interaction between and among academicians, practitioners and students, promote the development and understanding of basic and applied research and of sound financial practices, and to enhance the quality of education in finance.

FMA's members include finance practitioners and academicians and students who are interested in the techniques and advances which define the field of finance. Over 5,000 academicians and practitioners throughout the world are members of the FMA. The FMA publishes *Financial Management*, *Journal of Applied Finance* and *FMA Survey and Synthesis Series*.

European Economic Association (EEA)

http://www.eeassoc.org/   The EEA is an international scientific body, with membership open to all persons involved or interested in economics. The aims of the EEA are: to contribute to the development and application of economics as a science in Europe; to improve communication and exchange between teachers, researchers and students in economics in the different European countries; to develop and sponsor cooperation between teaching institutions of university level and research institutions in Europe. In pursuing these aims, the EEA is particularly eager to foster closer links between theory-oriented and policy-oriented economists, as well as between students and more senior economists, from all parts of Europe. The EEA holds annual congresses and summer schools. *The European Economic Review* is the official journal of the EEA.

European Financial Management Association (EFMA)

http://www.efmaefm.org/   The EMFA was founded in 1994 to encourage research and disseminate knowledge about financial decision making in all areas of finance as it relates to European corporations, financial institutions and capital markets. EFMA membership consists of academics, practitioners and students from Europe and the rest of the world who are interested in the practice of sound financial management techniques and are dedicated to understanding and solving financial problems. The EFMA holds annual meetings every June and publishes *European Financial Management*.

Royal Economic Society (RES)

http://www.res.org.uk   Now in its second century, the RES is one of the oldest economic associations in the world. Currently it has over 3,300 individual members, of whom 60 per cent live outside the United Kingdom. It is a professional association which promotes the encouragement of the study of economic science in academic life, government service, banking, industry and public affairs. The RES publishes *The Economic Journal*, which is one of the oldest in the world, and a new journal *The Econometrics Journal*.

American Real Estate and Urban Economics Association (AREUEA)

http://www.areuea.org/   The AREUEA was originated at the 1964 meeting of the Allied Social Science Association in Chicago. The AREUEA grew from discussions of individuals that recognised a need for more information and analysis in the fields of real estate development, planning and economics. The continuing efforts of this non-profit association have advanced the scope of knowledge in these disciplines and have facilitated the exchange of information and opinions among academic, professional and governmental people who are concerned with urban economics and real estate issues. The AREUEA's journal, *Real Estate Economics* (formerly *The American Real Estate and Urban Economics Association Journal*) is published quarterly and is distributed on a calendar year subscription basis. The journal contains research and scholarly studies of current and emerging real estate issues.

American Real Estate Society (ARES)

http://www.aresnet.org/   The ARES was founded in 1985 to serve the educational, informational and research needs of thought leaders in the real estate industry and real estate professors at colleges and universities. The ARES has several affiliated societies, with the largest, The International Real Estate Society (IRES), being founded in 1993. The ARES publishes *Journal of Real Estate Research*, *Journal of Real Estate Literature* and *Journal of Real Estate Portfolio Management*.

International Institute of Forecasters (IIF)

http://forecasting.cwru.edu/   The IIF's objectives are to stimulate the generation, distribution and use of knowledge on forecasting. The IIF was founded in 1981 as a non-profit organisation. The IIF sponsors an annual International Symposium of Forecasting every June and publishes the *International Journal of Forecasting*.

9.4   Organisations and institutions

9.4.1   International financial institutions and other organisations

International Monetary Fund (IMF)

http://www.imf.org   The IMF is an international organisation of 183 member countries, established to promote international monetary cooperation, exchange stability and orderly exchange arrangements; to foster economic growth and high levels of employment; and to provide temporary financial assistance to countries to help ease balance of payments adjustment. Since the IMF was established in 1946, its purposes have remained unchanged but its operations, which involve surveillance, financial assistance and technical assistance, have developed to meet the changing needs of its member countries in an evolving world economy.

World Bank

http://www.worldbank.org   The World Bank is the world's largest source of development assistance, providing nearly $16 billion in loans annually to its client countries. It uses its financial resources, highly trained staff and extensive knowledge base to help each developing country onto a path of stable, sustainable and equitable growth in the fight against poverty.

Organisation for Economic Cooperation and Development (OECD)

http://www.oecd.org   The OECD has been called a think tank and monitoring agency. The OECD groups 30 member countries in an organisation that, most importantly, provides governments with a setting in which to discuss, develop and perfect economic and social policy. It is rich, in that OECD countries produce two-thirds of the world's goods and services, but it is not an exclusive club. Essentially, membership is limited only by a country's commitment to a market economy and a pluralistic democracy. The core of original members has expanded from Europe and North America to include Japan, Australia, New Zealand, Finland, Mexico, the Czech Republic, Hungary, Poland and Korea. There are many more contacts with the rest of the world through programmes with countries in the former Soviet bloc, Asia and Latin America, which, in some cases, may lead to membership.

Exchanges between OECD governments flow from information and analysis provided by a Secretariat in Paris. Parts of the OECD Secretariat collect data, monitor trends, analyse and forecast economic developments, while others research social changes or evolving patterns in trade, environment, agriculture, technology, taxation and more. This work, in areas that mirror the policy-making structures in ministries of governments, is done in close consultation with policy makers who will use the analysis, and it underpins discussion by member countries when they meet in specialised committees of the OECD. Much of the research and analysis is published.

European Bank for Reconstruction and Development (EBRD)

http://www.ebrd.org/ The EBRD was established in 1991. It exists to foster the transition towards open market-oriented economies and to promote private and entrepreneurial initiative in the countries of central and eastern Europe and the Commonwealth of Independent States (CIS) committed to and applying the principles of multiparty democracy, pluralism and market economics.

Asian Development Bank (ADB)

http://www.adb.org The ADB is a multilateral development finance institution dedicated to reducing poverty in Asia and the Pacific. Established in 1966, the ADB is now owned by 59 members, mostly from the region. The ADB helps improve the quality of people's lives by providing loans and technical assistance for a broad range of development activities.

Bank for International Settlements (BIS)

http://www.bis.org This website has links to all central banks' websites except that for China http://www.pbc.gov.cn One of the reasons might be that the web of the People's Bank of China is a Chinese-language-only website. The BIS is an international organisation which fosters cooperation among central banks and other agencies in pursuit of monetary and financial stability. The BIS functions as: a forum for international monetary and financial cooperation where central bankers and others meet and where facilities are provided to support various committees, both standing and *ad hoc*; a bank for central banks, providing a broad range of financial services; a centre for monetary and economic research, contributing to a better understanding of international financial markets and the interaction of national monetary and financial policies; an agent or trustee, facilitating the implementation of various international financial agreements. The BIS operates the Financial Stability Institute (FSI) jointly with the Basel Committee on Banking Supervision. The BIS also hosts the secretariats of the Financial Stability Forum (FSF) and the International Association of Insurance Supervisors (IAIS).

9.4.2   *Major stock exchanges, option and futures exchanges and regulators*

New York Stock Exchange (NYSE)

http://www.nyse.com   The NYSE traces its origins to a founding agreement, the Buttonwood Agreement by 24 New York City stockbrokers and merchants, in 1792. The NYSE registered as a national securities exchange with the US Securities and Exchange Commission on 1 October 1934. The Governing Committee was the primary governing body until 1938, at which time the Exchange hired its first paid President and created a 33-member Board of Governors. The Board included Exchange members, non-member partners from both New York and out-of-town firms, as well as public representatives.

In 1971, the Exchange was incorporated as a not-for-profit corporation. In 1972, the members voted to replace the Board of Governors with a 25-member Board of Directors, comprised of a Chairman and CEO, 12 representatives of the public, and 12 representatives from the securities industry. Subject to the approval of the Board, the Chairman may appoint a President, who would serve as a Director. Additionally, at the board's discretion, they may elect an Executive Vice Chairman, who would also serve as a Director.

London Stock Exchange

http://www.londonstockexchange.com   The London Stock Exchange was formed in 1760 by 150 brokers as a club for share trading. It changed to the current name in 1773. Since 1986, trading has moved from being conducted face-to-face on a market floor to being performed via computer and telephone from separate dealing rooms. This is due to the introduction of SEAQ and SEAQ International, two computer systems displaying share price information in brokers' offices around the UK. The London Stock Exchange became a private limited company under the Companies Act 1985. In 1991, the Exchange replaced the governing Council of the Exchange with a Board of Directors drawn from the Exchange's executive, customer and user base. In recent years, there have been major changes in the Exchange: the role of the Exchange as UK listing authority with the Treasury was transferred to the Financial Services Authority in 2000; and the exchange became a PLC and has been listed since July 2001.

Tokyo Stock Exchange

http://www.tse.or.jp   In the 1870s, a securities system was introduced in Japan and public bond negotiation began. This resulted in the request for a public trading institution and the 'Stock Exchange Ordinance' was enacted in May 1878. Based on this ordinance, the 'Tokyo Stock Exchange Co. Ltd.' was established on 15 May 1878 and trading began on 1 June. The Tokyo Stock Exchange functions as a self-regulated, non-profit association. Established under a provision of the Securities and Exchange Law, the Tokyo Stock Exchange is managed and maintained by its members.

Chicago Board Options Exchange (CBOE)

http://www.cboe.com The CBOE was founded in 1973. Prior to that time, options were traded on an unregulated basis and did not have to adhere to the principle of 'fair and orderly markets'. At the opening on 26 April 1973, the CBOE traded call options on 16 underlying stocks. Put options were introduced in 1977. By 1975, options had become so popular that other securities exchanges began entering the business. The quick acceptance of listed options propelled CBOE to become the second-largest securities exchange in the country and the world's largest options exchange. In 1983, options on stock indices were introduced by the CBOE. Today, the CBOE accounts for more than 51 per cent of all US options trading and 91 per cent of all index options trading. The CBOE now lists options on over 1,200 widely traded stocks.

The CBOE was originally created by the Chicago Board of Trade (CBOT) but has always been managed and regulated as an independent entity. Due to increased volume in the early 1980s, the CBOE outgrew its trading facilities at the CBOT and moved into its own building in 1984.

Chicago Board of Trade (CBOT)

http://www.cbot.com The CBOT was established in 1848 and is the world's oldest derivatives exchange. More than 3,600 CBOT members trade 48 different futures and options products at the CBOT, resulting in an annual trading volume of more than 233 million contracts in 2000. In its early history the CBOT listed for trading only agricultural instruments, such as wheat, corn and oats. In 1975 the CBOT expanded its scope to include financial contracts, initially, the US Treasury Bond futures contract which is now one of the world's most actively traded.

The CBOT presently is a self-governing, self-regulated, not-for-profit, non-stock corporation that serves individuals and member firms. The governing body of the exchange consists of a Board of Directors that includes a Chairman, First Vice Chairman, Second Vice Chairman, 18 member directors, 5 public directors, and the President. The Exchange is administered by an executive staff headed by the President and Chief Executive Officer.

London International Financial Futures and Options Exchange (LIFFE)

http://www.liffe.com Unlike the case of the CBOT and CBOE where the latter was created by the former and they are now separated exchanges, the LIFFE was created when the original LIFFE, the London International Financial Futures Exchange, merged with the London options exchange. Notice that the acronym does not include the first letter of Options, though Options is in the full name. In February 1999, the LIFFE's shareholders voted unanimously for a corporate restructuring which progressed the LIFFE further towards becoming a profit-oriented commercial organisation. With effect from April 1999, the restructuring split the right to trade and membership from shareholding, simplified a complex share structure and enabled non-members to purchase shares in LIFFE (holdings) PLC.

Philadelphia Stock Exchange (PHLX)

http://www.phlx.com   The PHLX was founded in 1790 as the first organised stock exchange in the United States. The PHLX trades more than 2,200 stocks, 922 equity options, 10 index options and 100 currency pairs.

The PHLX is reputed for its invention of exchange traded currency options in 1982. By 1988, currency options were trading in volumes as high as $4 billion per day in underlying value. Currency options put the Exchange on international maps, bringing trading interest from Europe, the Pacific Rim and the Far East, and leading the Exchange to be the first securities exchange to open international offices in money centres overseas. Currency options made the PHLX an around-the-clock operation. In September 1987, Philadelphia was the first securities exchange in the US to introduce an evening trading session, chiefly to accommodate increasing demand for currency options in the Far East, and the exchange responded to growing European demand by adding an early morning session in January 1989. In September 1990, the PHLX became the first exchange in the world to offer around-the-clock trading by bridging the gap between the night session and the early morning hours. Although the exchange subsequently scaled back its trading hours, its current currency option trading hours from 2:30 a.m. to 2:30 p.m. (local time) are longer than any other open outcry auction marketplace.

Securities and Exchange Commission (SEC)

http://www.sec.gov   The SEC's foundation was laid in an era that was ripe for reform. Before the Great Crash of 1929, there was little support for federal regulation of the securities markets. This was particularly true during the post-First World War surge of securities activity. Proposals that the federal government require financial disclosure and prevent the fraudulent sale of stock were never seriously pursued. Tempted by promises of 'rags to riches' transformations and easy credit, most investors gave little thought to the dangers inherent in uncontrolled market operation. During the 1920s, approximately 20 million large and small shareholders took advantage of postwar prosperity and set out to make their fortunes in the stock market. It is estimated that of the $50 billion in new securities offered during this period, half became worthless.

The primary mission of the US Securities and Exchange Commission (SEC) is to protect investors and maintain the integrity of the securities markets. As more and more first-time investors turn to the markets to help secure their futures, pay for homes, and send children to college, these goals are more compelling than ever.

The laws and rules that govern the securities industry in the US derive from a simple and straightforward concept: all investors, whether large institutions or private individuals, should have access to certain basic facts about an investment prior to buying it. To achieve this, the SEC requires public companies to disclose meaningful financial and other information to the public, which provides a common pool of knowledge for all investors to use to judge for themselves if a company's securities are a good investment. Only through the steady flow of timely, comprehensive and accurate information can people make sound investment decisions. The SEC also oversees other key participants in the securities world, including stock exchanges, broker-dealers, investment advisers, mutual funds and public utility holding companies. Here again, the SEC is concerned primarily with promoting disclosure of important information, enforcing the securities laws and protecting investors who interact with these various organisations and individuals.

Crucial to the SEC's effectiveness is its enforcement authority. Each year the SEC brings between 400 and 500 civil enforcement actions against individuals and companies that break the securities laws. Typical infractions include insider trading, accounting fraud and providing false or misleading information about securities and the companies that issue them. Fighting securities fraud, however, requires teamwork. At the heart of effective investor protection is an educated and careful investor. The SEC offers the public a wealth of educational information on its Internet website at www.sec.gov. The website also includes the EDGAR database of disclosure documents that public companies are required to file with the Commission.

Though it is the primary overseer and regulator of the US securities markets, the SEC works closely with many other institutions, including Congress, other federal departments and agencies, the self-regulatory organisations (e.g. the stock exchanges), state securities regulators and various private sector organisations.

Financial Services Authority (FSA)

http://www.fsa.gov.uk   The FSA is a relatively new organisation, which was founded in 1997 when the government announced its decision to merge the supervision of banking and investment under one regulatory organisation. The FSA's predecessor was known as the Securities and Investments Board (SIB), created in May 1997 and changed to its current name in October 1997. The FSA is an independent, non-governmental body which employs 2,000 people. The FSA board is appointed by an Executive Chairman, with 3 managing directors and 11 non-executive directors.

The first stage of the recent reform of UK financial services regulation was completed in June 1998, when responsibility for banking supervision was transferred to the FSA from the Bank of England. The Financial Services and Markets Act of the UK, which received Royal Assent in June 2000 and was due to be implemented on 1 December 2001, transferred to the FSA the responsibilities of several other organisations: Building Societies Commission, Friendly Societies Commission, Investment Management Regulatory Organisation, Personal Investment Authority, Register of Friendly Societies and Securities and Futures Authority.

The FSA regulates the financial services industry and has four objectives under the Financial Services and Markets Act 2000: maintaining market confidence, promoting public understanding of the financial system, the protection of consumers and fighting financial crime. The FSA is the UK's financial watchdog, keeping an eye on the goings-on in the City. It regulates and oversees the financial system, and plays an important part in ensuring that training within the banking industry is up to scratch.

All companies in the financial services market, from banks to pension companies, must be FSA accredited. Then they are supervised and inspected on a regular basis. There are 7,700 accredited FSA companies, while in 2000, 23 companies had their accreditation revoked and 300 resigned. The FSA produced more than 750,000 fact sheets for the public in 2000/01 and recently launched a section on its website designed for consumers. The FSA imposes levies on accredited companies, equating to an annual budget of £158 million per year.

9.4.3   Central banks

Board of Governors of the Federal Reserve System

http://www.federalreserve.gov   The Federal Reserve, the central bank of the United States, was founded by Congress in 1913 to provide the nation with a safer, more flexible and more stable monetary and financial system. Today, the Federal Reserve's duties fall into four general areas: conducting the nation's monetary policy; supervising and regulating banking institutions and protecting the credit rights of consumers; maintaining the stability of the financial system; and providing certain financial services to the US government, the public, financial institutions and foreign official institutions.

The Federal Reserve System was designed to ensure its political independence and its sensitivity to divergent economic concerns. The Chairman and the six other members of the Board of Governors who oversee the Federal Reserve are nominated by the President of the United States and confirmed by the Senate. The President is directed by law to select governors who provide 'a fair representation of the financial, agricultural, industrial and geographical divisions of the country'.

Each Reserve Bank is headed by a President appointed by the bank's nine-member Board of Directors. Three of the directors represent the commercial banks in the Bank's region that are members of the Federal Reserve System. The other Directors are selected to represent the public with due consideration to the interest of agriculture, commerce, industry, services, labour and consumers. Three of these six directors are elected by member banks and the other three are chosen by the Board of Governors.

The 12 Reserve Banks supervise and regulate bank holding companies as well as state chartered banks in their District that are members of the Federal Reserve System. Each Reserve Bank provides services to depository institutions in its respective District and functions as a fiscal agent of the US government.

Federal Reserve Bank of New York

http://www.ny.frb.org The Federal Reserve Bank of New York is one of 12 regional Reserve Banks which, together with the Board of Governors in Washington, DC, comprise the Federal Reserve System. Stored inside the vaults of the New York Fed building are hundreds of billions of dollars of gold and securities. But what is unique and most significant about the Bank is its broad policy responsibilities and the effects of its operations on the US economy.

The New York Fed has supervisory jurisdiction over the Second Federal Reserve District, which encompasses New York State, the 12 northern counties of New Jersey, Fairfield County in Connecticut, Puerto Rico and the Virgin Islands. Though it serves a geographically small area compared with those of other Federal Reserve Banks, the New York Fed is the largest Reserve Bank in terms of assets and volume of activity.

European Central Bank (ECB)

http://www.ecb.int The European System of Central Banks (ESCB) is composed of the ECB and the national central banks (NCBs) of all 15 EU Member States. The 'Eurosystem' is the term used to refer to the ECB and the NCBs of the Member States which have adopted the euro. The NCBs of the Member States which do not participate in the euro area, however, are members of the ESCB with a special status – while they are allowed to conduct their respective national monetary policies, they do not take part in the decision making with regard to the single monetary policy for the euro area and the implementation of such decisions.

In accordance with the Treaty establishing the European Community (the 'Treaty') and the Statute of the European System of Central Banks and of the European Central Bank (the 'Statute'), the primary objective of the Eurosystem is to maintain price stability. Without prejudice to this objective, it will support the general economic policies in the Community and act in accordance with the principles of an open market economy.

The basic tasks to be carried out by the Eurosystem are: to define and implement the monetary policy of the euro area; to conduct foreign exchange operations; to hold and manage the official foreign reserves of the Member States; and to promote the smooth operation of payment systems.

Bank of Japan

http://www.boj.or.jp The role of the Bank of Japan is similar to that of the pre-1997 Bank of England in that the Treasury or the Ministry of Finance makes important decisions and monetary policy and the Bank implements monetary policy.

The Bank of Japan's missions are to maintain price stability and to ensure the stability of the financial system, thereby laying the foundations for sound economic development. To fulfil these two missions, the Bank conducts the following activities: issuance and management of banknotes; implementation of monetary policy;

providing settlement services and ensuring the stability of the financial system; treasury and government securities-related operations; international activities; and compilation of data, economic analyses and research activities.

Bank of Russia

http://www.cbr.ru   The Central Bank of the Russian Federation (Bank of Russia) was founded on 13 July 1990, on the basis of the Russian Republic Bank of the State Bank of the USSR. Accountable to the Supreme Soviet of the RSFSR, it was originally called the State Bank of the RSFSR. In November 1991, when the Commonwealth of Independent States was founded and Union structures dissolved, the Supreme Soviet of the RSFSR declared the Central Bank of the RSFSR to be the only body of state monetary and foreign exchange regulation in the RSFSR. The functions of the State Bank of the USSR in issuing money and setting the rouble exchange rate were transferred to it. The Central Bank of the RSFSR was instructed to assume before 1 January 1992 full control of the assets, technical facilities and other resources of the State Bank of the USSR and all its institutions, enterprises and organisations.

The Bank of Russia carries out its functions, which were established by the Constitution of the Russian Federation (Article 75) and the Law on the Central Bank of the Russian Federation (Bank of Russia) (Article 22), independently from the federal, regional and local government structures. In 1992–1995, to maintain the stability of the banking system, the Bank of Russia set up a system of supervision and inspection of commercial banks and a system of foreign exchange regulation and foreign exchange control. As an agent of the Ministry of Finance, it organised a government securities market, known as the GKO market, and began to participate in its operations.

People's Bank of China

http://www.pbc.gov.cn (this is a Chinese-language-version only website)   The central bank of the People's Republic of China is the People's Bank of China. In the early times of the People's Republic, the Bank, though a ministerial department of the State Council (the cabinet), was coordinated by the Ministry of Finance. It was largely a commercial bank with high street branches all over the country. During the 1980s, its commercial and corporate banking functions were reorganised and grouped into a new and separate bank, the Industrial and Commercial Bank of China, one of the largest of its kind in the world. Since then, the People's Bank solely plays the role of a central bank and is completely independent of the Ministry of Finance but is not separated from the Administration. The People's Bank used to have branches at provincial level (for regional monetary policy matters or the monitoring of monetary policy from Headquarters), but which have now been reorganised to form regional branches (covering several provinces/municipal cities), a structure similar to that of the US Federal Reserve System.

Schweizerische Nationalbank

http://www.snb.ch   German version only.

Bank of Canada

http://www.bankofcanada.ca
For all other central banks, the reader can refer to the BIS website.

Subject index

Name index